AGRICULTURE, CONSERVATION AND LAND USE

AGRICULTURE, CONSERVATION AND LAND USE

Law and Policy Issues for Rural Areas

edited by

WILLIAM HOWARTH
and
CHRISTOPHER P. RODGERS

UNIVERSITY OF WALES PRESS
CARDIFF
1992

© the contributors, 1992

Published by the University of Wales Press in collaboration with the Centre for Law in Rural Areas, University College of Wales, Aberystwyth.

British Library Cataloguing in Publication Data

Agriculture, conservation and land use: law and policy issues for rural areas.
  I. Howarth, William II. Rodgers, C. P. (Christopher Parker)
  344.10376
  ISBN 0-7083-1126-1

Typeset by Megaron, Cardiff

Printed in Great Britain by Billing and Sons Limited, Book Plan, Worcester

Preface

In recent years an increasing part of the research undertaken by the Department of Law at University College of Wales, Aberystwyth, has been concentrated upon legal issues which are of special importance to rural areas. As a step towards recognition of the distinctive problems faced by rural areas and the need for the co-ordinated study of law relating to those problems, it was decided to establish the Centre for Law in Rural Areas.

Although UCW Aberystwyth is well-placed to appreciate the difficulties presently experienced by rural areas, the legal concerns to which they give rise are not uniquely relevant to Mid Wales. Essentially, the same problems are shared by rural localities and communities throughout the United Kingdom. Moreover, frequently the law dealing with these issues has a particular character which calls for a special approach towards its description and evaluation. Legal issues of special concern to rural life are not readily categorized according to traditional legal subdivisions. Many well-established fields of legal research and practice, such as crime and property law, have relatively unacknowledged but distinctively rural dimensions. Most notably, rural law spans a range of topics within the field of agricultural and environmental law and also extends into criminology and social welfare law. In each case, however, conventional legal categories encompass bodies of law illustrating uniquely rural features.

Amongst the key purposes of the Centre for Law in Rural Areas is that of acting as a focal point for research on rural law. Rural law is broadly conceived to encompass theoretical, expository and empirical discussion of the law, and comparative and contextual research relating to rural localities, activities and communities. The ground which this general characterization of the subject area leaves open for more precise determination is to be covered in a series of publications dealing with particular issues in rural law. *Agriculture, Conservation and Land Use* is a collection of essays providing an initial delineation of some key topics within the sphere of rural law.

William Howarth
Christopher P. Rodgers   **Centre for Law in Rural Areas**

Contents

The Editors and Contributors

William Howarth BA, LLM is the Director of the Centre for Law in Rural Areas at the University College of Wales, Aberystwyth and a member of the United Kingdom Environmental Law Association. He has written widely on the law relating to the aquatic environment. Previous publications include *Freshwater Fishery Law* (1987), *Water Pollution Law* (1988), *The Law of Aquaculture* (1990), *The Law of the National Rivers Authority* (1990) and numerous articles concerning water law in legal journals.

Christopher P. Rodgers LLM, LLB is a solicitor and senior lecturer in law at the University College of Wales, Aberystwyth and a member of both the United Kingdom Environmental Law Association and the Agricultural Law Association. He has written widely on agricultural law topics and the law of landlord and tenant. His publications include *Agricultural Law* (1991), *The Housing Act 1988* (1989) conservation planning law sections in *Agricultural Law, Tax and Finance* (Longman Looseleaf, 1990) and numerous articles in legal journals.

Michael Gregory OBE LLB barrister, is a full-time writer since retiring as Chief Legal Adviser of the Country Landowners' Association (1977–90). He is a founder member of the Agricultural Law Association and a trustee of two charities for disabled people. His many publications include *Organisational Possibilities in Farming* (1968), *Joint Enterprises in Farming* (1968, 2nd edn 1973), *Angling and The Law* (1967, 2nd edn 1974), *Essential Law for Landowners and Farmers* (with Margaret Parrish 1980, 2nd edn 1987, 3rd edn with Angela Sydenham 1990) and numerous other books, booklets, and articles mainly on legal, countryside and Parliamentary subjects.

Allan Lennon MA, is a solicitor in private practice and is the President of the Agricultural Law Association. He is the general editor of *Agricultural Law, Tax and Finance* (Longman Looseleaf, 1990).

Fiona Reynolds BA, MPhil, was appointed Assistant Director (Policy) of the Council for the Protection of Rural England (CPRE) in 1987. She was previously Secretary of the Council for National Parks (1980–87). In 1990 she was awarded the Global 500 Award for outstanding achievement in protection and improvement of the environment from the United Nations Environment Programme (UNEP), and appointed a Member of the National Parks Review Panel by the Countryside Commission.

William Sheate BSc, MSc, DIC, was appointed Campaigns Officer of the Council for the Protection of Rural England (CPRE) in 1989, having worked previously as a consultant ecologist (1985–7) and then lecturing in environmental studies and biogeography at Kingston Polytechnic (1987–9). He has researched and published on environmental assessment and water resource issues, and has been involved in Parliamentary lobbying for CPRE on numerous bills, including the Water Bill (1989) and the Environmental Protection Bill (1990).

David Withrington worked in the Nature Conservancy Council's Sites and Pollution Policy Branch until March 1991. He is now Freshwater Policy Officer of English Nature, one of the NCC's successor bodies, based in Peterborough. He joined the NCC in 1978 as its author/editor and has written widely on environmental topics.

Wyn Jones BSc, is the Acquisitions Officer for English Nature and was previously the Site Safeguard Officer for the Nature Conservancy Council. He is a member of the United Kingdom Environmental Law Association and of its Nature Conservation Working Group.

J. D. C. Harte MA, Dip.Crim., is a barrister and lecturer in law at Newcastle Law School in the University of Newcastle Upon Tyne. He specializes in planning and environmental law with a particular interest in the conservation of the countryside and of natural resources. His previous publications include *Landscape Land Use and the Law* (1985). He is case notes editor for *Environmental Law*, the quarterly bulletin of the United Kingdom Environmental Law Association, and is a member of the editorial boards of the *Ecclesiastical Law Journal* and of the *Rights of Way Law Review*.

John Aitchison MA, PhD, is the Gregynog Professor of Human Geography at the University College of Wales, Aberystwyth. He is also Director of the Rural Surveys Research Unit in the Department of Geography and co-director of the recently established International

Centre for Protected Landscapes at Aberystwyth. His research ranges widely but relates in particular to environmental, conservation and rural development issues in Britain and France. He has a special interest in the geography of language change in Wales.

Gerald Gadsden Dip.Agric., LLB, PhD, is a retired former broadcaster and, most recently, lecturer in law at the Cardiff Law School. His publications include *The Law of Commons* (1988) and numerous articles in legal and other journals on the subject of common land.

Peter Wathern BSc, PhD, is Director of Studies in Environmental Impact Assessment in the Department of Biological Sciences, University College of Wales, Aberystwyth and senior lecturer in applied ecology. He has written widely on aspects of environmental management including EIA, environmental policy in the EC and derelict land reclamation. He edited *Environmental Impact Assessment: Theory and Practice* (1989) and has published many papers on environmental management.

Introduction

Changes in farming practices over recent years have been dramatic, and concerns about the cost of those practices to the environment have been forcefully expressed in the literature concerning conflicts in rural land use (see, for example, Pye-Smith and Rose, *Crisis and Conservation* (1984); Adams, *Nature's Place* (1986); Lowe, Cox, MacEwen, O'Riordan and Winter, *Countryside Conflicts* (1986); and Blunden and Curry, *A Future for Our Countryside* (1988)). The tasks of conserving flora and fauna, and the habitats upon which they depend, alongside the continuation of increasingly intensive forms of agriculture, are issues occupying the minds of specialists from a range of disciplines. At the very least, meeting conservational objectives depends upon sound science, effective administration and appropriate laws. This collection of essays places central emphasis upon the last of these three requirements. The policies which are the subject of deliberation between agriculturalists, ecologists, economists and, not least, politicians will, in the last resort, almost invariably need to be expressed and implemented in the form of legislation. Naturally, conservation legislation will require discussion and evaluation according to established legal criteria. Characteristically, lawyers will be primarily concerned with the workability and efficacy of the enacted legal rules to facilitate and contain agricultural activity within acceptable boundaries fixed on conservation grounds. In contrasting ways the essays in this collection are all concerned with that key problem.

Overall, the collection provides a description of nine different legal topics of central importance in relation to agricultural and conservational land use. In each case the author has sought to introduce the legal detail of the subject matter in a manner which makes it as accessible as possible both to lawyers and to non-lawyers with an interest in the topics under consideration. Beyond an exposition of the law the essays seek, where possible, to place their subject matter in perspective alongside broader agricultural and environmental concerns. In each chapter the objective has been both to describe and to evaluate the areas of law under discussion.

Whilst recognizing the existence of distinctively *legal* problems in reconciling agriculture with conservational objectives, the essays presented here also reflect the fact that there is little uniformity, even amongst legal commentators, as to the policy objectives to be sought. Accordingly, these essays do not seek to present any consensus, but rather to indicate the range of disparate views which are found amongst those concerned with both agricultural law and conservation law. Contributors range from those closely associated with organizations representing the interests of farmers to authors directly involved with conservation organizations. Other contributors occupy a middle ground between the two. Hopefully the range of interests represented is balanced and the different perspectives are clearly illustrated. If the collection serves only to draw attention to debate upon the distinctively *legal* issues of agriculture, conservation and land use it will have made the contribution to the study of rural law for which the editors had hoped. Beyond this, however, it is hoped that the contributors' differing evaluations of the implementation of agricultural policy may serve, particularly, to emphasize the need for a coherent and integrated legislative approach to environmental protection and land use. Clearly, one problem highlighted in a number of the essays is a tension between the public policy underlying much agricultural legislation, and that underlying a large part of recent conservation legislation.

The underlying rationale of much of the post-war agricultural legislation has been to encourage maximization of production and to promote the efficiency of agriculture. This is manifest not only in the system of agricultural grants, but in the privileged status accorded to agriculture under planning law, and the terms on which farm tenants are afforded protection under the agricultural holdings legislation. Clearly, any study of conservation and land use must take account of the impact of agricultural policy *per se*, and in particular the structure of agricultural grants. The European Community's Common Agricultural Policy has in recent years moved towards encouraging diversification of farm businesses and the 'set-aside' of land from production, in an effort to curb overproduction and reduce public subsidy. A study of the relevant domestic regulations will reveal few references to conservation and environmental protection. Yet, in making substantial grant aid available to encourage farmers to change land to a variety of non-agricultural uses, measures such as the set-aside regulations and the farm diversification scheme have a direct bearing upon conservation, and on issues of environmental protection. Following recent amendments, the set-aside regulations do now provide for enhanced grant payments if additional obligations of a conservational character are undertaken by participating farmers. The primary concern of the scheme, however, as with other diversification measures, remains agricultural rather than conservational in nature, that is, to reduce structural surpluses in agricultural production.

In contrast, the underlying philosophy of the agricultural holdings legislation remains that of maximizing production. Farm tenants enjoy extensive rights to security of tenure and control of rents under the agricultural holdings legislation. These rights are qualified, however, in that a tenant only has their full advantage while farming in accordance with the 'rules of good husbandry'. The latter presuppose that stocking levels and arable cropping are sustained at levels of optimum efficiency. As a consequence, legal problems of a special character arise where farmers who hold tenanted land apply for set-aside, or participate in land management agreements under conservation legislation. A further difficulty arises in relation to diversification, in that the tenancy laws apply only if the substantial user of a holding remains *agricultural*.

Previously, there has been a tendency to place legislation into one of two compartments, as being concerned with 'agriculture' or 'conservation', and to treat the two as separate and distinct. In fact they are interdependent, and the failure of the legislature to reconcile agricultural and conservation objectives in much of the relevant legislation is the source of many of the problems explored in the contributions presented in this volume. The essays all impinge on land use, and in particular the problems of controlling agricultural activity in the interests of conservation and environmental protection. Nevertheless, they can usefully be grouped under three broad headings; those more directly concerned with agricultural issues, those primarily concerned with conservation; and those focusing specifically on issues of land management and land use.

Agriculture

Conservation is not solely about preserving the status quo in the countryside. It goes hand in hand with the need to encourage those who rely on agriculture for their livelihood to establish alternative business activities and sources of income. Public policy in encouraging diversification of farm enterprises and, in some cases, the taking of land out of production altogether, is of central importance to a study of conservation law and its practical implementation. Diversification of agriculture produces two broad areas of concern. It promotes conservation, in that it is aimed at reducing intensive agricultural production. Where diversification into non-agricultural businesses is promoted on a large scale, however, its effect could clearly be antipathetic to conservation in the countryside, were there not effective legal regulation to dictate the kinds of diversified businesses permissible and to control the manner in which they are carried on. This involves a consideration, for instance, of the terms of the Farm Diversification Grant Scheme 1987, and the nature of planning control over the conduct of diversified farm businesses.

Two of the essays included in this volume address different problems created by diversification. Michael Gregory examines the various ways in which diversification of agricultural businesses can be achieved, and the financial support available under current legislation for different categories of diversified business. The legal framework within which diversified farm enterprises must operate is also considered in detail. This involves a consideration, for instance, of planning control over changes in the use of agricultural land and buildings, and problems arising where the farmer seeking to take advantage of new opportunities is a tenant farmer, share farmer or partner in a farm partnership.

Allan Lennon, on the other hand, focuses on problems in implementing European Community requirements as to the set-aside of arable land in the United Kingdom. Set-aside is, of course, but one particular manifestation of diversification policy. He considers the United Kingdom set-aside scheme alongside that operated by other EC Member States, and examines its effectiveness in taking arable land out of production. Environmental control of set-aside land is also considered, as are the distinctive legal problems encountered by farmers and landowners setting land aside for non-agricultural uses.

Perhaps the most immediate concerns about the effect of agricultural activity upon the environment arise in relation to pollution problems posed by increasingly intensified farming practices. The modern trend towards greater indoor containment of animals and consequent slurry accumulation, use of silage as feed, and applications of pesticides and fertilizers to land, each have damaging consequences to the environment, and particularly the watercourses which provide the eventual conduit for many kinds of farm waste. The legal response to the resultant damage to the aquatic environment is considered in William Howarth's essay dealing with the applications of the Water Act 1989 to agricultural contexts. The essay describes the application of the traditional offence of causing or knowingly permitting water pollution and contrasts this with the recent development of preventative approaches towards water pollution control such as the designation of nitrate sensitive areas.

Conservation

Laws must be backed up by an appropriate allocation of administrative responsibilities for matters such as law enforcement if their objectives are to be realized. The division of these responsibilities has recently attracted a good deal of attention, and Fiona Reynolds and William Sheate provide an incisive account of the background to the administrative reorganization introduced under Part VII of the Environmental Protection Act 1990. The administrative changes which have been brought about include the establishment of the Nature Conservancy Councils for England and Scotland, the Countryside Council for Wales and the Joint Nature Conservation Committee. The authors provide a critical examination of the political and Parliamentary background to these developments and the controversies that are likely to surround their future operation.

The new conservation bodies will acquire responsibilities for conservation law enforcement from the Nature Conservancy Council and will inherit a body of important experience of law enforcement from the Council. Specifically, the experiences of the Council in enforcing the Wildlife and Countryside Act 1981 in respect of Sites of Special Scientific Interest are informatively recounted by David Withrington and Wyn Jones. The discussion of various case studies in which prosecutions under the 1981 Act were sought provides a useful study of the shortcomings in the legislation in practice and the vital importance of devising a rigorous procedure for the enforcement of conservation law if acquittals on technicalities are to be avoided.

Land Use

Changes in agriculture over recent years have generated a new climate for the operation of planning law in the countryside. Responses to environmental concerns have brought about greater regulation of farming activity than previously, and indications are that more extensive controls upon agriculture will be introduced in the near future. David Harte considers the delicate balance which must be drawn between allowing farmers the freedom which they need to produce food most efficiently, and the increasingly pressing demands of conservation requiring protection of the rural environment. His essay examines both the ways in which controls of development can prevent degradation of the environment, as well as those respects in which a positive approach to planning controls can produce an effective *enhancement* of rural areas.

The long-term management of farmland in accordance with conservation objectives is currently achieved largely through the use of management agreements, concluded by conservation bodies with individual farmers and landowners. Management agreements provide the vehicle by which the voluntary participation of landowners in conservation and environmental protection measures is achieved. Agreements are available under a variety of statutes, and in different situations and different areas, e.g. in Environmentally Sensitive Areas, Sites of Special Scientific Interest and Nitrate Sensitive Areas. Christopher Rodgers examines the legal requirements for the conclusion of management agreements under the different conservation statutes, and looks at problems created by the lack of a coherent or unified approach to the implementation of management agreements under the relevant legislation. As well as arguing for a more integrated approach to the implementation of conservation policy, some options for improving the effectiveness of land management agreements and removing the anomalies in the current law, are examined in some detail.

Certain categories of land pose special problems of conservation management, and this is particularly the case in relation to common land. The formulation and implementation of conservation policy over common land has to take account of the diverse, and unique, legal interests which can subsist over a registered common, and the unique management problems that can arise where a multiplicity of common rights subsist in the land concerned. John Aitchison and Gerry Gadsden examine the legal framework within which the various categories of recognized common rights subsist, and the special problems of implementing land management policy where commons are concerned. Problems of protecting common rights, and preventing the deregistration and subsequent exploitation of common land, are also considered.

In the final contribution Peter Wathern takes a step back from the detail of the law and examines the broader policy objectives and implications for rural law of European Community environmental policy. In particular, cause for concern is found in the operation of Community legislation dealing with Less Favoured and Environmentally Sensitive Areas in that these designations have facilitated a range of undesirable environmental consequences. Although some improvements are to be discerned in the recent operation of the Environmentally Sensitive Areas programme, the conclusion is that there is an unacceptable discrepancy between environmental and production subsidies available to farmers in rural areas.

No claim to comprehensiveness of coverage is made for the collection of topics that are included in this volume, since there are broad areas of concern on which only incidental discussion has been provided. Many of the contributions are unreservedly committed to particular views as to the way in which identified conflicts between agriculture and conservation should be resolved, and no editorial discretion has been exercised to moderate the expression of these opinions. An important object in compiling the collection is that contributors with special knowledge and expertise on these aspects of rural law should have the opportunity to present the issues, describe the law, raise criticisms and suggest improvements as they think fit. As such, the essays provide a penetrating collection of insights into the state of the law, and a varied evaluation of its adequacy, which will be of interest to lawyers, administrators, and to others concerned with the regulation of agriculture and the protection of rural environments. The hope of the editors is that *Agriculture, Conservation and Land Use* will place a focus upon some central issues of rural law and serve as a point of reference for future research and debate.

William Howarth and Christopher Rodgers

Centre for Law in Rural Areas,
University College of Wales, Aberystwyth

1

The Implementation of Agricultural Diversification

MICHAEL GREGORY

The Road to Diversification*

Historians will undoubtedly designate ours as an Age of Lunacy in Europe — an age when farmers grew food in vast quantities not to be eaten, but to be hoarded in intervention stores, whilst great famines raged and half the world was underfed; an age when officially hoarded food became so great that farmers were condemned as sinners for growing it; an age when our island race, with the experience of two world wars in which every acre of productive land was precious, encouraged farmers to squander agricultural land, and bribed them not to produce food.

It will also be recorded as an age when plenty of the farming community were found to have the acumen to adapt and succeed as able businessmen in non-farming ventures, but others had neither the will nor the ability to do so.

The so-called surpluses

It is not surprising that European politicians have come slowly to tackle what they conceive to be the surplus produced from the soil. On a broad view, there has not been overproduction. Arguably, perceived 'surplus' production was simply food in the wrong place — warehoused in stores set up by politicians under rules inhibiting its dispersal. What may puzzle many is why the European Commission sought to solve the overstoring, not by devising a policy of distribution, but by treating it as a problem of overproduction.

* The following abbreviations are used in this essay ADAS = Agricultural Development and Advisory Service; FWS = Farm Woodland Scheme; MAFF = Ministry of Agriculture Fisheries and Food; and 'the scheme' = the Farm Diversification and Grant Scheme 1987 (unless the context is to the contrary).

British farmers have now been encouraged, by precept and bounty, to grow less of the foods in surplus, either by changing the use of farm land, or by diminishing the production from it. Uncomely terms have come into use. It may be useful to attempt some definitions:

Diversification — taking land out of growing or rearing produce normally practised on the farm, and putting the land to an alternative use, either agricultural or non-agricultural.

Extensification — a reduction of the annual quantity per hectare of agricultural produce from a given area of land.

Set-aside — taking all or some of the arable land on a farm out of production for a significant period.

Enter the Milk Quota

One of the surpluses most embarrassing to the EC was the 'butter mountain'. On 2 April 1984 milk quotas were introduced for the UK, as required by EC regulations. A national quota was allocated to each member state. Each was left to devise its own system for regulating its industry so as to keep dairy produce within the national quota.[1]

The UK played its hand quite cleverly. In effect the struggling dairy farmer was put out of his agony by being paid to give up, and those who continued had quotas allocated based on their production in 1983 (though other years could be the yardstick in certain special cases). The regulations were not flexible enough to avoid hard cases and perplexities, but prophecies of doom proved largely unfounded. When the dust settled, the dairy industry had a good degree of stability and viability.

Cereal and livestock farmers awaited their turn, but the idea of repeating a compulsory quota system gave place to voluntary schemes — the troika of diversification, set-aside and extensification. Taking these in reverse order, there is but a pilot scheme for extensification; set-aside is the subject of a separate essay in this work; and diversification will now be examined in depth.

The Legislative Backdrop

Grants under the Agriculture Act 1970

Grants from the public purse for one agricultural thing or another have come and gone in the post-Second World War years. They are not given to farmers out of benevolence, but to manipulate the industry in

---

[1] The principal regulations at the time of writing are the Dairy Produce Quota Regulations 1989, SI 1989 No. 380. The current EC legislation expires on 31 March 1992, but milk quotas are expected to continue thereafter.

the way the government of the day conceives to be in the national interest, or to compensate for losses caused by government action or edict.

Until the 1980s UK farmers were officially encouraged to increase production year by year, and creditably succeeded in doing so. Grant-aid was offered to spur them to this success. The time then came for encouraging farming failure rather than farming efficiency. When the weather vane swung this way, there remained on the statute-book an instrument for cajoling farmers, with carrots, to do the will of governments. The Agriculture Act 1970 allowed capital grants to be paid, under government schemes, 'towards expenditure incurred or to be incurred for the purposes of, or in connection with, the carrying on or the establishment of an agricultural business'.

Extending grants to diversified enterprises

In 1986 another Agriculture Bill was finding its way through Parliament. Among its measures it gave the Ministry of Agriculture, Fisheries and Food (MAFF) scope to widen its activities by supplying services relating to the production of food, the conservation and enhancement of the countryside and 'any other agricultural activity or other enterprise of benefit to the rural community'. It was to do this by giving advice, information and training, undertaking research, testing substances and by certain other means, for which they could charge a fee if they wanted to. These powers were to become useful pieces in the jigsaw of the diversification pattern which later emerged.

During the passage of the bill, the Country Landowners' Association made alternative submissions for advancing the cause of diversification. They persuaded Lord Peel to table a new clause in the House of Lords widening the scope of grant-aid. Parliamentary draftsmen brushed up the wording and it is now section 22 of the Agriculture Act 1986. It amends the Agriculture Act 1970 by extending the meaning of 'an agricultural business' which can be grant-aided. It includes any other business, of a kind to be specified in a statutory instrument, carried on by a person also carrying on an agricultural business on the same, or adjoining land. Only an Act of Parliament can make a non-agricultural business an agricultural business.

The Agriculture Act 1986, therefore, laid the foundations for encouraging diversification into farm-related enterprises which were not really farming. Given this springboard, more legislation followed — statutory instruments specifying what 'other businesses' would count for grant-aid,[2] setting out the Farm Diversification Grant Scheme,[3] the Farm Woodland Scheme,[4] the Set-Aside

[2] The Farm Business Specification Order 1987, S1 1987 No.1948.
[3] The Farm Diversification Grant Scheme 1987, S1 1987 No.1949.
[4] The Farm Woodland Scheme 1988, S1 1988 No.1291.

Regulations,[5] and the Farm Land and Rural Development Act 1988. The importance of this 1988 Act was that it paved the way for making grants for expenditure of a non-capital nature in the cause of diversification. Under it grants are given for feasibility studies, marketing plans, and the promotion of diversified businesses.

The Farm Diversification Grant Scheme

A comprehensive package

The Farm Diversification Grant Scheme 1987[3] ('the scheme') is the principal instrument for encouraging farmers to take part of their farms out of agricultural production and use it for a non-agricultural business. It is not given to every farmer to have the skill or the will to carry on non-farming businesses. Those who enter the scheme move into laws, practices and strategies likely to be unfamiliar to them. There is wisdom in the scheme being, as MAFF justly calls it, 'a comprehensive package of assistance'. Public money should be invested in success, not 'lame ducks'. It is therefore common sense for the scheme to require applicants to undertake good research and preparation before businesses are assisted.

Criteria

Some golden principles can be discerned in the scheme. Applicants for grants must be genuine farmers; the diversified business must be non-agricultural but farm-related; it must be commercially viable and a quality business; it must be lawful, well planned and not harmful to wildlife or damaging to the environment or landscape; it must be destined to last at least five years.

The grants

An overriding requirement is that grants will not be made available for works started before they have been approved for grant. The numerous enterprises eligible for the scheme, and the works towards which grants may be made, are outlined in the scheme.

At the time of writing, the grants for feasibility studies are 50 per cent of the cost, to a maximum grant of £3,000, provided the cost is at least £500. Where the project is a joint enterprise by a group of farmers, the maximum grant is £10,000.

The other non-capital grant is for certain marketing costs during the first three years of the new enterprise. The rate is 40 per cent in the first

[5] The Set-Aside Regulations 1988, SI 1988 No.1352.

year, decreasing to 30 per cent in the second and 20 per cent in the third. The minimum grant is £250 a year. The maximum is £3,000 a year for individuals and £10,000 for groups of farmers.

The capital grants are at a rate of 25 per cent of the cost of qualifying works up to £35,000 of expenditure, provided at least £750 is invested. Farmers under forty years of age, with suitable qualifications, receive a higher rate at 31.25 per cent. Farm partnerships need all the partners to be under forty to qualify for this higher rate.

Eligibility for grant

First, an applicant must be eligible for the scheme. He or she must be actively engaged in agriculture or horticulture, and must have been for at least five years, or otherwise must hold a training certificate. The applicant will not qualify unless he is currently engaged in agricultural activities on the holding for at least 1100 hours a year. MAFF must be satisfied he derives more than half of his annual income from his agricultural business (including, if there is one, any diversified business of a kind recognized by the scheme). Fish farming does not count as an agricultural activity qualifying the operator for the scheme.

The application

Applications are made on the official MAFF form.[6] It asks pertinent questions to establish whether the applicant is eligible, and is the right person to apply. The right person is the one responsible for the day-to-day running of the farm business. The applicant will not be able to complete the form until a good deal of homework has been done.

The homework and study grants

Applicants are expected to undertake sufficient market research to assess whether the new project would give a good enough return to justify the expenditure. Even more to the point, the proposed enterprise must be legally possible. All necessary investigations have to be made to see there is no stumbling block that cannot be got over. Planning permission may be needed, for example, or a landlord's consent, or there may be a relevant restrictive covenant on the land. One of the first things an applicant must say to himself is, 'Where am I?' The diversification plan may be thwarted if the farm is in an area of special designation, such as an environmentally sensitive area, a site of

---

[6] MAFF supplies application forms with an explanatory booklet, 'New Opportunities in the Countryside. Capital Grants for Diversification' (amended edition, 1990).

special scientific interest, a national park, a nature reserve or the Broads.

General advice on a project can be obtained free of charge from an Agricultural Development and Advisory Service (ADAS) adviser. ADAS is a branch of MAFF. It will prepare a feasibility study for a fee. So will plenty of other consultants. To get a grant for the study,[7] the consultant used must be qualified to MAFF's satisfaction, and the study must include data under the following headings: market research and strategy; capital requirements; projected income and expenditure; labour; effect on the agricultural business; statutory requirements; the recommendation. The study must be specific to one eligible business activity, though it may examine a number of options within that business. For example, if the idea is to make and sell pottery, the study could consider garden gnomes as well.

The diversifications

The enterprises eligble for grant are wide-ranging and will not be comprehensively listed here. In a nutshell, they embrace processing of farm produce; craft manufacture and repair; retailing through farm shops, stalls and pick-your-own projects; tourist accommodation; catering; recreational and sporting facilities; equine activities; and educational endeavours concerned with farming and the countryside.

Expressly ruled out of the scheme are primary agricultural, horticultural and forestry operations, and services and leasing of equipment for them; treatment and bottling of liquid cow's milk; wine production; horse and pony breeding; accommodation for domestic animals (kennels, catteries and the like); long-term accommodation for humans; and certain sports which might unduly disturb the peace or the conscience.

Something of the variety of diversifications will be apparent from a closer consideration of these enterprises (below), indicating the works to which grants can be directed. Only a portion of the imaginative enterprises into which farmers diversify are indicated by the scheme. Some of the forward-looking diversified long before this government scheme came into being, and much is done without grant-aid. Typically of the UK, it might be noted that there is a members' association, society or advisory agency for almost every form of activity farmers may choose — from the well-known Regional Tourist Boards to the less well-known British Sheep Dairying Association and the British Snail Farmers' Association.

[7] MAFF has a separate application form for feasibility study and marketing grants and an explanatory booklet, 'New Opportunities in the Countryside. Feasibility and Marketing Grants for Farm Diversification'.

Processing farm products

Grants are payable towards permanent fixed equipment and machinery necessary for carrying out the enterprise. The business may be preparation of food for human consumption, such as yoghurt, farm cheeses, pies, butchered joints, fancy meats, bread or take-away meals. It could be combined with a catering line on the farmstead — tea bars, cafés or licensed premises for alcoholic drinks to be consumed with food. Again, permanent fixed equipment and machinery will be eligible for grant-aid, including major freezing facilities and bakery equipment. Processed agricultural products which are not supposed to be eaten, also qualify — woolly jumpers, perhaps, leather goods, or Hallowe'en lamps made from turnips.

Farm shops

Farmers are finding that farm shops, concentrating on quality foods, tend to pull in the customers. A tenant farmer, David Bowtell, with a successful shop at East Tisted in Hampshire, for example, avows that the only way to make a living today from 150 acres, is to retail the farm produce through an attractive shop. Equally the shop of the large Chatsworth estate in Derbyshire, giving an outlet for local farm produce of high quality, and foods not found in supermarkets, attracts customers from a wide catchment.

To qualify for grant-aid, the majority of the produce and wares sold in a farm shop must have been produced on the farm. It can include craft wares, for example, and tourist souvenirs. The items eligible for the grant are standard shop fixtures and fittings of a permanent nature, but not movables, like cash registers and dispensing machines. In January 1991 MAFF announced that the expected return on the investment in a farm shop was 39 per cent per annum.[8]

'Pick-your-own'

Pick-your-own is a cunning and popular form of retailing, in which the customer not only contributes free labour, but tends to get carried away with enthusiasm and purchases more than intended — though the odd strawberry does get popped straight into the mouth. Grants will be paid towards car parks, toilets, roads, paths, fencing and hardstandings. The project is usually well-suited for combination with other grant-attracting ventures, like cafés, ice cream booths and children's playgrounds. MAFF's expected return on investment in pick-your-own was stated to be 29 per cent per annum.[8]

[8] MAFF News Release, 15 January 1991.

Farm accommodation

After two years of the scheme, the Ministry decided that the return on providing tourist accommodation did not justify continuance in the scheme after 15 January 1991, except for bunkhouse barns and camping barns,[9] though feasibility study grants and grants for marketing would continue for all types of accommodation. No doubt this pruning was not unconcerned with the beady eye of the Chancellor of the Exchequer, but it appears short-sighted in view of the importance of the tourist industry.

Sport and recreation

This covers a multitude of outdoor and indoor physical activities — games played on pitches, tables, courts or courses, with balls kicked, hit or thrown, water sports, archery, martial arts, and gentler exercises such as walking in gardens or along nature trails, or sitting and munching in picnic sites. Angling is included, but not field sports, or any activity involving the use of motor vehicles, firearms, air weapons or crossbows.

Grants will be paid towards changing-rooms, ablutions, shelters, seating stands, preparation of ground and sites, fixed equipment, drainage, and much more, but not unfixed equipment like goalposts, cricket nets, marquees and kit.

Equestrian activities, stabling and livery qualify to an extent for the scheme, but pony trekking and hiring of mounts is restricted to Less Favoured Areas. The grants will be offered towards stabling and ancillary buildings, electricity supply, car parks, hard-standings and associated fencing.

Generally

Applicants must be 'green'. Additional grants will sometimes be payable for conservation and amenity works associated with qualifying diversifications, such as harmonious cladding, building materials traditional to the locality, and some amenity tree planting. Way-marking signs, and boards like 'Ye Farme Shoppe', will be grant-aided, and also some fees of professionals acting in an expert advisory or supervising capacity.

Once a new business has been grant-aided under the scheme, the farmer is to an extent locked into it. If he changes the use of the buildings or facilities for which a grant has been paid, or if he sells them within five years from the end of the approved plan, he may be liable to

[9] The change is implemented by the Farm Diversification Grant (Variation) Scheme 1991, SI 1991 No.2.

repay the grants. The amount to be repaid is on a sliding scale, from 100 per cent if it occurs in the first twelve months, to 20 per cent in the fifth year.

Legislation

Each category of diversified business will be regulated by primary and subordinate legislation (regulations) which the farmer will need to take into acount and comply with. The preliminary advice and feasibility studies should deal with it. For example, farmers will be familiar with some of the food laws, but retailing and catering brings into play laws concerned with hygiene, packaging, labelling, trade descriptions, health and safety at work, weights and measures, rating and town and country planning, to mention but some.

Marketing grants

These non-capital grants are for the engagement of suitably qualified personnel or agents employed for new marketing ventures. To attract grant there needs to be a three-year marketing plan, describing and estimating the quantity and value of the goods or services to be marketed or promoted, and specifying how the markets will be found and supplied. The grants will be towards the fees or salaries of the personnel and agents, and costs of design and printing of promotion material, but not travelling costs or advertising in the media.[7]

The Farm Woodland Scheme

An ambitious aspiration is to get farmers to diversify into planting woodlands. The Farm Woodland Scheme (FWS)[4] aims to persuade farmers to plant new woodlands, broad-leaved as well as conifers, on productive agricultural land.

It can only be supposed it would need more than faith, hope and charity to see the tree take over from the barley to any extent, and the FWS is notably tentative. The total that can be approved for planting in the UK is 36,000 hectares. The take-up has been disappointing, and at one time it was thought the Minister might be singing in his bath, 'I think that I shall never see/A poem lovely as a tree.'[10] The scheme was introduced on 1 October 1988. After the first two years no more than 12,000 of the 36,000 hectares had been taken up, and the FWS is currently under review. About 75 per cent of the approved plantings is for broad-leaved woodlands. This is good from the environmental point of view, and, significantly, it also suits shooting.

[10] Joyce Kilmer (1888–1918). The song concludes, 'Poems are made by fools like me/But only God can make a tree'.

The grants

To a farmer used to an annual harvest, the drawback in planting woodlands is that no return can be expected for a good number of years (when thinnings may be exploited) and even then it might hardly be worth waiting for. The FWS grants are meant to abate the farmer's loss of income during that period. Currently the rate of grant is £190 per hectare per annum in lowlands, £150 in Disadvantaged Areas and £100 in Severely Disadvantaged Areas.

The land planted

The maximum area that may be planted under the FWS is 40 ha. The minimum is 3 ha. With the object of preventing applicants selecting the unproductive corners of their farms for planting the trees, the FWS requires the planting to take place in blocks of at least 1 ha, on land that has been arable since before 31 December 1987, or has been improved grassland for the same period. As an exception, planting is allowed on unimproved land in Less Favoured Areas, though at a lower rate of grant. As permanent pasture cannot be utilized, the FWS virtually excludes England's West Country.

Period of grant-aid

The grants are for differing periods according to the type of tree planted. They are for as much as forty years for pure oak and beech, and for as little as ten years for coppice. The participant will need confidence that the FWS will continue for the time promised, and that the payments will be frequently revised to keep up their value. He is certainly being asked to put his trust in princes.

Forestry Commission's role

The Forestry Commission exercises some control. The applicant must agree a plan of operations with the Commission, and FWS grants are conditional upon the applicant receiving, in addition, planting grants.[11] If the participant fails to comply with the arrangements agreed with the Commission, the FWS grants will cease. Grants already paid may be recovered, depending on the circumstances of the failure.

Tenants

Tenant farmers are eligible for the FWS, though it is difficult to imagine tenants investing in such a long-term enterprise, unless the tenancy is

[11] Details of planting grants are obtainable from Forestry Commission, 23 Corstorphine Road, Edinburgh EH12 7AT.

under a family arrangement, or the tenant is virtually the owner (e.g. under a long lease, or where the tenant is the owner's company). The perils of the tenant being in breach of tenancy are obviated by the FWS requiring tenants to obtain consent from their landlords for their participation.

The Business Medium

The solitary reaper syndrome

Whilst joint enterprise has been a feature of commerce and the professions for centuries, the farmer has tended to 'plough his furrow alone'[12] and fairly imitate Wordsworth's 'Solitary Reaper'. He has favoured sole control. Equally the sole responsibility and liability is his in the event of debts, difficulties and disasters. Moving out of the furrow into a brave new world of diversification, it is worth considering whether there are not advantages in combined operations. In individual cases tax planning considerations may deter change and unscrambling existing arrangements may be too difficult, but the conception of a new business activity gives an opportunity to stand back and consider what business medium to employ.

Limited companies

Trading by means of a limited company enables the farmer to limit his business liability. It also gives an opportunity to bring into the enterprise others who may invest in it and contribute knowledge and experience of non-agricultural businesses the farmer may lack. The company will make its profits or losses, as the case may be, as a legal body separate from its shareholders and directors. They will derive their income by directors' fees and dividends.

Grants are obtainable for corporate bodies under the Farm Diversification Grant Scheme,[3] provided the diversified business is not run as a company separate from the farm business. The general drawbacks of a company can be lived with, namely compliance with the paperwork and other requirements of the Companies Acts,[13] and some loss of privacy due to information about the company being open to public inspection on the companies register.

Partnerships

A partnership does not offer the safeguards against liability to be found in a company.[14] Unlike a company, a partnership in England and

[12] Earl of Rosebery (1847–1929), 'I must plough my furrow alone' (speech on 19 July 1901).
[13] The main legislation is the Companies Act 1985.
[14] Partnerships are still governed by the venerable Partnership Act 1890.

Wales (it is otherwise in Scotland) is not a legal entity of its own, distinct from the partners. Partners share the profits and losses of the firm in accordance with the partnership deed. In dealings with the outside world any one partner can be sued for the whole of a partnership debt, and there is joint and several liability between the partners for any torts (wrongdoings) of the firm. There is an exception for limited partners. They are 'sleeping partners', merely investors in the partnership. Provided they stay asleep, taking no part in the affairs of the firm, their liability will be limited to their investment.[15]

Partners can obtain grants under the Diversification Scheme, through the partner responsible for the day-to-day running of the farm. Farming partnerships are most commonly family arrangements.

Share farming[16]

A share farming agreement is not a partnership. It is a joint enterprise in which the parties retain their separate businesses, contribute inputs as agreed between them, and share, not profits and losses, but gross output. Share farmers are eligible for the Diversification Grant Scheme. MAFF requires that if one party is the landowner and the other works the farm (the typical case), they must agree in writing to continue for seven years.

Tenancies

The farm tenant can obtain grants under the scheme, but as he is occupying another person's land under a contract to farm it, and, as agricultural holdings are governed by special legislation,[17] diversification throws up important and interesting points deserving separate treatment.

Farm Tenants and Diversification

The tenancy contract

An agricultural tenancy is a contract. The land is let by the owner to a tenant who agrees to farm it. In all likelihood it will be a tenancy from year to year, protected and governed by the Agricultural Holdings Act 1986 ('the 1986 Act'). The 1986 Act gives the tenant security of tenure, virtually for life, and allows him freedom to crop the arable land as he likes except possibly in the last year of the tenancy. If the tenant persists in breaches of tenancy, and, in particular, if he is guilty of bad husbandry, there can be dire consequences for his security and his

[15] Limited Partnerships Act 1907.

[16] The main thing to know about the law of share farming is that there is not any.

[17] The main legislation is the Agricultural Holdings Act 1986.

pocket. The 1986 Act incorporates Rules of Good Husbandry[18] which it uses as a yardstick.

Alternative crops

Diversification by growing unfamiliar crops on the arable land — say, evening primrose or fenugreek — would not be a breach of tenancy, no matter what the tenancy agreement says about cropping, except that any cropping provision in the agreement must be complied with in the last year of the tenancy.[19] Where a tenant considers growing alternative crops, however, he must have regard to good husbandry and the well-being of the holding.[20] The 1986 Act provides that if the tenant exercises his right of freedom of cropping 'in such a manner as to, or to be likely to, injure or deteriorate the holding', the landlord has the right, if the case so requires, to obtain an injunction to stop it, and to recover damages at the end of the tenancy.[21]

Grassland

The tenant does not have the same freedom as regards grassland. The 1986 Act states what may be thought obvious, that the arable land for which the tenant has freedom of cropping 'does not include land in grass which, by the terms of a contract of tenancy, is to be retained in the same condition throughout the tenancy'.[22] Tenancy agreements are sometimes encountered which require the holding to be farmed as a dairy farm, or stock rearing farm, and contain restrictions on ploughing up grassland. The tenant can go to arbitration asking for the area he is required to maintain as permanent pasture to be reduced, but this can only be done where 'it is expedient in order to secure the full and efficient farming of the holding'.[23] The wording of the tenancy agreement is therefore crucial where a tenant has alternative plans for the grassland. The landlord's consent may be needed.

Non-agricultural diversification

Diversification by putting some or all of the agricultural land to a non-agricultural use, without the consent of the landlord, would, unless the tenancy expressly allowed it, be a breach of tenancy. Even if it is not stated, it is an implied term at common law that the farm tenant shall farm the land to a good standard of husbandry.

[18] The Rules of Good Husbandry are set out in the Agriculture Act 1947, s.11.
[19] Agricultural Holdings Act 1986, s.15(2).
[20] Ibid. s.15(4).
[21] Ibid. s.15(5).
[22] Ibid. s.15(7).
[23] Ibid. s.14(2).

The rules of good husbandry

The Rules of Good Husbandry[18] have no fear for the good farm tenant, until he plans to diversify into something non-agricultural. They start with a general rule:

> the occupier of an agricultural unit shall be deemed to fulfil his responsibilities to farm it in accordance with the rules of good husbandry in so far as the extent to which and the manner in which the unit is being farmed (as respects both the kind of operations carried out and the way they are carried out) is such that, having regard to the character and situation of the unit, the standard of management thereof by the owner and other relevant circumstances, the occupier is maintaining a reasonable standard of efficient production, as respects both the kind of produce and the quality and quantity thereof, while keeping the unit in a condition to enable such a standard to be maintained in the future.

The rules go on to set out particular tests for determining whether the unit is being farmed in this way. There is no need to give them here. It will be seen from the general rule that taking productive land out of production to any significant extent is bound to be against the rules, unless it is for a good agricultural reason (e.g. temporary fallow, or the eradication of disease).

The consequences of failing to comply with the Rules of Good Husbandry are that it may lead to the tenancy being ended by a notice to quit from the landlord. The tenant will lose his security of tenure if the landlord obtains a certificate of bad husbandry from the Agricultural Land Tribunal,[24] or if the failure to comply with the rules results in the landlord's interest in the holding being 'materially prejudiced'.[25] Another possible misfortune is that the tenant may receive from his landlord a notice to remedy his breaches of tenancy. Failure to comply with a valid notice to remedy would give grounds for terminating the tenancy.[26]

Co-operation of the landlord

It can be seen that the landlord's consent will be needed for a non-agricultural diversification project by the tenant on the agricultural land, unless it is already envisaged in the tenancy agreement. Should the owner want the land to continue in farming, and gentle persuasion does not alter his mind, the tenant proceeds with the diversification at his peril.

[24] Agricultural Holdings Act 1986, Sched.3, Case C.
[25] Ibid. Sched.3, Case E.
[26] Sched.3, Case D. Note the ramifications in s.28.

It would appear that tenants have rarely been unreasonably frustrated by landlords. A well-conceived diversification may be the best course for the occupier of the farm, and what is best for the tenant will often be best for the landlord. A landlord does not want a tenant on the breadline, struggling to make ends meet, neglecting the maintenance of the land and buildings, always late with his rent. A prosperous tenant is good for the farm, a penurious tenant bad for it. The prudent landlord will weigh up the situation carefully. Is the project wild, reckless, a gamble? Or is it likely to be profitable for the occupier? Would it benefit both landlord and tenant to carry out a new business on the holding as a joint enterprise? There are undoubtedly instances where a joint venture between landlord and tenant is the ideal solution.

As mentioned above, a tenant applying for the Farm Woodland Scheme requires his landlord's consent. There is no such requirement for the Farm Diversification Grant Scheme, but tenants are warned in MAFF's brochure to consult their landlords. It would be a better safeguard for tenants if the application form required the tenant to state whether his landlord consented.

Will the 1986 Act still apply?

A degree of non-agricultural business on a let farm does not necessarily take the tenancy outside the protection and governance of the Agricultural Holdings Act 1986. The 1986 Act applies to 'agricultural holdings'. The definition of 'agricultural holding' in the Act envisages that it can include non-agricultural land. It starts by stating it 'means the aggregate of the land (whether agricultural or not) comprised in a contract for an agricultural tenancy . . .' To get the full meaning it is necessary to examine the definitions of some of its ingredients. It is then apparent that if the land is let to be used for agriculture as a business, any parts of the holding not so used will not deprive it of its status as an agricultural holding, so long as the non-agricultural parts 'do not substantially affect the character of the tenancy'.[27]

Before the 1986 Act replaced the previous statutory definition with a more elaborate version, courts employed the 'predominant user' test. They also held that the land in the tenancy was *all* an agricultural holding, or all not. Where the use was predominantly agricultural, it was an agricultural holding, including the non-agricultural parts.[28] The intention was to give effect to the predominant user test in the 1986 definition, though the intention has not been entirely fulfilled. Even so the courts are likely to follow a similar line as before. A substantial

[27] The definition of 'agricultural holding' and of the ingredients referred to are in s.1. Other definitions can be found in s.96.

[28] *Howkins* v. *Jardine* [1951] 1 KB 614 shed light on these points.

change away from the agricultural character of the holding, by a diversification, acquiesced in by the landlord, would take the holding outside the Act.

The decision in the leading case of *Short* v. *Greeves*[29] in 1988 illustrates that an agricultural holding does not readily lose its character when diversified enterprises are carried out on it. In that case the financial turnover from garden equipment and knick-knacks sold from a garden centre — gnomes, seats, hanging baskets, sheds etc. — exceeded that of agricultural and horticultural products grown on the holding. The court held that the character of the premises remained substantially agricultural and the holding was still subject to the 1986 Act.

Although one of the national bodies has advocated it, it is nonsensical to apply the 1986 Act when the land is no longer substantially agricultural in character. It is impracticable. The Act is about agriculture and husbandry. The parties could not carry out their obligations if husbandry was not practised on the land. The question must again be asked: how could a tenant keep to the Rules of Good Husbandry if the land was no longer farmed?

Business premises code

It is also pointless, where the tenant by agreement changes the character of the holding from agricultural to non-agricultural use, to carry on under a tenancy agreement fashioned for an agricultural holding. The sensible thing is for the parties to enter into a new agreement tailored for the new enterprise. The business premises code in Part II of the Landlord and Tenant Act 1954 ('the 1954 Act') is likely to come into play. The code does not apply to agricultural holdings, but it does apply to most other tenancies 'where the property comprised in the tenancy is or includes premises which are so occupied for the purposes of a business carried on by him or for those and other purposes'.

An important difference between the business premises code in the 1954 Act and the agricultural holdings code in the 1986 Act, is that the parties can contract out of the 1954 Act entirely, subject only to the leave of the court.

Where the business premises code applies, the tenant has a right to claim a new lease when the tenancy is terminated. If he claims a new lease, the landlord can resist it only by proving one of the statutory grounds in the Act — for example, that the tenant has been a bad tenant, or that the landlord requires the premises for his own business purposes or as his residence.

[29] [1988] 1 EGLR 1 (CA). See also (1988) 137 NLJ 329 (Wilkinson); and (1988) Conv. 430 (Rodgers).

Tenant's fixtures and improvements

Where the land remains an agricultural holding the tenant will have the right to remove tenant's fixtures. The right of removal extends to both agricultural and non-agricultural fixtures. In outline the law provides that any engine, machinery, fencing or other fixture of whatever description affixed to the holding by the tenant, and any building erected by him, remains his property and may be removed during or at the end of the tenancy, provided it was not installed as a term of the tenancy. Before removing fixtures the tenant must have paid all rent due, fulfilled his other tenancy duties and given the landlord an opportunity to purchase the fixtures concerned.[30]

These rules give the tenant farmer confidence that he can go ahead with capital investment in a diversified business, in the knowledge that if the tenancy ends he will not have to gift his fixed equipment to the landlord. A more difficult question is whether he could claim compensation at the end of the tenancy under the 1986 Act for tenant's improvements carried out for a non-agricultural business on the holding.

It is open to landlord and tenant to come to their own agreement about improvements and compensation for the tenant. On this score they *can* contract out of the Agricultural Holdings Act 1986. Where it is left to the Act, the tenant is entitled to compensation at the end of the tenancy willy-nilly for certain improvements listed in the 1986 Act, all of which are farming operations.[31] The Act also lists other improvements for which tenants are only entitled to compensation if they are carried out with the written consent of the landlord.[32] There is yet another list for which the tenant can claim compensation if they are carried out either with the landlord's consent, or with the approval of the Agricultural Land Tribunal.[33]

Although most of the improvements in these lists are entirely agricultural, there are some which might feature in a diversified non-farming project. A few examples are 'making gardens', 'erection, alteration or enlargement of buildings', 'erection or construction of loading platforms, ramps, or hard standings for vehicles', 'making improvements of roads or bridges'.

Undoubtedly the 1986 Act allows the tenant to claim for such improvements done in connection with a diversified business on an agricultural holding, but it is arguable that the measure of compensation set out in the Act would entitle him to little or none. The Act states that the compensation 'shall be an amount equal to the increase

[30] Agricultural Holdings Act 1986, s.10.
[31] Ibid. Sched.8.
[32] Ibid. Sched.7, Part I.
[33] Ibid. Sched.7, Part II.

attributable to the improvement in the value of the agricultural holding as a holding, having regard to the character and situation of the holding *and the average requirements of tenants reasonably skilled in husbandry*'.[34]

There is no undue difficulty in assessing the compensation for improvements which enhance farming efficiency — but does, say, an athletics stadium, or a war games battleground, meet any requirements of a tenant skilled in husbandry? If improvements of this kind are more profitable than farming, they will have value for any tenant capable of exploiting them, but the words 'reasonably skilled in husbandry' are there in the section and must be accorded significance.

The moral is that landlord and tenant would do well to come to a thoroughgoing new agreement for any diversification on the holding, dealing with the improvements to be carried out. It may also need to provide for rent reviews.

The rent

An advantage of having a new and, if necessary, separate lease for the diversified business, is that the parties can agree an appropriate formula for rent reviews. Otherwise — assuming the holding remains subject to the Agricultural Holdings Act 1986 — they will have to make do with a statutory formula designed for agriculture.

Under the 1986 Act either party can, at no more than three-yearly intervals, ask an arbitrator to settle 'the rent properly payable' for the holding. A wordy formula is set out by which the arbitrator is to make his assessment.[35] It states 'The rent properly payable . . . shall be the rent at which the holding might reasonably be expected to be let by a prudent and willing landlord to a prudent and willing tenant.' In calculating this the arbitrator is told to take into account 'all relevant factors' and certain particular factors set out in the formula.

The particular factors are not much help where the tenant carries on one or more non-agricultural businesses on the holding. In truth they are not much help when he does not. Aribtrators do not need to be told what factors to take into account in assessing rents. The attempt to do so has given lawyers 'field days' (sometimes eight or nine) at arbitrations which, under the pre-1984 short formula, rarely took more than a few hours in addition to a visit to the farm.

The factors in the present formula are the terms of the tenancy, the character and situation of the holding, and 'the productive capacity of the holding and its related earning capacity, and the current level of rents for comparable holdings'. 'Productive capacity' and 'related earning capacity' are then defined. As the definitions refer to 'a

[34] Ibid s.66.
[35] Ibid. Sched.2.

competent tenant practising a system of farming suitable to the holding', it has been questioned whether the earning capacity from non-farming enterprises should be taken into account in assessing the rent of the holding.

The question indicates the foolishness of statutes trying to tell rent arbitrators how to do the job for which they are trained. The earning capacity of the land from any source reasonably available to the tenant, agricultural or otherwise, is clearly a 'relevant factor', and is no less so because the Act tries to spell out the agricultural potential to be taken into account. Monies paid to the occupier, whether under a grant-aid scheme, or out of the pockets of customers, are relevant so long as they enhance the rental value of the holding to a hypothetical prudent and willing tenant. This is not unfair, because an increase in rental value is not to be taken into account in the rent if it is due to tenant's improvements or fixtures.[36]

Where the earning capacity of the holding is enhanced solely by the tenant spending money (with or without grand-aid) on, say, buildings, car parks, new accesses and tennis courts, for a diversified project, the landlord is not entitled on a rent review to claim part of the takings as rent. At the same time, the rental value reflects the potential of the holding, and if planning permission has been granted for a valuable change of use, and if goodwill attaches to the holding by reason of its use, these factors may affect the rent property payable.

Succession tenancies

On the death, or the retirement at age 65 or later, of the tenant of an agricultural holding, a close relative can obtain, under the 1986 Act,[37] a tenancy of the holding in succession to the deceased or retired tenant, provided he or she is an 'eligible person'. To be eligible the close relative has to be within certain degrees of kindred, must not be the occupier of a commercial holding elsewhere, and must satisfy a 'principal source of livelihood' test.

There is no statutory succession to other types of business tenancy, and so, when a farm ceases to be an agricultural holding upon the tenant diversifying, the succession chances of close relatives also cease.

Tenants' families clearly need to plan for succession, if they can, where the tenanted land remains an agricultural holding after diversification.[38] To be eligible under the principal source of livelihood test, referred to above, an applicant for a succession tenancy must show that in five out of the seven years immediately before the death or

[36] Ibid. Sched.2, para.2.

[37] The succession tenancy provisions in all their complexity are in ibid. Part IV and Sched.6.

[38] See (1990) Sol. Jo. 1032 (H. Hargreave).

retirement of the tenant, he derived his only or principal source of livelihood 'from his agricultural work on the holding or on an agricultural work on the holding or on an agricultural unit of which the holding forms part'.

If, therefore, the tenant hopes that a son working with him will get a succession tenancy, it may be important to see that the son's main income from the business is for agricultural work, and not from work on a non-agricultural side of the enterprise. There is scope for a little flexibility. The 'principal source of livelihood' test is not an absolute rule. The Tribunal which decides on eligibility is given a discretion to treat a close relative as eligible, even if the test is not fully met, provided it 'is satisfied to a material extent'.[39]

Planning and Other Permissions

Development permission

A diversification to a non-agricultural use of land will bring the farmer within the ambit of the planning legislation. Planning permission is required under the Town and Country Planning Act 1990 for 'development', including 'any material change of use', unless it is exempted by the General Development Order.[40]

The *use* of land or buildings for the purposes of agriculture or forestry is excepted from the definition of development. Nevertheless, it is unlikely that the farmer will be encountering the planners for the first time when he proposes a diversification. Getting planning permission is one of the key requirements in a diversification. Its implications are merely touched on here, as the operation of the planning laws is the subject of a separate essay in this work.

The importance of preliminary studies by the prospective diversifier has already been emphasized. One of the first steps will be to consider whether planning permission can be obtained where it is needed. Informal discussions with the planning officer before an application is made, and with the parish council — they will be consulted — will be time well spent.

The planning role

For their part, the planners must recognize the changes with which the farming community are trying to live, the policies of the EC and the UK in encouraging diversification, the need of farmers to make a livelihood, and the ways in which the public can be served by new rural

[39] Ibid s.41.
[40] Currently the Town and Country Planning (General Development) Order 1988, SI 1988 No.1813. On planning law generally see Ch. 6 below.

enterprises. For too long planning authorities appeared to conceive their role as preventing changes in the countryside. Planning, however, must be positive, enabling things to happen. Fortunately this is now largely recognized.

An illustration — creating a fishery

The regulatory edicts into which the diversifier is likely to run will usually be more than the town and country planning laws. This is one reason why feasibility studies are essential. As an illustration, let us take the case of a farmer who conceives the idea of creating a fishing lake on his land. He will need sundry kinds of consents, and will have to comply with a number of statutory requirements.

Because the construction of the lake will involve 'engineering works', planning permission will be required. It may also be required for other features in the plan, such as a fishing hut and drying room for anglers. An impounding licence from the National Rivers Authority (NRA) will be needed before the lake is constructed.[41] When the lake has been created and is ready for stocking, consent from the NRA will be required to introduce fish or spawn into it,[42] and will be needed every time there is stocking. Once stocked, no angler could lawfully fish there without a licence from the NRA, unless a general licence for the fishery was obtained.[43] There will be by-laws to be observed in constructing the lake, and fishery by-laws in fishing it. If the lake is a large one, the onerous provisions of the Reservoirs Acts will have to be complied with and an official certificate held under these Acts. The fishery may also be rated.

Occupiers' Liability

The countryside is full of hazards, with plenty for the visitor to fall over, into or off, get stuck in, or have fall on him. What if customers invited to take part in war games, or orienteering, or to walk a nature trail, have mishaps?

The Occupiers' Liability Act 1957 imposes on the occupier of premises a 'common duty of care' owed to visitors. It falls far short of an absolute responsibility for their safety. It is 'a duty to take such care as in all the circumstances of the case is reasonable to see that the visitor shall be reasonably safe in using the premises for the purposes for which he is invited or permitted by the occupier to be there'.

The duty may be restricted, modified or even excluded by agreement, but where there is 'business liability' the Unfair Contract Terms Act

---

[41] Water Resources Act 1963, s.36.
[42] Salmon and Freshwater Fisheries Act 1975, s.30.
[43] Ibid. s.25.

1977 steps in to stop the businessman saying to his paying customers 'enter at your own risk'. He may not contract out of liability for death or personal injury caused by his own negligence. Contracting out of liability for other sorts of loss or damage will only be effective if it is 'fair and reasonable' in the circumstances.

The occupier should give adequate warning of at least the less obvious dangers to which visitors have access, and greater care is expected where children are allowed on the land. The Occupiers' Liability Act 1984 expressly permits the occupier to say 'enter at your own risk' to visitors going on to the premises for recreational or educational purposes, but here again this exclusion of liability does not apply if the access to the land 'falls within the business purposes of the occupier'. Much turns therefore on whether the visitor is a paying customer.

Rating and Community Charges

Land is a rateable hereditament, but by the Local Government Finance Act 1988 ('the 1988 Act') agricultural land and agricultural buildings are exempt from rating.[44] The farmer diversifying out of agriculture is likely to be diversifying into rating, unless it is for planting trees. Rating liability is therefore one of the important factors to weigh in the balance when making a feasibility study. The definition of 'agricultural land' in the 1988 Act[45] includes 'land used for a plantation or a wood or for the growth of saleable underwood'.

The definition does not include

land occupied together with a house as a park
gardens (other than market gardens)
pleasure grounds
land used mainly or exclusively for purposes of sport or recreation
land used as a racecourse

and so they may be rated.

Some forms of diversification raise special rating considerations.

Tourist accommodation

Domestic rating was abolished by the 1988 Act when the community charge was introduced. Business rating is retained. These reforms were so inadequately thought out that the Government is making frequent changes. Anything written here could become rapidly out of date, especially as regards holiday accommodation.

[44] Local Government Finance Act 1988, s.51 and Sched.5, para.1
[45] Ibid. Sched.5, para.2.

The personal community charge is the 'poll tax, every adult (except exempt persons) has to pay as a personal tax, unrelated to his or her dwelling. The standard community charge is different and often more onerous. It is payable on dwellings which are nobody's sole or main residence. The local authority fixes the amount, subject to the Secretary of State putting a ceiling on particular categories of dwelling. It can be up to twice the poll tax.

At the time of writing, cottages and chalets let for holidays will be rated if the letting to holiday makers is for at least 140 days in the year. They will be subject to the standard community charge (probably twice the poll tax for the district) if let for less than 140 days.

Occupied farm houses, being the sole or main residence of the farmer, are subject to neither rating nor the standard community charge, but may be partly rated if a business is carried on in them. If it is bed and breakfast, under a new rule from 1 April 1991 the bed and breakfast accommodation will not be rated so long as it is offered to no more than six persons.

Fish farms

Fish farming is not eligible for diversification grants, but it is a common form of diversification. Land and buildings 'used solely for or in connection with fish farming' are exempt from rating, whether the fish are reared for direct human consumption or for stocking fisheries.[46]

Studs and stables

In 1988 the House of Lords, hearing an appeal, caused something of a stir by holding that stables, studs and associated buildings were not agricultural and were therefore rateable, though the pastures on which the horses grazed were exempt agricultural land.[47] The impact of this decision has been mitigated for farmers diversifying into equine activities by an Order exempting from rates the first £2,500 of the rateable value of buildings used wholly or in part for the breeding or rearing of horses and ponies, provided the buildings are occupied together with agricultural land or buildings.[48]

Sporting rights

Sporting rights are rateable only when 'severed from the occupation of the land on which the right is exercisable'.[49] Whether they are severed

[46] Ibid. Sched.5, para.9.
[47] *Hemens v. Whitsbury Farm and Stud Ltd* [1988] 1 All ER 72.
[48] The Non-Domestic Rating (Stud Farms) Order 1989, SI 1989 No.2331.
[49] Local Government Finance Act 1988, s.64(4)(d).

turns on legal technicalities, one of which is that the letting of sporting rights by the landowner does not sever them from the occupation of the land, unless the letting is by deed. Rating is therefore frequently avoidable if the farmer wishes to exploit fishing or shooting rights. If the sporting rights are not rateable, they may enhance the rateable value of the land, but it does not arise where the land, or land covered by water, is agricultural land, because agricultural land is exempt from rating.[44]

Bee keeping

A final sweet note. A building used solely in connection with the keeping of bees counts as an agricultural building exempt from rating.[50]

L'Envoi

Farm diversification fits the mode of the times. The working population in the UK is gaining more leisure time, tends to retire at an earlier age than heretofore and lives longer. Town folk look increasingly to the countryside to be their playground, and they expect country folk to conserve its amenities. The countryside is not a museum. It would advantage nobody if it were preserved as such. It lives. It is inhabited. It is inhabited by people who love it and make their livelihood there. It is becoming harder for farmers to make a livelihood from the land. By their enterprise they can provide not only food, but also opportunities for recreation. A happy advance in diversification is becoming manifest, in that it is being recognized that farmers can serve the cause of conservation, and achieve income for themselves, by making it their business to provide environmental services to the public.

---

[50] Local Government Finance Act 1988, Sched.5, para.6.

2

Set-aside of Agricultural Land: policy, practice and problems

ALLAN A. LENNON

Introduction

The farmers of Great Britain have to date stood up as unflinchingly to the vagaries of politicians as they have done to the uncertainties of the British climate. Since 1939 the British farmer has found himself, in turn, exhorted to produce as much as the land could stand to save the country from famine during the Second World War; exposed to competition thereafter; incited by scientists and merchants of agro-chemicals to get ever better production out of his soil by the use of new chemicals and seeds; criticized for doing so by those keen on nature conservancy and environmentalists; exhorted yet again to produce less and by more natural means; first of all cocooned by the Common Agricultural Policy with the normal subsidies, producing the normal surpluses, and then when these have grown too great and become too expensive attacked yet again. His livelihood is threatened and he is exhorted to reduce the amount of his land used for cereal production. Add to this the problems arising out of the present round of GATT talks, where the subvention of Community farmers puts in danger the entire world trade equilibrium, and consider just for a moment the never-ending threats of famine to a great proportion of our world at a time when other sectors of it are actually encouraging farmers to produce less, and you have (paraphrasing Shakespeare) 'stuff such as nightmares are made of'.

It is in this context that one has to look at the 'set-aside' regulations of the EC.[1] The principal aim of the Community regulations is to lay down detailed rules for applying the set-aside incentive scheme for arable land. Basically the scheme provides for the voluntary taking out of arable production by farmers (whether owners or tenants), for a

---

[1] Commission Regulation (EEC) No.1272/88 of 29 April 1988.

period of five years, of land being of no less than one hectare per holding and an area which must represent at least 20 per cent of the arable land on the holding at the time the application for aid is submitted. The land which has so been set-aside may be left fallow either permanently or in a rotation system, or used for extensive (as opposed to intensive) grazing; it may be used for planting woodland or it may be used for non-agricultural purposes. The land may also be used for growing lentils, chickpeas or vetch, but in this case (as also where there is extensive stock grazing) there must be a reduction of aid by 40 to 60 per cent. Generally speaking, the aid given to the farmers who participate in this scheme as originally laid down could vary between 100 and 600 ECUs. The aim is to compensate the farmer for the loss he would be making by not growing cereals upon that land.

Since this is only a beginning, there is also under consideration the question of taking land out of production permanently with suitable compensation — as is the possibility of growing industrial agricultural products on land taken out of agricultural production.

As is usual with EC directives, member states are left with a great deal of autonomy as to how to apply the mandatory portions of the regulations and how, if at all, to phase in the various permissible uses etc. Thus the United Kingdom, for instance, in the first two years when the scheme became applicable here, did not allow any extensive grazing and only brought in this provision in 1990/1. The UK continues to make no provision for the growing of lentils, chickpeas or vetch.

The United Kingdom is one of the first countries within the Community to bring in its own regulations as to set-aside to implement the Community policy.

The Area

As at June 1988 the total area of agricultural land in the UK was 18.6 million ha, some 77 per cent of the total land area of the UK. Excluding minor holdings, there were 252,000 holdings. The average total area per holding was 105 acres. Of these holdings, 95,100, occupying 3,893,000 ha, were devoted to cereals (excluding maize).

Finance

Approximately £11 million had been allocated for payments for set-aside for 1988/9, the first year of the scheme. Payments are made annually in arrears. Feoga reimbursement (from the European Agricultural Guidance and Guarantee Fund) is set by the EC rules at 50 per cent for the first £140 per hectare per annum; 25 per cent for payments between £140 and £280, and 15 per cent for payments between £280 and £240. For the UK this meant reimbursement of 125 ECUs (£83) per hectare per annum, or 42 per cent of UK expenditure.

Administrative function

Central government in the person of the Minister of Agriculture, Fisheries and Food, and civil servants of his Ministry acting on his behalf, decide policy in relation to the implementation and administration of set-aside in England. Policy and administration for Wales, Scotland and Northern Ireland are decided by the respective agriculture departments for those countries in consultation with the Ministry of Agriculture, Fisheries and Food (MAFF).

Day-to-day administration of the scheme, including the distribution and processing of applications and claim forms and arrangements for payment of claims, is carried out by the Ministry's nineteen divisional offices in England in consultation with the five regional offices and MAFF, as necessary, with similar arrangements operating in Wales, Scotland and Northern Ireland.

There are two principal sets of regulations to implement Community policy and restrict the production of cereal crops on arable land, namely the Set-Aside Regulations 1988[2] and the Set-Aside (Amendment) Regulations 1990.[3] These regulations, which apply to Great Britain, provide for payment of aid to farmers who undertake for a period of five years ('the set-aside period') to withdraw from agricultural production an area of land equal in size to at least 20 per cent of the area of land on the holding[4] used in the reference period (period commencing 1 July 1987 and ending 30 June 1988)[5] for producing 'relevant' arable crops.[6] Relevant crops include the following: wheat, durum wheat, rye, barley, oats, grain, maize, buckwheat, millet, canary seed, triticale, fresh vegetables, peas and beans harvested in dried form for human or animal consumption, sugarbeet, hops, oilseed rape, linseed, castor seed, safflower, sunflower seed, flax, potatoes, forage roots and tubers, lucerne/alfalfa, sainfoin, clover, lupins, vetches, fodder, kale rape and maize.

Set-aside land may be 100 per cent of the farmer's arable land used for growing the relevant crops, but in any event must include either one whole field amounting to 1 ha (approximately 2.5 acres) or an area consisting of adjacent whole fields and amounting to at least 1 ha.

[2] Set-Aside Regulations 1988, SI 1988 No.1352.
[3] Set-Aside (Amendment) Regulations, 1990, SI 1990 No.1716.
[4] SI 1988 No.1352, reg. 3(i)(a).
[5] Ibid. reg. 2(b).
[6] Ibid. reg. 2(b) List A Sched.1.

Providing this minimum 1 ha unit has been set-aside, additional land can consist of strips, but these must be at least 15 m wide.[7]

In the first two years this scheme was run, i.e. 1988/9 and 1989/90, the farmer who wished to set land aside under these regulations could do so for either permanent or rotational fallow, for permitted non-agricultural use or for woodland.[8] As from 1990/1 and from then on, new regulations[3] have been brought in whereby 'grazing fallow' has been added to the fallow alternatives,[9] and in addition farmers who joined in that year and those who, having joined in previous years, decide to abide by new regulations relating to conservancy will receive higher payments than for identical uses in 1989/90. In other words farmers joining for 1990/1 will in any event be subject to the new rules and the new payments which are set out later (see Appendix), but those who had already joined in previous years will have the option of either continuing with the previous remuneration and more limited obligations, or of undertaking the more onerous obligations but getting paid more. The grazed fallow obligations had in fact always been permissible under the EC Regulations for set-aside but simply had not previously been implemented in the United Kingdom.

Fallow Land

Where a farmer chooses to set the land aside, such land must be left fallow either for the whole of the set-aside period or as part of the arable rotation (i.e. different parcels of land each year can be set-aside as part of the normal arable process). The authority must be notified annually in advance which land the farmer intends to set-aside when he submits a claim for payment. The payment for rotational fallow is lower than for permanent fallow to take account of the benefit this brings by increasing the yield on the following crop, or for land used for woodland or for non-agricultural purposes. In addition, farmers entering the scheme must undertake to restrict the area of land used for growing relevant arable crops during the set-aside period (in other words they cannot set-aside land which had been used for this purpose previously and commence using other land which had not been so used for that purpose whilst drawing compensation for having set land aside).

Fallowed set-aside land and land awaiting conversion to woodland or to use for non-agricultural purposes must be managed in accordance with the requirements in the Regulations with a view to

[7] Ibid. reg. 4(1) and (2).
[8] Ibid. reg. 3(i) and (b).
[9] SI 1990 No.1716 5, 7a and 9.

keeping it in good agronomic condition and to protecting the environment.[10]

Grazed Fallow

The grazed fallow option provides that farmers who kept livestock in the base year 1987/8 would be able to graze animals on fallow land to a limit of the number of livestock units on the holding in the base year.[11] Where no such livestock was kept a farmer can still use the fallow land as grazed fallow for deer or goats providing the number of livestock units on his holding does not exceed one livestock unit per hectare or the forage area of his holding.[12] There are also regulations aiming at environmental appearance and protection. The new regulations require the plant cover on fallow set-aside land to be cut twice a year instead of once only as previously laid down, and a new set of regulations had to be brought in regarding the grazed fallow. Provision is made as to how the grassland to be grazed is to be sown and managed. Unlike the situation regarding the other two types of fallow where cuttings cannot be used for any agricultural purpose including the feeding of animals, where grazed fallow option is used the grass can only be cut once a year but the cuttings can be used to feed the livestock.[13]

For the preservation of the environment the beneficiaries must maintain all existing hedges and rows of trees (including hedgerow trees), all existing lakes, lochs, water courses, ponds and pools, all existing unimproved grassland, moorland, and heath, and all existing vernacular (defined as traditionally found in the locality) buildings and stone walls.

Finally, provision is made by the 1990 Regulations regarding land set aside for rotational fallow, whereby farmers are allowed to offset reductions in the area set-aside in one year with increases in the previous year. The effect of this is that the farmers must not increase or reduce the area of the land set-aside for rotational fallow by more than 10 per cent; reduce that area below 20 per cent of the relevant arable land on the holding in the reference period; or increase it to more than the area of relevant arable land on the holding in the reference period.

Except as provided above for grazing fallow, any agricultural production is prohibited on set-aside land. This means the farmer may not graze farm livestock or produce (either for sale or on-farm use) fodder crops (e.g. hay and silage) for feeding to farm livestock. Where horses are kept as part of a non-agricultural enterprise the farmer is

[10] Ibid. reg. 8.
[11] Ibid. reg. 7A(i).
[12] Ibid. reg. 7A(2).
[13] Ibid. Sched.3.

allowed to graze them on set-aside land without endangering the subsidy.

The set-aside land used for fallow or rotational fallow must establish plant cover immediately after the commencement of the set-aside period and retain it during the period where the requirements apply to the land. Destruction of that plant cover by cultivation is allowed only in specific cases. The plant cover has to be cut at least once in every year, and the cuttings may not be used for feeding livestock nor sold. The application of fertilizer and pesticide is prohibited as a general rule. The land may be managed for environmental or conservation purposes. Existing trees, hedges, water courses, ponds and pools on or next to the land set-aside must be maintained.[14]

Non-Agricultural Use

Where a farmer elects to use set-aside land for non-agricultural use he may use it for activities such as tourist facilities, caravan and camping sites, car parks, football pitches, tennis courts, golf courses, riding schools, livery stables and game and nature reserves. He may not use it for any form of agricultural production, mineral extraction (including open cast coalmining) any permanent building or structure to be used for industrial processes, sale of goods by retail or wholesale, use as a storage or distribution centre, housing or other residential use including hotels or office use.[15] Exceptions to the above are those allowed in the Farm Diversification Grant Scheme (e.g. farm shops selling solely products grown on the farm) provided that the new use continues to form part of the diversified agricultural business of the holding.

Woodland

A farmer who wishes to plant trees on set-aside land can do so either through the scheme directly under the set-aside regulations for woodland or through the Farm Woodland Scheme.[16] Under either option he has to obtain approval for planting the land concerned under the terms of the Forestry Commissions Woodland Scheme.[17] The exceptions to these are areas of less than 0.25 ha and planting of short-rotation coppice. The planting of fruit trees and orchards, Christmas trees or hardy nursery stock for sale is not permitted under the set-aside scheme. Whilst the farmer is waiting for approval for tree planting he must maintain the land as fallow and is paid at the appropriate rate during that period.

[14] Generally see SI 1988 No.1352 Sched.4.
[15] Ibid. reg. 9(2).
[16] Farm Woodland Scheme 1988 SI 1988 No.1291.
[17] SI 1988 No.1352, reg.8.

The current rates payable by the Forestry Commission for approved planting under the Woodland Grant Scheme at the rate per hectare depending on the size of each block of woodland are as follows:

Area approved (ha)	Conifers	Broadleaved trees
0.25–0.9	£1,005	£1,575
1.0–2.9	£880	£1,375
3.0–9.9	£795	£1,175
10.0 and over	£615	£975

Under this scheme in addition to planting grants (above) the farmer will receive the woodland set-aside payments of £180 on land in less favoured areas (LFAs)[18] and £200 elsewhere. Such payment will continue for the duration of the farmer's set-aside agreement only.

Under the second option through the Farm Woodland Scheme the rates are as follows:

Area approved (ha)	Conifers	Broadleaved trees
1.0–2.9	£505	£1,375
3.0–9.9	£420	£1,175
10.0 and over	£240	£975

In addition to the above payments, which are planting grants, the farmer will receive annual payments at Farm Woodland Scheme rates which are £150 in disadvantaged areas, £100 in severely disadvantaged areas and £190 elsewhere. These payments continue for a different number of years depending on the type of trees planted.

Administration of Land

During the first three years the beneficiary may change the use of the land unless it has been converted to woodland. If the change is from permanent to rotational fallow he may have to repay the difference between the two amounts in payments already received.

The farmer may increase the amount of land but may not decrease it. The increase can consist of either newly acquired arable land or arable land forming part of the original holding.

Transfer of Ownership

Set-aside obligations are tied to the beneficiary, not to the land. The beneficiary can sell or lease some or all of his holding at any time during his participation in the scheme. The new owner or tenant may take on the set-aside obligations, if he is eligible, but he is not required to do

[18] Ibid. reg. 2, 'less favoured area'.

so.[19] If he does not, and the original beneficiary does not set-aside an equivalent area of land, action may be taken to recover any payments already made and withhold any still due to him.

Succession on Death

If the beneficiary was a tenant and the tenancy is legally terminated by the landlord following the tenant's death, the set-aside obligations cease without an obligation on the estate or new occupier to repay any set-aside payments already received or to forfeit payments still due.[20] If the beneficiary was an owner-occupier, or the tenancy is passed on to a legal successor, Regulation 12 requires that the set-aside obligation must either be taken on by the new occupier or tenant, or action may be taken to recover any set-aside payments already made and to withhold any payments still due.

Administrative Control

Divisional offices do a thorough check on information contained in applications including, if necessary, field inspections and/or checking against satellite imagery or aerial photographs. The beneficiary must allow visits at all reasonable times by officials to inspect land, documents or records.[21]

If a beneficiary is in breach of his obligations he may either have some or all of the aid withheld or may be forced to repay any aid already received, and the Minister has powers in such an event to charge interest on such payments already made.[22] Additionally, a new criminal offence is created for recklessly or knowingly making false statements, and the penalty for this is a fine not exceeding £2,000.[23]

Consequences of the Set-aside on the Agricultural Character of the Land Withdrawn from Agricultural Use

Status of land

The legal status of land set-aside will depend on the use to which it is put. If fallowed, it is likely generally to continue to be regarded as agricultural land, but woodland or a non-agricultural use (such as a golf course or a riding stable) could affect its agricultural status. This could have implications, for instance, on the occupier's protected status under the Agricultural Holdings Act 1986 if he is a tenant.

---

[19] Ibid. generally reg. 12.
[20] Ibid. reg. 12(7)(b).
[21] Ibid. reg. 15(1).
[22] Ibid. reg. 16.
[23] Ibid. reg. 17.

Effect of taxation

Capital Taxes. Participation in the set-aside *fallow* option is unlikely to affect the eligibility of land for relief from capital taxes. Consequently land set-aside to fallow will (1) continue to be regarded as occupied for the purposes of agriculture for Inheritance Tax Agricultural Property Relief, and (2) be regarded as occupied for agricultural trade purposes for Capital Gains Tax roll-over and retirement relief.

Woodland will be treated in the same way as other woodlands. Non-agricultural use is likely to affect eligibility for agricultural relief depending on individual circumstances, including the type of use to which the land is put.

Income Tax. Set-aside payments are likely to be regarded as agricultural income where land is fallowed, even if the whole farm is set-aside. Payments where the land is put to woodland or non-agricultural use are likely to be similarly treated except where the whole farm is converted to these uses.

VAT. The VAT status of set-aside payments is currently under consideration by Customs and Excise. If VAT is chargeable, farmers will be able to charge it to MAFF.

Rates. Agricultural land and buildings are exempt from rating; agricultural dwellings are not. Land set-aside under the fallow option is likely to be regarded as agricultural land and therefore to continue to qualify for exemption from rating. Land used for other purposes could be liable for rates but this will depend on the individual circumstances.

Continued eligiblity for area-based grants

The area set-aside will not count towards the Hill Livestock Compensatory Allowances 1989 (HLCA) financial ceiling. Since HLCA payments are based on a maximum payment for each hectare this could in some circumstances lead to a reduction in HLCA payments. Participants who retain less than 3 ha of usable agricultural land (which is a condition of receiving HLCA payments) will no longer be eligible for HLCAs.

Ministers may refuse set-aside payments on land in Environmentally Sensitive Areas (ESAs)[24] where there is a risk of double funding. Regulation 13[5] allows deduction of ESA payments for set-aside payments where there is a degree of overlap between the two schemes.

Problems of Set-Aside

In setting up the set-aside scheme the Government has not enacted any legislation affecting the prospective participants' obligations under

[24] Ibid. reg. 6(5).

civil law. The participant must therefore ensure that in entering the scheme he will not be in breach of any civil obligations (e.g. under his tenancy agreement (if a tenant), mortgage or other borrowing agreements, and producer/buyer contracts) and that he is not in breach of any planning regulations.

Tenancy. As far as tenancy agreements are concerned, the scheme gives the landlord the right to prevent a tenant from entering set-aside under the woodland or non-agricultural use options. Although in the case of fallow the tenant needs merely to inform the landlord, he would be well-advised to consider carefully his tenancy agreement. Such agreements vary widely, and even on taking up the fallow option, the tenant could expose himself to an action by the landlord to repossess the land, for instance if the latter alleges that he is not complying with the Rules of Good Husbandry in section II of the Agriculture Act 1947.

Rent Review. The tenant should also consider possible effects on future rent reviews under the Agricultural Holdings Act 1986. The arbitrator, for instance, would there have to take account of all relevant factors, including the productive capacity of the holding and its related earning capacity.

Agricultural Tenancy Status. Also, if a great proportion of the land is turned to a non-agricultural use, there is the possibility that even though the landlord's consent for this had been obtained, the tenant could find himself no longer an agricultural tenant — with ill effects on his security of tenure and deprived of the benefit of the agricultural tenancy succession rules. No effect on agricultural co-operatives has as yet been reported.

Share Farming. In the case of share farmers, only the landowner, as legal occupier of the land, is eligible for the scheme, and only then if the share farming contract has come to an end or he has the agreement of his share farming partner. The share farming partner cannot enter the scheme in his own right, as he does not 'occupy' the land in the required sense.

Production Contracts. As far as contracts between producers and buyers are concerned, the farmer has to make certain that by entering the scheme he will not make it impossible for himself to satisfy any existing agreement of that nature, thereby exposing himself to an action for breach of contract.

Employment. The effect on contracts of employment is limited to redundancy payments.

Borrowing. Borrowers will have to look carefully at their agreements and the actual terms of any mortgage etc. It would obviously be prudent to consult the lender before participating in the scheme. It is unlikely that there would be any difficulties since presumably the participant would not be entering upon the scheme unless it was likely to prove more profitable than to continue farming that particular part of the land. The lender however might consider that participation might in the long term affect the value of his security.

Afforestation. If the area to be planted exceeds 2.5 ha the applicant must first obtain approval for tree-planting grants under the Forestry Commission's Woodland Grant Scheme (WGS). All applications for such grants are scrutinized with regard to landscape and nature conservation as well as timber production and silviculture, with a view to achieving environmental benefits and avoiding environmental damage. A beneficiary who has entered the woodland option may not switch to another option unless he has failed to obtain approval for planting grants.

Trees planted under the WGS may be felled only with a felling licence from the Forestry Commission. For woodlands planted under the Farm Woodland Scheme or set-aside, there will be a presumption in favour of granting licences without any replanting condition. At the end of the five year set-aside period any trees planted under the set-aside scheme would almost certainly be below the licensing size. However, under the rules of the WGS the owner is obliged to repay the planting grants if the trees are removed within ten years or are not properly maintained during that period.

Non-Agricultural Use. Apart from possible failure to obtain the landlord's consent, there are two further restrictions on non-agricultural use. First of all the Statutory Instrument sets out a list of non-permissible uses.[25] Secondly, even if such uses are allowed by the Statutory Instrument, an applicant may fail to obtain planning permission if this is required. Under the Town and Country Planning Act 1990, permission for 'development' must be sought. 'Development' includes 'the making of any material change in the use of any building or other land'. Land ownership carries with it only the bare right to continue to use land for its existing purposes. An owner has no right to build on his land and no right to change its use. However agricultural land is favoured. The use of land for agriculture, and the use for such purpose of any building occupied with land so used, do not constitute development. Automatic permission is granted for the carrying out of building or engineering operations reasonably necessary for the purposes of agriculture on agricultural land of more than one acre (0.4 ha) which is comprised in an agricultural unit. Planning permission must be sought and obtained for development which does not fall within the ambit of the automatic permission above. Problems arise as to the meaning of 'requisite for the purposes of agriculture', e.g. the building of a packing station for farm-grown produce has been allowed, but a building for the processing of produce

---

[25] Ibid. reg. 9.

was not. Similar problems arise in relation to the words 'use for agriculture'. A farm shop selling horticultural produce grown only on the holding does not constitute development, but the sale of any produce brought in from outside is not a 'use for agriculture' and therefore is a development requiring planning permission.

Ability to return land to agricultural production at the end of the set-aside period would depend on the type of use taken up and any conditions applied by the Planning Authorities initially.

The Environment

Although this scheme has as its primary purpose the reduction of surplus production of cereals and other crops, it has always been intended that it should also protect the environment and, where possible, go further than that and lead to environmental improvements. It obviously makes good sense that agricultural policy should embody environmental measures wherever possible.

When answering questions in Parliament on the introduction of the first scheme the then Minister of Agriculture was asked whether the scheme did anything for the environment. The reply was that it does. The scheme provides, for instance, that fallowed land has to be kept in good agricultural condition with a green cover crop cut once a year (as has been said, this has now been improved to twice a year); hedgerows, shelter belts and other features on the set-aside land have to be maintained; use of fertilizers is prohibited and pesticides only permitted on special authorization and in special circumstances. Since marginal strips are permitted for set-aside land these do give opportunity for game and wildlife conservation, country paths, bridleways etc., and set-aside land may be used for wildlife parks, nature reserves, woodlands etc. It should also be mentioned that of course organic farming is encouraged indirectly by the fallow scheme, which prepares the land for a switch of farming methods. Less intensive farming is also encouraged by the grazing fallow 'extensive' scheme.

The most recent regulations have extended the accent on environmental protection not merely by providing that fallow set-aside land should be cut twice a year so as to improve its appearance, but also by extending the list of environmental features which farmers participating in this scheme will have to maintain and protect, and these now include stone walls, 'vernacular' buildings, unimproved grassland, moorland and heath.[26]

Equivalent changes were made to the Countryside Commission's Countryside Premium Scheme,[27] which is available in addition to the

[26] SI 1990 No.1716 reg. 15 and Sched.1.
[27] Countryside Premium for Set-Aside Land (Countryside Commission,

set-aside payments to farmers in Norfolk, Suffolk, Essex, Hertfordshire, Bedfordshire, Cambridgeshire and Northamptonshire. The scheme applies in addition to set-aside for land which has already been accepted for permanent fallow land and the normal set-aside scheme. Land accepted under this scheme runs side by side with the MAFF scheme, and there are five options which involve special management of wooded margins or meadowland, or wildlife fallow, or Brent Geese pasture, or habitat restoration. We may have different options exercised on the same farm and the payment per hectare varies depending on which one a farmer is accepted for. Clearly the land has to be appropriate for the purpose for which it is intended. For example, Brent Geese Pasture option is available only within three miles of the coast, and the wildlife fallow option available only on light free-draining soils.

In general the land will obviously benefit from restrictions on the use of harmful fertilizers and pesticides and encouragement of headlands. Moreover, land set aside for agricultural use may not be developed for industrial, retail or residential purposes, nor for mineral extraction.

How Successful?

The Ministry reported in its first two years that over three thousand farmers had applied to set-aside 110,000 ha, i.e. 250,000 acres of arable land (54,630 ha in 1988, 55,431 in 1989 – about 2.3 per cent of eligible land in the UK). Of these, 80 per cent have taken the permanent fallow option, 9 per cent rotational fallow, 2 per cent woodland, and 9 per cent non-agricultural use. In the EC as a whole about 500,000 ha were set-aside in 1989, reducing the production of cereals by some 1 to 2 million tonnes.

In the statistical table the United Kingdom seemed fairly typical in the preference of farmers for fallow, and came about half way in the league table for the amount of land set-aside. Top of the league (prior to the inclusion in Germany of East Germany) was West Germany, where similar schemes had already been started before 1988, and where the nature of farming lent itself to this type of pursuit. This is dealt with more fully below. For statistics as to the comparision of the application and success of this scheme in the first year that it was applied in the various countries of the Community, the report by the Commission published in Brussels on 12 September 1989 (COM(89)353 Final) is recommended.

In a written answer given by Mr Curry relating to set-aside (reported Hansard 1 March 1990) to a question put by Dr David Clark as to what proportion of land in the non-agricultural use option of the set-aside scheme is being used for enterprises connected with tourism, recreation

Torrington House, 13–15 Hills Road, Cambridge CB2 1NL, 1990 edition).

and leisure, Mr Curry replied that the information that he did have, which did not in fact cover all the question, suggested that the majority of the land set-aside to non-agricultural purposes is being used for horse-based activities, golf courses and sports fields.

Further, a break-down showing statistical tables for the entire country by counties and also by countries (i.e. England, Scotland, Wales and Northern Ireland), shows that in 1988 the United Kingdom had 1,746 farm entrants and in 1989 the number was 1,350. The hectares of land set-aside in 1988 numbered 54,630, and in 1989 were 55,431. Thus roughly the same number of hectares was set-aside in each of those two years. Both in 1988 and 1989 the favoured set-aside option was permanent fallow.

At the Fifteenth European Congress on Agricultural Law, organized by the CEDR (European Committee for Agricultural Law) in Ghent in October 1989, the participating nations (which include all the nations in the EC and in addition Austria, Switzerland and Norway) submitted reports on the working, during its first year, of the set-aside policy in those countries where it was applicable.[28] Professor Wolfgang Winkler of the Institute of Agricultural Law in Göttingen was the General Rapporteur and produced an excellent report based on the various national contributions.[29] As may be expected, since so many of the provisions of the EC Directive do not have much flexibility, there is considerable similarity between the various participating countries in the regulations which they have brought in governing payments to those who participate. There is an interesting difference in administration depending upon the political structures of the participating nations. The most interesting and considerable difference, however, arises in the amounts which the various participating states decided to pay by way of aid within the boundaries set by the EC (100–600 ECUs), and the distribution of such payments as between participators. This of course was the area where the directive gave the participants the greatest flexibility. First of all there are nations such as the Netherlands, Ireland, and Luxemburg, where there is a uniform premium paid per hectare irrespective of what option (i.e. fallow, woodland or non-agricultural) is taken. In others, the premium is graduated: in some, depending upon the type of soil (Belgium), intensity of irrigation (Spain and Greece), yield index figure (Germany), different groups of *départements* (France) and finally, on a totally different basis in Great Britain, where although there is a differentiation between the advantaged areas and others, the rotation depends on different types of fallow, forestation and other uses.

[28] The author was UK rapporteur at the Ghent Conference.
[29] Reports of the Fifteenth European Agricultural Law Congress, Ghent, Belgium, 2–6 October 1989, Vol. II, p.717. Obtainable from: R. E. O. Mackay, Hon. Sec., Agricultural Law Association, Nunton Cottage, Nunton, Salisbury, Wilts. SP5 4HW.

It is to be remembered that in the case of extensive pasture farming the Community calls for a reduction of 40–60 per cent in premiums paid to allow for the income which farmers will obtain from such grazing. It is left to the participating nations as to how much this reduction should be. Again, the size of premiums paid for non-agricultural use differs between those countries which have laid down a permanent amount and those where such premium is reduced by the actual amount of income achieved from the non-agricultural use (Germany, Belgium, Ireland).

The general conclusion to be reached was not very different from that reached by the Community itself, namely that there was an enormous difference in the application of the same rules in the various countries participating; that a great deal of cheating could go on with lands being withdrawn which were not, strictly speaking, in production but where farmers were being compensated for giving up completely worthless, unproductive lands; and that there was such a great difference in the amount of compensation being paid by the various national schemes that obviously the results must be considerably influenced by these figures. All in all, however, it was felt that the incentive to farmers to withdraw from production was not sufficient on the existing financial compensation permitted. A start has certainly been made, but it was merely scratching the surface; and indeed with the ever-increasing efficiency of farming in most countries, due not least to the ever better agrochemical aids available to them, and the constant improvement of various cereal and seed strains which become better-yielding and more resistant to various diseases, it is quite possible that, despite the withdrawal of certain quantities of arable land from production, those still remaining are in fact more than compensating for such withdrawal. Many participants could report that the set-aside scheme in their respective countries had shown itself to be more attractive to those farmers with large areas of land under cultivation, who could quite happily sacrifice certain quantities of it and receive compensation in the certainty that the remainder of the land under cultivation, particularly whenever better methods could be used for production, would more than compensate for any production loss caused by the set-aside.

Dr Winkler's report also deals with the implementation by Germany and Greece of EC Order No.1096.88 of 25 April 1988 on the introduction of a Community arrangement to promote the discontinuation of agricultural activity. This order, unlike that applying to set-aside, did not make it obligatory on member states to introduce such a scheme, but left it entirely to the individual decision. As only Germany and Greece have done anything about it so far, there is insufficient material on which to carry out comparisons, but there has been a great deal already of learned writing on the subject, particularly contemplating the more far-reaching results on any permanent withdrawal of agricultural land from production, not least looking at it from the point of view of ecology and structural changes.

Use of Agricultural Commodities in the Non-Food Sector

The Commission reported to the Council on non-food products in January 1990.[30] This research arises from the fact that all objective studies accept that non-food use of agricultural products can grow in importance in the medium and long term. Because of their chemical and physical properties, agricultural commodities are potential sources for the production of a wide range of non-food products. Despite this, the quantities of agricultural products concerned must be relatively limited when compared with the present surpluses, and even more so with the surpluses which could arise if agricultural production were not to be checked.

Obviously very many factors would be at play in this. The progressive exhaustion of finite fossil resources will improve the prospects for using renewable raw materials for industrial purposes. Technical developments are likely to concentrate on this as the financial climate makes this more viable. At the same time one must also consider what will be the prospective financial reward to landowners for using the land for other non-agricultural uses such as leisure activities. What the land is ultimately used for will very much depend upon what brings the greater reward.

At present the Community's outputs of items such as starches, sugar, alcohol, flax fibre and tobacco, are small in relation to agricultural output. Not counting forests, non-food use employs less than 1 per cent of the land area of Europe, and less than a quarter even when forests are included. Looking at the future, even optimistically assuming that for example bio-degradable products could take 10 per cent of the market, their outlet would still represent only a very small fraction of the Community's annual cereals surplus.

The Commission's report shows a very impressive development in Community policy, including research and demonstration projects, and it is particularly the latter which could be developed in connection with agricultural crops such as castors, rape, high oleic acid, sunflower varieties, flax and hemp, various fibres and lupins. It is particularly important to obtain the active participation of farmers in these projects.

The annexes to this report are particularly interesting. Pilot projects already in existence shown in annex 1 range from the establishment of a

[30] Report from the Commission to the Council COM(89)597 Final for amending Council Regulation (EEC) No.797/85.

goat-rearing enterprise for cashmere production in Scotland, at a cost of 656,000 ECUs to the establishment of a pilot scheme for intensive woodcropping from fast-growing trees (poplars) on land currently under grass in the Alderburg region of Germany (cost 950,000 ECUs).

Annex 2 deals with illustrations of specific industrial projects, for instance, in the chemical industry, the castor bean producing castor oil on a large scale for the manufacture of polyamide 11, which cannot be manufactured from petrochemicals. High erucic rape oil is at present mainly supplied from Eastern Bloc countries (of very variable quantity and quality); the potential for this market is about double the present output.

The paper industry potentially gives a great market for high-quality fibres not coming from the use of wood. Kenaf, at present imported from China and Thailand, produces both long and short fibres which can be used in the paper industry and also for insulation boards in place of glass fibre etc. Other plants which can be used in the paper industry are miscanthus and fibre sorgum.

The potential proposal here would be for an additional set-aside provision whereby farmers who put aside a minimum of 30 per cent of their arable land would be allowed to produce cereals for non-food uses on at most half as much land as has been set-aside, and would be granted a certain premium. However, this would be subject to the production of a contract concluded between any industrial company and individual farmers (or groups of farmers), and the processor would have to guarantee that the product would not be used for food or feed manufacture.

A MAFF survey amongst interested parties in the United Kingdom for such a new Regulation produced a rather mixed response. It would appear that most of the participants in the survey thought that the greatest potential use of cereals in a non-food capacity would be in Biothanol. The costs of producing plants for the manufacture of this commodity out of cereals would be prohibitive when one bears in mind that a set-aside scheme would run only for some five years. Nabim considered that there would be a considerable distortion of the cereal market, BP Chemicals thought that there would be no market unless crude oil rose to the range of US$30–40 per barrel (but what about wars like the one in the Gulf?). The CLA (Country Landowners Association) believed that the demonstration projects are a necessary and effective link between research, farmers and processors. UKASTA (United Kingdom Agricultural Supply Trade Association) feared the heavy expense necessary initially to set up a new and efficient industry and the length of time required to bring such an industry into operation; and of course the conservation bodies and the game conservancy unanimously regretted that such new proposals would not expand on environmental implications, and indeed could be counterproductive to the existing promotion of the environment.

What of the Future?

Part of a potential trend can be seen in the consideration above of the employment of land set-aside from cereal production for agricultural production to cereal production for non-agricultural purposes. Whilst all this goes on, however, the Common Agricultural Policy is under enormous stress, not least because of the 1991 round of GATT talks. Will the voices within the CAP prevail which are intent on producing changes which will structurally worst affect large farmers who are efficient, like those in the United Kingdom? Will, in the long run, these proposals yet come to naught? This remains to be seen.

However, there is a very grave danger that some proposals, such as those before the Commissioners at present for the lowering of agricultural prices and the introduction of an aid per hectare system, will come to be implemented. Aid would be in the form of a deficiency payment per hectare to all farmers, but with percentage reductions for farmers over the first 50 ha (25 per cent reduction) and over the first 30 ha (35 per cent reduction). The first 30 ha would not have any reduction applied. Although participation in the aid scheme for the crops would yet again not be compulsory, producers who did participate would be required to set-aside a predetermined percentage of the total area of cereals, oil seeds and pulses as temporary fallow. This would range from 0 per cent for up to 30 ha; 25 per cent for the next 50 ha; 35 per cent for areas over the first 80 ha.

The reduction in milk quotas to 95 million tonnes would also not be applied uniformly since there would be no quota reduction for the smaller or medium farms with an annual production of less than 200,000 kg. However, 150,000 large and very large farms with an annual production of 200,000 kg or more would have the quota reduced by 10 per cent. As can be seen, these new proposals would be yet again a heavy blow against UK farmers. These are all measures against size and efficiency.

No wonder the future for farmers in this country is now looking bleaker than ever. Farmers, already suffering from great reduction in the values of their land, which in turn leads to banks calling in overdrafts, as they are no longer secured, and receiving smaller subsidies from the Community, face disaster. There is a unanimous opinion that smaller farms will become entirely unviable and will disappear. The larger farms will encounter even greater pressures to become as highly intensively productive and efficient as possible in order to survive. This of course will, in the longer term, have a completely counter-productive effect on ecology and the environment.

APPENDIX

1990/1 UK Set-Aside Payments

		LFAs (£)	Other (£)
1	Permanent fallow		
	New management provisions		
	(a) Normal rates		
	(1) existing participants	190	210
	(2) new participants	202	222
	(b) Differential rates		
	(1) existing participants	140	160
	(2) new participants	152	172
	Existing management provisions	180	200
2	Rotational fallow		
	(a) Normal rates		
	(1) existing participants	170	190
	(2) new participants	182	202
	(b) Differential rates		
	(1) existing participants	120	140
	(2) new participants	132	152
	Existing management provisions		
3	Grazed fallow	100	110
4	Non-agricultural purposes	130	150
5	Woodland (other than under the provisions of the Farm Woodland Scheme)	180	200

Agricultural Pollution and the Aquatic Environment

WILLIAM HOWARTH

Farm pollution incidents seem to be a growing phenomenon with often serious effects on water quality. While we would accept that the vast majority of farmers are highly responsible in their approach to preventing water pollution on their farms, effective action is still needed as a matter of urgency to deal with the irresponsible minority causing the problems. If this minority is less than one per cent of all farmers it should not be difficult to apply firm measures to bring them into line. (House of Commons Environment Committee Report 1987)[1]

The Nature of Agricultural Pollution

Until recently there was a fairly widespread belief that farming, as an activity conducted almost since the dawn of humanity, must be an environmentally benign operation, if only for the reason that, if it were not, the adverse effects would have been noticed long ago. Historically it may be true that the most dramatic consequences of environmental pollution have been by-products of industrialization, and that an environmental legacy from Victorian manufacturers remains in the form of contaminated land and highly toxic sediments which form the beds of many rivers and estuaries. Whilst the environmental record of industry has shown encouraging improvements, however, agriculture has become increasingly prominent as a cause of pollution, and especially the pollution of watercourses.[2]

[1] House of Commons Environment Committee, Third Report, *Pollution of Rivers and Estuaries*, 1987, House of Commons Paper 183 para. 67.

[2] Generally see Royal Commission on Environment Pollution, Seventh Report, *Agriculture and Pollution*, 1979, Cmnd. 7644; Institution of Water and Environmental Management, Annual Symposium 1989, *Agriculture and the Environment*, 1989; Nitrate Conservancy Council, *Nature Conservation and Pollution from Farm Wastes*, 1991.

A major reason for this disturbing trend lies in the intensification of agricultural production techniques which has taken place over recent years. Modern methods of animal husbandry, involving the indoor containment of stock to a greater extent than in traditional agricultural practice, have greatly increased the potential for water pollution where animal waste is not adequately contained. A large proportion of agricultural pollution incidents occur because slurry containment facilities are improperly constructed, or poorly maintained, and permit effluent to escape into watercourses. The deoxygenating effect of slurry is considerable, and may be as much as 100 times as polluting as domestic sewage. A related problem stemming from agricultural intensification is the developing trend for farmers to produce a greater amount of silage rather than hay for animal fodder, partially because of its higher nutritional value, and partially because of the greater need for food for animals over-wintering indoors. Silage production is also capable of producing a highly deoxygenating liquid effluent, which is capable of being as much as 200 times as polluting as untreated domestic sewage.[3]

Other water pollution problems generated by agriculture arise because of the application of nitrogenous fertilizers and pesticides to land, and the application of pesticides to animals as, for example, in sheep dipping.[4] The eventual seepage of these chemicals into watercourses is a major source of pollution and the presence of nitrate in particular has been a special cause of concern in the relation to waters which serve as a source of water supply. In agricultural contexts the traditional offences relating to water pollution have severe limitations in relation to diffuse forms of pollution and various forms of preventative measures are required as a legal mechanism for effective pollution control. Hence, for the purpose of protecting waters from the entry of polluting substances, provision exists for the enactment of precautionary regulations and the designation of specified areas as water protection zones, or nitrate sensitive areas. The object of this essay is to note the difficulties with the traditional legal approach to agricultural water pollution, and to outline some of the improvements in the law of England and Wales which will allow the problems involved to be dealt with more appropriately in future.

[3] House of Commons Environment Committee, Third Report, *Pollution of Rivers and Estuaries* 1987, House of Commons Paper 183 para. 65.

[4] On pesticides generally see, Part III Food and Environment Protection Act 1985; Ministry of Agriculture, Fisheries and Food/Health and Safety Executive, *Code of Practice for the Safe Use of Pesticides on Farms and Holdings*, 1990; and Gilbert and Macrory, *Pesticide Related Law*, 1990.

The Extent of Agricultural Pollution

From the outset the extent of the problem of agricultural pollution of watercourses must be placed in perspective alongside other major causes of pollution. An authoritative source of information about the extent of agricultural pollution is the annual publication *Water Pollution from Farm Waste*, produced jointly by the National Rivers Authority and the Ministry of Agriculture, Fisheries and Food, the most recent edition of which includes information relating to the period up to the end of 1989. The report recognizes that in relation to the other major causes of water pollution, industrial and sewage pollution, agriculture gives rise to a lesser number of pollution incidents. Hence in 1988, the most recent year for which full information is available, of a total of 24,153 reported pollution incidents of all kinds, 34 per cent were of industrial origin, 20 per cent arose through sewage pollution and 17 per cent from farm pollution, with 29 per cent being categorized as 'others'.[5] None the less, the 17 per cent of pollution incidents originating from agricultural activity amounted to 4,141 distinct incidents. Assuming that the seriousness of a pollution incident is reflected in the likelihood of legal proceedings ensuing from it, agricultural pollution included a disproportionate number of the most serious incidents in that 56 per cent of the prosecutions brought for water pollution offences fell into this category. It is arguable, therefore, that in 1988 agriculture constituted the most damaging single activity in relation to water quality.

The figures for the number of agricultural pollution incidents taking place in 1989 showed a significant improvement over 1988. In 1989 there were 2,889 reported incidents, representing a reduction of 30 per cent from the previous year's figure, the lowest total since 1984 and the first fall in the number of incidents since 1979. Regrettably, however, this improvement has not been attributed to improvements in farming practice but rather to the exceptionally dry weather conditions that were experienced in 1989, which had the effect of reducing the volume of farm waste and facilitating its safe disposal. Accordingly, Baroness Trumpington, the Minister of State at the Ministry of Agriculture, Fisheries and Food, took the view that 'it would be premature to conclude from this that we have reversed the alarming upward trend in reported farm pollution incidents', and Lord Crickhowell, the chairman of the National Rivers Authority, expressed similar reservation as to the underlying trend of agricultural pollution incidents.[6]

Of the 2,889 agricultural pollution incidents which took place in 1989, 18 per cent were classified as 'serious' and 163 prosecutions were

[5] *Water Pollution from Farm Waste 1989*, 1990, p.2.
[6] Ibid., foreword.

pursued. Clearly the use of the criminal law is relatively infrequent in relation to this kind of offence in that legal proceedings were undertaken in only 5.6 per cent of the total number of incidents. In respect of the 163 offences which were prosecuted, the major causes of pollution incidents were slurry stores and collection tanks, which accounted for eighty of the incidents. Specific problems with slurry storage giving rise to these incidents were listed as inadequate storage capacity, leaking stores, problems with sluices and valves and poor storage operation. Of second greatest significance were incidents involving silage, which accounted for twenty-nine incidents arising through inadequate effluent storage, leaking silos and drains. Thereafter problems with land run-off gave rise to twenty-two incidents, yard washings ten, and the remaining incidents were listed in a range of miscellaneous categories each containing only a small number of incidents. The evidence provides a clear identification of the storage of slurry and silage as the agricultural operations causing the most serious problems in relation to water pollution.

Criminal Offences concerning Water Pollution

Although special offences may arise in relation to the pollution of water where this involves damage to a fishery,[7] the main water pollution offences which are likely to be committed in respect of agricultural pollution incidents are now provided for under the Water Act 1989. This enactment establishes the National Rivers Authority and sets out its powers and duties in relation to its principal functions.[8] The specific powers and duties of the Authority in respect of the control of water pollution, and the key offences, are provided for under Chapter 1 of Part III of the Act.[9] The particular offences which it specifies arise in relation to waters referred to as 'controlled waters', a term incorporating the subcategory 'inland waters', which are those most likely to feature in connection with pollution from farms.[10] Inland waters are defined as the waters of any relevant lake or pond or of so much of any relevant river or watercourse as is above the fresh-water limit.[11] 'Relevant lake or pond' means any lake or pond, whether it is natural or artificial, above or below ground, which discharges into a relevant river or watercourse or into another lake or pond which is itself a relevant lake or pond. 'Relevant river or watercourse' means any river or watercourse, including an underground watercourse and an artificial river or watercourse, which is neither a public sewer nor a

[7] See s.4 Salmon and Freshwater Fisheries Act 1975.
[8] Generally see Howarth, *The Law of the National Rivers Authority*, 1990.
[9] Ss.103 to 124 Water Act 1989
[10] The subcategories of *controlled waters* are defined in s.103 Water Act 1989.
[11] Ibid. s.103(1)(c).

sewer or drain which drains into a public sewer.[12] In either of these cases the Secretary of State has the power to modify these definitions by providing that particular waters are, or are not, relevant lakes or ponds or relevant rivers or watercourses.[13] The general picture is that almost all flowing waters and stillwaters with an outflow will come within the definition of 'controlled waters' and be subject to regulation under the 1989 Act in instances of pollution.

In the agricultural context there are two formulations of the offence of polluting controlled waters which are most likely to be of relevance. First, there is the offence of causing or knowingly permitting any poisonous, noxious or polluting matter or any solid waste matter to enter any controlled waters.[14] Although, the expression 'poisonous, noxious or polluting' is not statutorily defined, it is clear that it encompasses many kinds of farm waste, including slurry and silage liquor. Second, there is the offence of causing or knowingly permitting any trade effluent to be discharged into controlled waters. 'Trade effluent' is defined to include any effluent which is discharged from premises used for the carrying on of any trade or industry, other than surface water or domestic sewage, and premises wholly or mainly used for agricultural purposes, whether for profit or not, are deemed to be premises used for carrying on a trade.[15]

Common to both of the water pollution offences which may arise in agricultural contexts is the requirement of 'causing or knowingly permitting' the entry or discharge of the polluting matter or effluent,[16] and in most cases the principal difficulty for the prosecution lies in establishing that the accused either caused or knowingly permitted the entry or discharge into controlled waters. The requirement of showing that the entry of polluting matter into waters is 'caused or knowingly permitted' is to be found in a series of previous enactments providing for essentially the same offence,[17] and a sizeable body of case law provides guidance as to the meaning of the phrase.[18] In the most general terms some key principles are usefully distilled from past decisions.[19] First, the disjunctive form of the phrase envisages two distinct matters, causing pollution *or* knowingly permitting it. Second, a person *knowingly permits* pollution where he fails to prevent

[12] Ibid. s.103(4).
[13] Ibid. s.103(5).
[14] Ibid. s.107(1)(a).
[15] Ibid. s.124(1) and (3).
[16] Ibid. s.107(1).
[17] See ss.2 to 5 Rivers Pollution Prevention Act 1876; s.2(1) Rivers (Prevention of Pollution) Act 1951; and ss.31(1) and 32(1) Control of Pollution Act 1974.
[18] Generally see Howarth, 'Causing, Knowingly Permitting and Preventing Pollution', *Utilities Law Review* (1990), 105.
[19] Generally see Howarth, *Water Pollution Law*, 1988.

pollution where that failure is accompanied by knowledge.[20] Third, the offence of *causing* pollution is an offence of strict liability for which there is no requirement that the accused acted intentionally or negligently: it is enough that a positive and deliberate act leads to pollution for it to have been 'caused' within the meaning of the provision.[21] Fourth, as a counterpart of this, a passive looking on will not amount to causing pollution, though it may amount to knowingly permitting pollution in some circumstances. For this reason it is vitally important that prosecutions are pursued under the correct limb of the disjunction.[22] Fifth, it is possible that the chain of causation may be broken by the act of a third party, or an act of God, so that the accused may properly be said not to have *caused* the pollution.[23] Finally, where collaborative activities involving more than one party give rise to pollution it is vital that the correctly formulated offence is pursued *against the appropriate party*.[24]

The Pegrum *case*

Some of the above principles are illustrated by the recent example of a water pollution offence in an agricultural context provided by *Southern Water Authority* v. *Pegrum and Pegrum*.[25] The defendants in this case were pig farmers, and effluent produced by the pigs was transferred into a lagoon from which it was emptied four or five times a year by contractors and spread on fields as manure. Because of the wet summer in 1987, the sediment from the lagoon had not been removed for some eighteen months, and as a result the storm drains had become clogged. After a period of four days of rain the lagoon overflowed and some of its contents escaped into a stream which flowed into the River Medway, resulting in a serious pollution incident. The farmers were charged with the offence of causing polluting matter to enter the stream.[26]

Magistrates acquitted the farmers on the ground that, in order to be guilty of 'causing' pollution, it had to be shown that there was a positive act resulting in pollution. As a point of fact it was found that the ingress of rainwater was an intervening event which broke the chain of causation between the farming activities and the pollution. The prosecution appealed against this decision.

[20] *Alphacell Ltd* v. *Woodward* [1972] 2 All ER 475, at p. 479.

[21] Ibid., and *Wrothwell Ltd* v. *Yorkshire Water Authority* [1984] Crim. L R 43.

[22] *Price* v. *Cromack* [1975] 2 All ER 113.

[23] *Impress (Worcester) Ltd* v. *Rees* [1971] 2 All ER 357.

[24] *Price* v. *Cromack* [1975] 2 All ER 113; and *Welsh Water Authority* v. *Williams Motors (Cymru) Ltd* (1988) Unreported CO/1080/88.

[25] (1989) 153 JP 581.

[26] Under s.31(1) Control of Pollution Act 1974, the precursor of s.107(1)(a) Water Act 1989.

On the basis of the leading authority of *Alphacell Ltd* v. *Woodward*[27] and other decisions, Henry J. took the view that the following principles were applicable to the circumstances. First, where a defendant conducts some active operation involving storage, use or creation of material capable of polluting a river should it escape, then if it does escape and pollute, the defendant is liable if he causes that escape. Second, 'causing' must be construed in a common-sense way. Third, a defendant may be found to have caused an escape even though he did not intend it and even if he was not negligent. Fourth, it is a defence if the defendant can show that the escape was due to an intervening act of a third party or an act of God. Fifth, in deciding whether an intervening act was a defence on the general principles of causation, the general question was whether that intervening factor was some activity outside the defendant's control, such as the action of a trespasser or an act of God, and was of so powerful a nature that the defendant's conduct was not a cause at all but was merely a part of the surrounding circumstances.

On the facts of the case, Henry J. found that the ingress of rainwater was the causative factor. The storage and release of effluent was within the active operation of the farm. In order to conclude that the ingress of rainwater was an act of God it had to be so unpredictable as to excuse the farmers of all liability, but there was nothing so extraordinary about the amount of rain that had fallen since it was not so great that it could not have been contemplated. Nor was it possible to argue that the blocked drains were an intervening cause since these fell within the responsibility of the farmers. Consequently, the appeal by the Water Authority was allowed and the case remitted to the magistrates with a direction to convict.

Penalties for Agricultural Pollution

Although the *Pegrum* case, considered above, serves as a useful illustration of the operation of the relevant principles of law in an agricultural context, the effectiveness of the law as a deterrent to agricultural pollution must in some part be evaluated in terms of the levels of punishments which courts are prepared to impose in this kind of case. Over the first year of existence of the National Rivers Authority, since September 1989, a number of significant convictions were secured in respect of agricultural pollution incidents. The two most serious of these concerned pollution of watercourses by pig slurry. In the first case, proceedings brought by the Anglian Region of the Authority resulted in a fine of £10,000 imposed by the Crown Court, along with an award of £20,000 costs, against a farmer who

[27] [1972] AC 824.

allowed some three million gallons of pig slurry to pour into the River Sapiston killing some 10,000 adult fish. In addition, the Authority sought compensation of £27,000 for the cost of restocking the river with fish.[28] In a second case a Leicestershire pig farmer was fined £10,000 for polluting a tributary of the River Soar with slurry and causing extensive fish mortality. Leicester Crown Court was informed that a pollution control officer had found the brook grey, and with an oxygen level 80 per cent lower than it should have been, as a result of a land drain taking slurry from 4,000 pigs through an irrigation ditch and directly into the watercourse.[29]

During the calendar year of 1989, the total of 163 prosecutions recorded included convictions arising from a diverse range of agricultural pollution offences. Marked differences in the numbers of prosecutions are discernible between the ten different regions of the National Rivers Authority ranging from only three convictions recorded during the year at the lower extreme to forty-three convictions at the higher. These differences are possibly attributable to different levels of agricultural activity taking place in different parts of England and Wales. Less readily explicable are the variations between levels of fines imposed in agricultural water pollution cases. The average levels of fines imposed by Magistrates and Crown Courts in the different regions ranged between £105 recorded at the lower extreme and £1,421 at the higher.[30]

Concern has been expressed on a number of occasions that the law operates with insufficient stringency in relation to agricultural pollution offences. Hence, a recent report of the House of Commons Public Accounts Committee expressed the view that prosecutions were too infrequent, fines were too low and did not generally reflect the severity of the pollution caused. More specifically, the MPs were disturbed that the 'polluter pays' strategy was not being effectively applied in relation to agricultural pollution, were openly critical that the courts were not playing their full part, and urged the Ministry of Agriculture, Fisheries and Food and the National Rivers Authority to take a firm line on prosecutions.[31] Perhaps with more general concerns in mind as to the inadequate levels of fines imposed in water pollution cases, the maximum fine which may be imposed on summary conviction was

[28] *Water Guardians* (the newspaper of the National Rivers Authority), 1 (1990), 2.
[29] *Water Guardians*, 9 (1990), 2.
[30] *Water Pollution from Farm Waste 1989*, 1990, table 7. The House of Commons Environment Committee also noted, 'considerable variations in the levels of fine for apparently similar offences around the country', Third Report, *Pollution of Rivers and Estuaries*, 1987, House of Commons Paper 183 para.45.
[31] House of Commons Committee of Public Accounts, Seventeenth Report, *Grants to Aid the Structure of Agriculture in Britain*, 1990, House of Commons Paper 150 para.28.

increased from £2,000 to £20,000 from 1 January 1990.[32] From that date a person found guilty of the offence of polluting controlled waters will be liable, on summary conviction, to imprisonment for a term not exceeding three months, or to a fine not exceeding £20,000 or both, and on conviction on indictment, to imprisonment for a term not exceeding two years or to a fine of unlimited amount or both.[33]

Alongside the statement of the penalties which may be imposed for pollution of controlled waters it may be noted that the situations which give rise to prosecutions in agricultural contexts occasionally involve inadequate effluent storage facilities which the farmer concerned would incur considerable expense in rectifying. Indeed, there may be situations where the amount of any fine that might reasonably be imposed is markedly less than the cost of repairing or renewing the facility which is the root of the problem. In such situations there are strong arguments for enabling a court to require the offender to carry out specified work to prevent future pollution, either in addition to, or as an alternative to, any fine that might be imposed in relation to the particular incident which is before the court. A clear legal parallel may be drawn with the provisions under Part I of the Environmental Protection Act 1990 providing for integrated pollution control over the most environmentally harmful forms of industrial processes. Under these provisions the regulatory body concerned, Her Majesty's Inspectorate of Pollution, may withdraw the authorization necessary for an offending activity to continue, and a court convicting a person of conducting the process without authorization may, in addition to or instead of a punishment, order the offender to take specified steps to remedy matters which it is in his power to remedy.[34] Similarly in relation to some instances of agricultural pollution, tackling the root of the problem might hold considerable environmental benefits over the imposition of punishment for its consequences.

Good Agricultural Practice

Prior to the enactment of the Water Act 1989, a defence existed to the offence of causing or knowingly permitting the entry of polluting matter into controlled waters so that no offence was committed if the entry in question was attributable to an act or omission which was in accordance with 'good agricultural practice'.[35] This was a reference to

[32] S.107(6) Water Act 1989 as amended by s.145(1) Environmental Protection Act 1990.

[33] S.107(6) Water Act 1989, as amended. In practice no instance of custodial sentences being imposed for the offence have ever been recorded.

[34] See ss.13, 14 and 26(1) Environmental Protection Act 1990.

[35] S.31(2)(c) Control of Pollution Act 1974.

a code formulated by the Minister of Agriculture, Fisheries and Food and deemed to be good agricultural practice, without prejudice to any evidence that any further practice was good agricultural practice.[36] The principal document constituting the Code was introduced in 1985 and covered matters such as the storage, application and disposal of inorganic and synthetic fertilizers; organic manures, slurries and waste waters; silage effluent; and pesticides. In addition to the principal document, however, a range of miscellaneous pamphlets was issued dealing with particular problems in pollution control, and these were also deemed to be a part of the Code. In respect of all of the matters contained in these documents adherence to the practices described provided the farmer with a special defence to a water pollution offence unless the Secretary of State served a notice directing the recipient to desist from practices leading to the entry of polluting matter into controlled waters.[37]

Although it has been suggested that the good agricultural practice defence was relatively infrequently pleaded in practice,[38] the availability of a special defence for farmers who caused water pollution was the subject of considerable controversy. The House of Commons Environment Committee[39] recognized that though the concept of a code was a good one, its operation in practice did not withstand close scrutiny and failure to observe it was widespread. The Committee was unable to conceive of any circumstances where the pollution of a stream by a farm could justifiably be excused on the grounds that 'it accorded with good agricultural practice' since the two were mutually exclusive. It was concluded that, in the light of the growing tide of farm pollution incidents, the special defence provided to farmers should be repealed. Beyond the repeal of the Code as a defence, the Committee recommended that consideration should be given to revision of the Code and providing it with statutory force, so that it would become an offence for a farmer to fail to follow the code regardless of whether or not this gave rise to any incident of water pollution.

With this background of controversy it was inevitable that the continuation of the good agricultural practice defence should be subject to modification during the passage of the Water Act 1989. The Act brought about the removal of good agricultural practice as a defence to the water pollution offence but retained the Code of Good Agricultural Practice albeit with a different legal status. The Secretary

[36] Ibid. s.31(9).
[37] Ibid, s.51.
[38] Observations of the Government on the Third Report of the Environment Committee, *Pollution of Rivers and Estuaries*, 1988, House of Commons Paper 543 para.3.6.
[39] House of Commons Environment Committee, Third Report, *Pollution of Rivers and Estuaries*, 1987, House of Commons Paper 183 paras.63 to 78.

of State and the Minister of Agriculture, Fisheries and Food are now empowered to approve a code of practice for the purpose of giving practical guidance to persons engaged in agriculture with respect to activities that may affect controlled waters, and promoting what appear to them to be desirable practices for avoiding or minimizing the pollution of controlled waters.[40]

The new status of the Code of Agricultural Practice is such that its contravention is not to give rise to any criminal or civil liability, but the National Rivers Authority is to take into account whether there has been, or is likely to be, any contravention in determining when and how it should exercise its powers. Specifically, a contravention of the Code is to be taken into account in relation to the exercise of the Authority's power to impose a relevant prohibition prohibiting certain kinds of discharge,[41] or any powers conferred on the Authority by regulations[42] requiring precautions to be taken against pollution.[43] In practical terms the effect of the changes which have taken place is that the existing Code will continue to have effect under the 1989 Act, to the extent that it has not been superseded by new provisions,[44] but with a significantly different legal status.

At the time of writing it is evident that a revision of the Code of Good Agricultural Practice is imminent. The Ministry of Agriculture, Fisheries and Food is in the process of preparing a revised free advisory package of Codes of Good Agricultural Practice,[45] and the first of these, relating to the protection of water, was issued in draft form for consultation in January 1991.[46] The draft revised Code contains much of the information already found in the existing Code and associated booklets, but updates it in line with current technology and policies and presents it in its full form in a single volume. In particular the draft Code contains practical and detailed advice to farmers on how to avoid pollution of water from farm wastes, fertilizers, nitrate, fuel oil, sheep dip, carcase disposal and pesticides.

Alongside the information on water pollution prevention that is provided by the Code of Good Agricultural Practice it is pertinent to note that measures which are undertaken by a farmer to prevent water pollution may attract substantial grant-aid. Under the Farm and Conservation Grant Scheme introduced in 1989, 50 per cent grants are available in respect of providing, replacing or improving facilities for the storage, treatment and disposal of agricultural wastes and silage

[40] S.116(1) Water Act 1989.
[41] Under ibid. s.107(2)(a) or (b).
[42] Under ibid. s.110.
[43] Ibid. s.116(2).
[44] Ibid. Sched.26, para.21.
[45] Announced in *This Common Inheritance*, 1990, Cm. 1200, para.12.16.
[46] Draft codes are also in preparation to advise farmers on air and soil protection.

effluent. Accordingly, it was recently announced that the Ministry of Agriculture, Fisheries and Food had committed £50 million of grant-aid, over the first three years of the scheme, to encourage the agricultural industry to reduce the number of pollution incidents.[47]

Counteracting Agricultural Pollution

Despite the imposition of strict liability in relation to the offence of causing or knowingly permitting water pollution, the greater readiness of the National Rivers Authority to pursue legal proceedings than previous authorities, and the significant increase in the levels of fines that may be imposed in certain cases, the problem of agricultural pollution remains. Indeed, it is possible that it may be worsening. Although an increase in any form of undesirable behaviour is not always a good reason to conclude that there is a defect in the law relating to it, in this context there may be grounds to suppose that the traditional legal perception of the environmentally damaging activity may be misconceived.

Traditionally the law has conceived of the problem of agricultural pollution of watercourses in terms of a discrete and identifiable entry of polluting matter into a watercourse causing a dramatic and sudden change in water quality and, usually, obvious environmental consequences such as the death of large numbers of fish. This picture may be typified by those kinds of cases which are most likely to feature amongst the small proportion of farm pollution incidents that result in convictions. However, the overall decline in the state of river water quality which has taken place over recent years is not solely due to such incidents but also to the more serious, pervasive and intractable difficulties which arise through the gradual transmission of diffuse pollutants into watercourses. For example, animal waste may wash from yards gradually as rainwater run-off, and other agricultural pollutants such as pesticides and fertilizers may pass into watercourses from the land to which they are applied by imperceptible percolation through soil. Although these kinds of problem feature only rarely as the basis of criminal proceedings, it is clear that they constitute a substantial part of the overall problem of declining water quality. Moreover, it is evident that they constitute a problem which requires a different kind of approach from that which is traditionally employed in relation to agricultural pollution. Effective control of water pollution from these sources requires proactive controls upon potentially polluting agricultural land use rather than reactive legal proceedings

---

[47] House of Commons Committee of Public Accounts, Seventeenth Report, *Grants to Aid the Structure of Agriculture in Great Britain*, 1990, House of Commons Paper 150 para.18.

being pursued after a pollution incident has taken place and inflicted damage upon the aquatic environment.

Fortunately the inadequacies of the traditional approach to the regulation of agricultural water pollution have been recognized through the provision of enabling powers facilitating the enactment of regulations to counteract those agricultural land uses which constitute a water pollution hazard.[48] Specifically, the Water Act 1989 provides for three distinct forms of proactive regulation in respect of agricultural water pollution: precautionary regulations, water protection zones and nitrate sensitive areas.[49] The implications of these are considered in the following sections.

Precautionary regulations

In environmental terms, the prosecution of a farmer for a water pollution incident is no substitute for preventing the incident occurring in the first place. Moreover, the fact that an incident has taken place is frequently a recognition that inadequate preventative measures were taken. The imposition of a fine may serve as a deterrent to prevent recurrence of incidents of the same kind but does nothing to restore the watercourse to its former state. Even where a criminal court exercises its power to grant a compensation order to a person who has been harmed by a pollution incident,[50] or where civil proceedings give rise to the payment of compensation,[51] the difficulty remains that, once damaged, aquatic ecosystems cannot be simply costed out and repurchased in the manner that redress is sought to be provided in other branches of the law.

Environmentally, prevention is always better than cure, and this principle is clearly acknowledged at a European Community level by the reaffirmation that Community action relating to the environment is to be based on the principles, amongst others, that preventative action should be taken wherever possible and that environmental damage should be rectified at source.[52] Although, in England and Wales, provision has existed for some years for regulations to be enacted under previous legislation requiring precautions to be taken by persons having the custody or control of any poisonous, noxious or polluting matter for the purpose of preventing the matter from entering

---

[48] Although provision previously existed for preventative regulations to be enacted and water protection areas to be designated, under ss.31(4) and (5) Control of Pollution Act 1974, no use was ever made of these powers.

[49] Provided for under ss.110 to 112 Water Act 1989.

[50] Under Powers of the Criminal Courts Act 1973.

[51] Generally see, Howarth, *Water Pollution Law*, 1988, Chapter 3.

[52] See also art.130R Treaty of Rome 1957, inserted by the Single European Act 1987.

waters,[53] no use has ever been made of these powers. A similar power to make precautionary regulations incorporated into the Water Act 1989 has, however, been exercised and regulations recently made.

The Secretary of State for the Environment, in relation to England, and the Secretary of State for Wales, in relation to Wales, are empowered to make regulations providing for preventative measures in relation to water pollution. In particular, they may exercise this power to prohibit a person from having custody or control of any poisonous, noxious or polluting matter unless prescribed works, precautions and other steps have been taken for the purpose of preventing or controlling the entry of the matter into any controlled waters. Similarly, they may require a person who already has custody or control of, or makes use of, poisonous, noxious or polluting matter, to carry out works and take precautions for the same purpose.[54] Precautionary regulations may confer power on the National Rivers Authority to determine and specify the circumstances in which a person is required to carry out works or take precautions or other steps to prevent water pollution. Regulations may also provide for appeals to the Secretary of State against notices served by the Authority in pursuance of its power to determine preventative measures. Contravention of precautionary requirements is to be an offence the maximum penalty for which is not to exceed the penalties provided for in relation to the principal offence of polluting controlled waters.[55]

Precautionary regulations on agricultural pollution

Precautionary regulations in respect of agricultural water pollution have recently been enacted following the Department of the Environment and the Welsh Office consultation paper on proposed regulations to control silage, slurry and agricultural fuel oil installations.[56] The Regulations are the Control of Pollution (Silage, Slurry and Agricultural Fuel Oil) Regulations 1991[57] and, in general terms, they introduce controls and set standards for the construction of silage stores, slurry installations and agricultural fuel oil stores for all farms in England and Wales.

When the Regulations came into force, on 1 September 1991, they made it an offence for any person to have custody or control of any crop that is being made into silage unless it is stored in a silo which conforms with specifications set out in Schedule 1 to the Regulations.

[53] See s.31(4) Control of Pollution Act 1974, now repealed.

[54] S.110(1)(a) and (b) Water Act 1989.

[55] Ibid. s.110(2).

[56] Department of the Environment, Public Consultation on *Proposed Regulations to Control Silage, Slurry and Agriculture Fuel Oil Installations*, 1990.

[57] SI 1991 No.324.

Silage is to be stored in bales which are individually wrapped and sealed within an impermeable membrane and stored at least 10 m from any watercourse, and bales are not to be unpacked within 10 m of any watercourse which silage effluent could enter. Schedule 1 to the Regulations sets out a range of requirements in respect of the construction of silage silos, such as requirements in respect of maximum loading capacity, an impermeable base, a prohibition on any part of the silo being constructed within 10 m of any watercourse and a requirement that silos are to be designed and constructed so that, with proper maintenance, they are likely to satisfy other requirements of the Schedule for at least twenty years.

In relation to the storage of animal slurry, the Regulations require that a person having custody or control of slurry is to store it in a reception pit or a slurry storage tank which conforms to requirements set out in Schedule 2 to the Regulations. Schedule 2 imposes requirements to the effect that the slurry storage tanks are to be constructed with an impermeable base and walls capable of withstanding specified loads. Storage tanks are to have adequate storage capacity for the quantity of slurry produced on the premises, an amount which is presumed in the absence of evidence to the contrary, to be the maximum quantity of slurry which is likely to be produced in any continuous four-month period taking into account the amount of rainfall which may enter the tank. Again, no tank is to be situated within 10 m of any watercourse, and tanks are to be designed and constructed so that with proper maintenance they are likely to satisfy the requirements of the Schedule for twenty years.

In relation to the storage of fuel oil on farms, no person is to have custody or control of such oil in a quantity exceeding 1,500 litres unless it is stored in a storage tank within a storage area which satisfies requirements set out in Schedule 3 to the Regulations. This Schedule includes requirements for oil storage tanks to be surrounded by an impervious bund which will retain 110 per cent of the capacity of the tank in the event of an escape of its contents. Discharging taps from the tank must be within the bund and kept locked shut when not in use, and no part of the bund is to be situated within 10 m of any watercourse which fuel oil could enter if it escaped.

The prohibitions which the Regulations impose on silage silos, slurry storage tanks and fuel storage tanks are applicable to all such facilities other than 'exempt structures'. This term encompasses facilities which were in use or constructed before 1 March 1991, or contracted to be constructed before that date and completed before 1 September 1991. However, provision is made for the loss of exemption by a structure where it is substantially enlarged or reconstructed. Alternatively, exemption may be forfeited where the National Rivers

Authority is satisfied that there is a significant risk of pollution and it serves a notice upon a person having custody or control of the structure requiring works to be carried out and appropriate precautions taken and, thereafter, the notice is not complied with. Notices requiring works to exempt structures are to describe the works to be conducted and specify a reasonable period within which requirements are to be complied with. Appeals against the service of a notice may be brought to the Secretary of State.

In the last resort, contravention of the Regulations amounts to a criminal offence which is punishable, on summary conviction, by a fine not exceeding the statutory maximum, presently £2,000, or on conviction on indictment by a fine of an unlimited amount. Moreover, in all instances contravention of the Regulations constitutes an offence notwithstanding that no actual pollution of water takes place, and this does not detract from the need to avoid water pollution. The essence of the new Regulations is that a *failure to take precautions* to prevent pollution is in itself to become a punishable offence. It would seem that this provides a powerful means to counteract the problems arising from the main kinds of agricultural water pollution, and it is to be hoped that the proposed Regulations prove effective in achieving this.

Water protection zones

A separate mechanism for the prevention of agricultural water pollution is provided by the power to designate water protection zones provided for under the Water Act 1989.[58] Whilst the enactment of precautionary regulations allows for the control of polluting *substances*, the power to designate water protection zones is a facility for the prevention of water pollution which is related to *areas* that are particularly vulnerable to water pollution. Although not restricted in its use to agricultural contexts, the power to regulate specified activities in designated areas for the purpose of water pollution prevention is an important one, particularly for the protection of sensitive water resources such as underground water used for abstraction,[59] where agricultural activities are as capable as industrial activities of causing a hazard to such supplies.

The Secretary of State for the Environment may designate a water protection zone in England after consultation with the Minister of Agriculture, Fisheries and Food. In relation to Wales designation is a matter for the Secretary of State for Wales. Designation may take place where it is appropriate, with a view to preventing or controlling the

---

[58] S.111 Water Act 1989.

[59] Department of the Environment, *The Water Environment: the Next Steps*, 1986, para.5.7.

entry of any poisonous, noxious or polluting matter into controlled waters, or to prohibit or restrict the carrying on of activities which are likely to result in the pollution of those waters. The effect of designation is to enable the prohibition or restriction of activities specified or described in the order in the designated area.[60]

An order designating a water protection zone may confer power on the National Rivers Authority to determine the circumstances in which an activity is prohibited or restricted and determine the activities to which a prohibition applies. Alternatively, an order may apply a prohibition or restriction in respect of any activities which are carried on without the consent of the Authority or in contravention of any conditions subject to which consent is given. An order may also provide that contravention of a prohibition or restriction, or of a condition of a consent, is to be an offence the maximum penalty for which is not to exceed those provided for in relation to the main water pollution offence.[61] Matters falling to be determined by the Authority may be determined in accordance with a procedure and by reference to matters and the opinion of persons specified in the order. This is subject to the power of the Secretary of State to make separate provision by regulations with respect to applications, conditions and revocation or variation of consents, and appeals against the determination of any application. Provision may also be made for the exercise by the Secretary of State of any power conferred on the Authority along with administrative matters, including the imposition of charges for applications and consents, and the power to require registration of an application or consent.[62]

Although, at the time of writing, no water protection zones have so far been designated the potential of the powers provided for in the agricultural context is clear. If, for example, it were discovered that the excessive use of pesticides by farmers in a catchment area serving a source of drinking water supply was causing contamination of the supply, then the designation of the area as a water protection zone, with the imposition of appropriate conditions relating to the use of pesticides, would be an appropriate legal mechanism with which to tackle the difficulty.

Nitrate Sensitive Areas

The problem of pollution of watercourses by nitrate originating from fertilizer and manure applied to agricultural land is an especially serious one. As a result of surface water run-off and percolation

[60] S.111(1) Water Act 1989.
[61] Ibid. s.111(2).
[62] Ibid. s.111(4).

through the soil there takes place, frequently over long intervals of time, the gradual leaching of nitrate causing nutrient enrichment of watercourses, termed 'eutrophication', and ultimately the contamination of surface and underground sources of water supply. Given the dependence of much of the agricultural industry upon nitrate fertilizers alongside the vital need to maintain the purity of potable supplies, the problem represents a serious and formidable practical difficulty.[63] In legal terms it is also an urgent problem, given the prospect of proceedings being brought against the United Kingdom by the European Commission[64] for failure to meet the requirements of Community directives relating to drinking water quality in respect of nitrate content exceeding the limit value of 50 mg/l in some areas.[65] The important and distinctive features of the nitrate pollution problem are such that it has been specially provided for by a facility for the designation of nitrate sensitive areas. Accordingly, the measures concerning water protection zones, discussed above, are explicitly stated not to be applicable to the entry of nitrate into waters as a result of the use of any land for agricultural purposes.[66]

Powers provided under the Water Act 1989 enable the designation of a nitrate sensitive area where the 'relevant Minister' considers it appropriate to do so to prevent or control the entry of nitrate into controlled waters as a result of, or anything done in connection with, the use of any land for agricultural purposes.[67] Where designation of a nitrate sensitive area is brought about, and the Minister considers it appropriate to do so to prevent or control the entry of nitrate into controlled waters, he is provided with various powers either to enter into voluntary agreements with farmers in the area concerned, or to impose mandatory orders upon farmers within the area either with or without the payment of compensation.

[63] See Department of the Environment, *Nitrate in Water*, 1986; and Department of the Environment, *The Nitrate Issue*, 1988.

[64] See *Water Law*, (1990) 5.

[65] On the Community quality requirements for drinking water see 75/440/EEC directive concerning the quality required of surface water intended for the abstraction of drinking water in the member states; 79/869/EEC directive concerning the frequency of sampling and analysis of surface water intended for abstraction for drinking in the member states; and 80/778/EEC directive on the quality of water intended for human consumption. A Council directive has also been proposed (Document No.4136/89 COM (88) 708 Final) directly to control the entry of nitrate into water sources.

[66] S.111(5) Water Act 1989.

[67] S.112(1) and Schedule 11 Water Act 1989. The 'relevant Minister' for these purposes is the Secretary of State for Wales in relation to an area which is wholly in Wales. In relation to land which is wholly in England, or partly in England and partly in Wales, designation is by the Minister of Agriculture, Fisheries and Food and the Secretary of State for the Environment acting jointly (s.112(9)(a) and (b)).

In respect of the power to enter into voluntary agreements, the ministerial power enables him to enter into agreements with the owner of the freehold interest in the land, or any person having an interest in the land where the consent of the freeholder has been given. The substance of agreements of this kind is that, in consideration of compensatory payments to be made by the relevant Minister, the other party accepts obligations with respect to the management of the land imposed under the agreement.[68] An agreement of this kind will bind all persons deriving title to the land from the person entering into the agreement with the Minister.[69]

In addition to compensation agreements with landholders, provisions allow the Minister to make a mandatory order in respect of a nitrate sensitive area for the imposition of requirements, prohibitions or restrictions to prevent the entry of nitrate into controlled waters in relation to the carrying on of specified activities on agricultural land. Where this is done the order may provide for specified or determined amounts of compensation to be paid, if any, in respect of the obligations imposed under the order.[70]

A mandatory order in relation to a nitrate sensitive area may confer powers upon the appropriate Minister to determine the circumstances in which the carrying on of any activity is required, prohibited or restricted. In addition the order may apply a prohibition or restriction in respect of activities which may only be carried on subject to ministerial consent and in accordance with conditions subject to which the consent is given. Contravention of a requirement, prohibition or restriction in an order of this kind, or of a condition of a consent, is an offence which is punishable subject to penalties which are not to exceed those provided for in respect of the principal water pollution offence.[71]

The pilot nitrate scheme

The legal powers to create nitrate sensitive areas provided for under the Water Act 1989 have been exercised by the Minister of Agriculture, Fisheries and Food under the 'Pilot Nitrate Scheme' brought about, in part, by the Nitrate Sensitive Areas (Designation) Order 1990.[72] The objective of the scheme has been to select specific areas where nitrate concentrations in water sources exceed, or are at risk of exceeding, the limit of 50 mg/l specified in the European Community Drinking Water

[68] Ibid. s.112(2).
[69] Ibid. s.112(3).
[70] Ibid. s.112(4).
[71] Ibid. s.112(5).
[72] SI 1990 No.1013, as amended by Nitrate Sensitive Areas (Designation) (Amendment) Order, SI 1990 No.1187. Generally, see, Ministry of Agriculture, Fisheries and Food, *Nitrate Sensitive Areas Scheme*, 1989.

Directive, and to control the entry of nitrate from agricultural land into water sources in the area in order to ascertain the effect of such controls upon water quality. The particular locations within the scheme have been selected on the basis that they will serve as *pilot* areas in the sense that they will provide a means of evaluating the effectiveness of limiting nitrate use as a prelude to the general introduction of such schemes. For that reason the areas chosen represent a broad range of agricultural practices and hydrological conditions, but will provide a reasonably rapid response so that the effectiveness of the measures involved can be assessed in a relatively short period of time.

In part, the Pilot Nitrate Scheme involves the selection of nine 'advisory areas' which are to be subject to an intensive advisory campaign providing farmers with free advice on methods of reducing nitrate leaching. Beyond this, however, use has been made of the power under the Water Act 1989 to designate nitrate sensitive areas so that voluntary agreements can be entered into between farmers and the Minister. The Government has expressed a strong preference for a voluntary approach to nitrate reduction as an initial measure, but it has conceded that this may be succeeded by compulsory measures only if voluntary arrangements prove to be ineffective. The Nitrate Sensitive Areas (Designation) Order 1990 serves to designate ten pilot Nitrate Sensitive Areas in England. The ten areas, which are identified precisely by maps attached to the Order, are the following; Sleaford (Lincolnshire); Branston Booths (Lincolnshire); Ogbourne St George (Wiltshire); Old Chalford (Oxfordshire); Egford (Somerset); Broughton (Nottinghamshire); Wildmoor (Hereford and Worcestershire); Wellings (Staffordshire); Tom Hill (Staffordshire and Shropshire); and Kilham (Humberside). The total area covered by the ten sites is approximately 15,000 ha.

Within the ten designated Nitrate Sensitive Areas farmers will get free advice on ways to reduce the risk of nitrate leaching into water. More significantly, on application, farmers may enter into an agreement with the Minister, subject to certain conditions, allowing for payment of compensation to the farmer in return for an assurance that farming practices will be adopted which involve the application of reduced amounts of nitrate to the land. The detailed provisions regarding payments under Nitrate Sensitive Area agreements are rather intricate, but broadly two distinct schemes of payment are provided for under the Order, the 'basic scheme' and the 'premium scheme'. These are distinguished according to the burden of the obligations involved. For example, the obligations arising under a basic scheme agreement primarily concern limitations upon the maximum amounts of organic and inorganic nitrogen which may be added to the land and the times at which it may be added. By contrast, premium scheme agreements commit farmers to more fundamental changes in land use involving the conversion of arable land to low-intensity grassland of various descriptions. Because of the greater extent of the duties involved, the rates of payment arising under the premium scheme are considerably higher, though under both schemes the rates of payment vary according to the particular Nitrate Sensitive Area concerned.

All nitrate sensitive area agreements will contain a provision allowing the Minister to monitor compliance with the agreement or to assess the effectiveness of the agreement in preventing the entry of nitrate into controlled waters. Accordingly monitoring provisions will allow entry upon the land in question, the taking of samples, the installation of equipment and the examination of records. Where a farmer fails, without reasonable excuse, to comply with the provisions of an agreement the Minister may terminate the agreement and withhold the whole or any part of the payment payable to the farmer, and recover any payment already made to him. Provision is made for questions arising under Nitrate Sensitive Area agreements to be determined by arbitration in accordance with the Arbitration Acts 1950 to 1979.

The Pilot Nitrate Scheme is a first step, but a highly significant first step, in a direction which will unavoidably need to be followed to greater lengths in the future. The widespread control of land use as a means to the prevention of water pollution represents a major change in environmental policy and strategy. However, the 15,000 ha so far designated as Nitrate Sensitive Areas are insignificant by comparison to the extent of the problem of nitrate contamination of water supplies which presently exists. The likelihood that the problem will be exacerbated by the increased use of nitrate fertilizers which has taken place over recent years means that further measures will be inevitable. The findings of the pilot study will need to be urgently assessed with a view to achieving a considerable extension of the designated land in the manner which best realizes the objective of nitrate reduction. It is to be hoped that farmers will be co-operative in entering voluntary agreements of the kind presently provided for, but if this is not the case, the need to reduce nitrates is of such paramount importance that the introduction of a mandatory scheme, with or without compensation, will be unavoidable.

Conclusion

The developments which have been discussed make it evident that the law relating to agricultural pollution is changing rapidly. The progression beyond the traditional water pollution offences to the collection of proactive measures that have been described involves an appropriate and welcome recharacterization of the problems. If the new measures are properly implemented and enforced in the near future, they will make a significant contribution to improvements upon the poor recent record of agricultural pollution of the aquatic environment.

4

Reorganization of the Conservation Authorities

FIONA REYNOLDS AND WILLIAM R. SHEATE

On 11 July 1989 Nicholas Ridley, then Secretary of State for the Environment, announced without prior warning or consultation that he intended to carry out the biggest shake-up of the Government's conservation agencies in Great Britain since their establishment in 1949. The plans, to break up the Nature Conservancy Council and Countryside Commission, provoked a near-unanimous reaction of hostility from voluntary and statutory conservation organizations alike.

Less than eighteen months later these plans — only slightly amended — were implemented in Part VII of the 1990 Environmental Protection Act. In less than two years new bodies began to operate in England and Wales, with special Scottish legislation only months behind. The story of the shake-up is instructive both politically and as an indication of the varying fortunes of environmental concern at the hands of politicians in Britain.

The Ridley Proposals

Split-up

Nicholas Ridley's proposals were published in a written answer[1] in the closing days of the summer 1989 Parliamentary session — hardly de- signed to maximize attention. They were, in essence, to split the Nature Conservancy Council (NCC — then operating with a GB remit) into three separate bodies, one for each of England, Scotland and Wales; and the Countryside Commission (CC) for England and Wales into two. The CC in Wales and NCC Wales would

[1] House of Commons Hansard, col. 482, 11 July 1989; also DoE Press Release 383.

simultaneously be merged into a new 'Countryside Council for Wales' and later legislation (which was introduced into Parliament in October 1990) was promised to merge the previously separate Countryside Commission for Scotland with NCC Scotland, to form a new Natural Heritage Agency for Scotland. NCC England and the new English Countryside Commission would remain separate 'in view of the much greater density of population and consequent pressure on the land'. The intention and main driving force behind the proposals, the Government said, was to devolve the functions of the NCC so that nature conservation would be delivered closer to the ground.

The proposals were primarily associated with Nicholas Ridley, a Secretary of State for the Environment whose dislike of quangos was well known. But the decision to make the changes was a Cabinet one and was apparently discussed no less than three times before gaining approval. It rapidly became clear that the Scottish (Malcolm Rifkind) and Welsh (Peter Walker) Secretaries of State were equally implicated in the decision, and may even have been prime architects of it.

Whatever was said publicly about the benefits of devolution for its own sake, it must be acknowledged that a prime motivation for the reforms was the unpopularity of the NCC in Scotland. During the 1980s tension had grown between well-meaning, but possibly less than tactful, NCC officials and Scottish landowners over certain instances of SSSI designation or proposed controls over potentially damaging operations. The well-publicized and bitter dispute over afforestation of the Flow Country may have proved to be the last straw. Nicholas Ridley and Malcolm Rifkind were persuaded that an independent and Scottish-based NCC rather than a UK organization based in Peterborough, England was likely to be less antagonistic to the Scottish people and Scottish interests, and more likely to carry those interests with them in discharging their functions. Others feared that while this might indeed be the case, protection of the Flow Country and other internationally important habitats might not be given such high priority under such a body.

Merger

Once proposals for devolution in Scotland were aired within the Government system, it became politically necessary to consider devolution in Wales also. But NCC's Welsh Office was much smaller than the Scottish operation, and Peter Walker is credited with the idea of merging it with the Countryside Commission's Welsh office to create a separate and new Countryside Agency in Wales, reporting to the Welsh Office. In turn, the idea of merging the new Scottish NCC with the already independent Countryside Commission for Scotland was mooted.

These proposals had the undeniable advantage of turning a simple break-up of the NCC (which, it was recognized, was bound to be strongly opposed) into a much more constructive proposal for the integration of countryside and nature conservation interests: interests which were artificially separated in the UK, unlike elsewhere in Europe, under the 1949 National Parks and Access to the Countryside Act which had first established the quangos.

To a large degree, this tactic worked. The separation of the NCC and CC had long been regarded as illogical if not disadvantageous, and many commentators greeted the plans for integration of the NCC and CC as one of the most important — if not the only — benefit flowing from the Government's proposals.

But integration was not planned in England, and this illogicality dogged the Government's proposals from their earliest days. The justification for keeping the NCC and CC separate in England — that of greater population density — was delivered with less than confidence and proved to be far from convincing when examined in detail during the passage of the Environmental Protection Bill. And while the Scottish and Welsh wings of all political parties and many other Scottish and Welsh organizations greeted the new proposals with enthusiasm, the discontinuity in England left both English and UK bodies bemused, and appears to have remained a cause for private concern even within the Department of the Environment.

Among the voluntary conservation movement, the proposals as a whole were greeted with dismay. No matter how much debate had gone on behind the scenes, the proposals as presented appeared ill-conceived and ill-thought out. Few believed the new structures would work, never mind deliver effective conservation advice to Government.[2]

Consultation

Lack of consultation was the source of the most bitter reaction to the proposals, and here the Government both misunderstood and misjudged the strength of feeling. Although the conservation agencies are the Government's own advisers and therefore technically the Government's to do with as it wishes, the quangos are inextricably linked with the voluntary sector bodies. First, their very creation in the 1940s had been due to voluntary sector pressure; second, key individuals within the quangos over their forty-year history had voluntary sector roots and/or close connections; and third but not least, the quangos had worked closely with the voluntary sector since

[2] 'Lords Petitioned to Halt Conservation Split', Wildlife Link Press Release on behalf of eighty conservation groups and twenty senior conservationists, 4 July 1990.

their inception, recognizing the enormous multiplier effect voluntary activity has on their own efforts. To break these bodies up — whatever the motive — cut at the heart of voluntary bodies' own roots and pre-occupations.

That the motive was largely perceived as a political one doubled the anxieties felt. Most conservation bodies claimed that they would have recognized the case for devolution in some form and of some functions had they been given the opportunity to comment on proposed reforms. What angered them was devolution for the sake of it, when it was clear that the proposals were too crudely formulated to deliver the Government's promise of more effective conservation, simply delivered closer to the ground.

The fact that the quangos themselves were not consulted led to deeper scepticism of the Government's motives. In fact, the NCC had drawn up its own 'federal' model which it was on the point of implementing when the Government announced its proposals. And within weeks of the announcement, a new Secretary of State for the Environment (Chris Patten) was promising a more open and consultative approach to the Government's most ambitious ever environmental exercise — the Environment White Paper.

In fact, although there was no consultation whatever prior to the Government's announcement, the decision to conduct the reorganization in Scotland in two phases — establishment of a separate NCC (Scotland) and then merger, a year later, with the Scottish Countryside Commission — provided the Scottish Office with an opportunity to consult on how this might best be achieved. Speaking to the Royal Society of Edinburgh in February 1990, Malcolm Rifkind made a virtue of this, saying:

> To achieve [something really worthwhile for conservation and the protection of the countryside] we need the right organisation capable of an integrated approach to wildlife and to landscape. It is important to take time to get it right. That is why we have taken a different approach in Scotland to our colleagues in England and Wales . . . The two stage process we have adopted gives us time to collect ideas, consult informed opinion and to develop a practical and effective agency.[3]

Two consultation papers were published by the Scottish Office and, although they did not permit the principle of reorganization to be challenged (a principle which tended not to be challenged in Scotland

[3] Scottish Office Press Release and text of speech to the Royal Society in Edinburgh by Rt Hon. Malcolm Rifkind QC MP, on 'Scotland's Natural Heritage', Monday 26 February 1990.

in any case), the exercises achieved much in establishing consensus within Scotland about how the merger should best be achieved.

This was in marked contrast to the enforced merger in Wales, where the Countryside Council was to be operational within six months of the Act's Royal Assent. Concerned about 'getting it right', the Countryside Commission attempted to establish a new mandate for the CCW (Countryside Council for Wales) rather than requiring it simply to inherit the cobbled-together statutory duties of the two previous bodies. This was resisted by the Government and only very late in the day was a very unsatisfactory clause inserted into the bill in a grudging attempt to remedy this.

The UK dimension

What particularly dismayed the conservation bodies was the complete void in the Government's proposals at UK level — the four new agencies were apparently expected to work entirely independently, with no reference to any national and/or international dimensions to their work. This suggested that each country would be able to adopt different standards or approaches to conservation activity, reinforcing fears about weakening conservation in Scotland and Wales. Two concerns dominated the debate: the break-up of the NCC's 'science base' (in particular, its Chief Scientist's division); and fears that the much valued UK-wide designation systems — National Nature Reserves (NNRs), Sites of Special Scientific Interest (SSSIs) and National Parks (NPs in England and Wales) would be designated, protected and managed under different criteria in each country. Only days after the initial announcement, the Government was forced to recognize this vacuum, acknowledging that proper co-operation between the new bodies would be essential and that all work would need to be underpinned by 'rigorous science', in recognition of the data and expertise which the NCC had built up over forty years.

The absence of provision for UK-wide standards or overview in the Government's proposals was thus very quickly characterized in terms of a threat to the NCC's 'science base', and responded to by the Government in those terms. This occurred despite NCC's ready acknowledgement that its science base had been eroded long ago with the splitting off of the Natural Environment Research Council, and that science and policy were integrally related — in both its vertical and horizontal structures — in its work throughout the UK. Nevertheless, concern for 'science' led to the establishment of a House of Lords Science and Technology Committee inquiry and became the rallying cry for the campaign for a UK dimension to reorganization.

The Patten Amendments

The appointment of a new, environmentally-friendly Secretary of State for the Environment only days after the plans were announced in July 1989 led to hopes that the reforms could be stopped or at least considerably amended. Chris Patten's immediate actions on appointment were to reassure a public dismayed by a series of decisions made by Nicholas Ridley: he dismissed plans for a new town at Foxley Wood in Hampshire and took immediate steps to rebuild public confidence in the planning system. But — not least because of Cabinet endorsement of the reorganization plans — he took no steps to withdraw them.

He could, as an alternative, have agreed to implement the reforms at a slower pace, allowing for example consultation in Wales over the most effective means of merging the NCC and CC, and time to reconsider the illogicality of not implementing a merger in England. He chose to do neither.

A joint co-ordinating committee

Rather, Chris Patten addressed only the most gaping hole in the proposals — the absence of a UK dimension. He announced on 23 November (the day the Environmental Protection Bill was published) that there would be a statutory duty placed on the new conservation bodies to form a Joint Co-ordinating Committee through which they would be required to fulfil certain of their functions.[4] These included providing advice to Government on nature conservation issues having a GB or international dimension; and the establishment of common standards for designation, research, monitoring and data analysis.

Chris Patten rejected NCC's suggestion that the Joint Committee should have an independent chairman, only to change his mind three weeks later. On 20 December, when the bill received its Second Reading in the Commons, Chris Patten announced that there would be an independent chairman for the Joint Committee, later confirmed as Professor (now Sir) Fred Holliday.

A contested bill

The passage of the bill through Parliament was characterized by acrimonious disputes between those bodies (largely those based in Scotland and Wales, plus the pro-devolutionists of all political parties) in favour of the proposals, and those (largely the voluntary sector conservation bodies, including many with Scottish or Welsh arms or

[4] House of Commons Hansard, col. 16, 23 November 1989; also DoE Press Release 636.

based in Scotland and Wales) who were against them in principle or detail.

From the voluntary conservation organizations' perspective, a number of key issues dominated the passage of the bill:

the fact that the plans were announced without prior consultation with either the voluntary sector or the agencies themselves;

the Government's desire to rush the plans through Parliament without allowing sufficient time for proper consultation, scrutiny or formulation;

the lack of any indication by the Government right up to the very last stages of the bill of the costs of reorganization;

the proposals' different arrangements in England, Scotland and Wales, and the lack of clarity in the arrangements for the UK perspective;

the selective application of the Government's logic for integration, with poor explanations given for the decision to merge the functions of the NCC and CCs in Scotland and in Wales, but not in England;

there was no analysis of the best level at which responsibilities should be carried out, whether at the national, regional or UK level. The proposals simply devolved all functions to the country bodies and required a few to be carried out via the Joint Committee;

the Government's proposals failed to recognize the UK dimension of the Countryside Commission's work in relation to landscape conservation and public enjoyment.

Although many of the voluntary bodies opposed the reforms as drafted and called for their withdrawal from the Environmental Protection Bill, constructive amendments were also tabled around which vital debates of principle took place. Disappointingly, the Government was steadfast that its proposals alone would improve the delivery of conservation.

The 'Carver' Committee

Conversely, the Government hung most of its hopes for getting the bill through Parliament on the report of the sub-Committee of the House of Lords Select Committee on Science and Technology. The sub-Committee was chaired by Lord Carver and its report,[5] published on 1 March 1990 during the House of Commons Committee stages of the bill, proved to be influential within its remit.

[5] Report of the House of Lords Select Committee on Science and Technology, 'Nature Conservancy Council', HL Paper 33-I, 1 March 1990, Session 1989–90, 2nd Report, HMSO.

The so-called 'Carver Committee' took as its remit the task of examining the effect of the Government's proposals on the scientific base of the NCC. These narrowly defined terms of reference were of considerable significance for the final outcome of the reorganization proposals. The Committee did not see its task as to examine, nor did it take a view on, the merits or otherwise of the Government's proposals *per se*; nor did it stray far beyond the central importance it attached to 'science'.

However, the Committee could not confine those giving evidence to this narrow remit, and it heard a great deal of criticism of the Government's proposals. In spite of the usually moderate language of the House of Lords Select Committees, the Committee's conclusion was that 'the reorganisation could have been better handled', and it aired the criticism that

> the policy had not been thought through: the original announcement did not make satisfactory provision for the scientific base of nature conservation, and the incomplete mergers of the NCC and Countryside Commission are illogical. The manner and timing of the announcement raised suspicions about the Government's motives, particularly in the voluntary sector: this has made a successful reorganisation more difficult. Then the fact that a consultation exercise — albeit a rather superficial one — was held in Scotland while no consultation was held in England made matters worse.

The Carver Committee made a number of recommendations, some more far-reaching than others. Their main thrust was the need to strengthen the role and effectiveness of the Joint Committee, to achieve full integration of the NCC and CC within England *and* at the level of the Joint Committee (though this latter argument was poorly developed) and to ensure that the new structures as a whole were adequately staffed and funded.

The Government in responding[6] accepted many of its recommendations, though most of these were not particularly arduous, and were more or less essential if the proposals were to be workable (see Table 4.1). Notably, it did not accept the recommendations for integration within England or the Joint Committee — not only the Carver Committee's most ambitious recommendations, but also those which would have lent some coherence and a genuinely forward-looking vision to the proposals as a whole.

[6] Government Response to the Report by the House of Lords Select Committee on Science and Technology on the Nature Conservancy Council, 17 May 1990; published the evening before Second Reading of the Bill in the House of Lords, 18 May 1990.

Table 4.1   *Main recommendations of the Carver Committee and Government responses*

Carver recommendations	Government response
JC to have 11 voting members	Accepted recommendation
JC to include an independent chairman, 3 independent members appointed by Secs. of State, and the Chairman of the Countryside Commission for England	Accepted
Reps. from N. Ireland on JC (non-voting)	Accepted — 2 representatives
JC remit also to cover countryside and landscape conservation	Rejected[1]
JC to have *c.*20 professional staff	Did not commit itself[2]
JC to supervise quality of scientific work	Rejected
Councils and JC to give annual reports to Parliament	Accepted for councils but not at this stage for JC[3]
Consultation — amalgamate CC and NCC in England	No amalgamation, though to be considered in future
Decisions of JC should be binding on country councils	JC can vote but decisions not binding
Scottish Dev. Department should be renamed to reflect conservation and countryside responsibilities	Accepted in principle

Notes

[1] The Government later renamed the Joint Committee as the Joint Nature Conservation Committee to stress its limited remit.

[2] Actual staff number is 51 (February 1991).

[3] The publication of an annual report by the Joint Committee was eventually accepted on amendment in the House of Lords.

The Joint Committee

Arguments over the form and responsibilities of the Joint Committee were central to the reorganization proposals. In simple terms, the recognition that a Joint Committee was necessary at all reflected a major concession against the interests of those who wanted in-dependent country agencies because there were, as the Government had put it at the beginning, 'increasing feelings that [existing] arrangements are inefficient, insensitive and mean that conservation issues in both Scotland and Wales are determined with too little regard for the particular requirements in these countries'.

Yet to give the Joint Committee more than a co-ordinating role, as most of the voluntary conservation movement argued was necessary, would be to reinvoke decision-making at a level remote from Scotland and Wales. As things turned out, the events surrounding the Government's establishment of a Joint Committee (later renamed the Joint Nature Conservation Committee (JNCC), as if to emphasize the fact that integration at the UK level was not to be provided) revealed the extent to which the reorganization plans were decided 'on the hoof' as problems and inconsistencies emerged.

At the heart of the matter was the extent to which the Joint Committee was to be a creature of the new country agencies, only operating through them and with their full agreement; or was to take an independent view to which it could require the country agencies to adhere. Valuable though the Carver Committee's report was, it fudged this vitally important question. On the one hand, it recommended that the Joint Committee should 'be the means through which the country councils work together . . . [and] should not be an independent quango'. On the other, it stressed that the Joint Committee should 'be strong enough to drive forward the cause of conservation at a national level' and 'in the event of a disagreement between the Councils . . . the decision of the Joint Committee should be binding'.

How could the circle be squared? Was the Joint Committee to take decisions and resolve disputes, or could it only speak when there was unanimity among the country agencies? The debates on the Joint Committee's functions and powers during the House of Commons Committee stage produced some extraordinary scenes of disarray on the Government front bench, the Under-Secretary of State (David Heathcoat-Amory) backing himself into a particularly awkward corner from which he took two days to extricate himself.

During the afternoon of 8 March and the morning of 13 March 1990 the Minister treated the Standing Committee to a long and elaborate explanation of the powers of the proposed Joint Committee in the event of a dispute between the committee and the country councils. The Government had always argued that the Joint Committee should be a 'servant' of the country councils, and the means through which the country councils would deal with national and international issues. Who would decide what was a national/international issue, i.e. of significance to the UK/GB as a whole, as opposed to only England, Scotland or Wales? Would the Joint Committee be able to vote, and if so would such a decision be binding on the country councils? Above all — and returning to the controversy which underlay the whole process — would the Flow Country be regarded as a purely Scottish matter, or one in which the Joint Committee could legitimately intervene?

This, of course, raised the fundamental principle of the degree of devolution that the proposals would actually deliver. In the event of an issue or project being deemed by the Joint Committee to be of UK/GB importance, and therefore requiring funds from all the country councils, would the Joint Committee be able to require each council to provide the necessary funds? If a council was not directly affected by the project, e.g. Wales in relation to the North Sea, it might not wish to provide funds. Could it be forced to? If not, what would be the point of the Joint Committee being able to vote in the event of a dispute?

The summing-up comments from Bryan Gould MP, Opposition spokesman on the Environment, illustrate the difficulty that MPs of all parties faced, forced to choose between a strong Joint Committee (and thus incomplete devolution) or a weak Joint Committee but referral of disputes up to an *English* Secretary of State for the Environment, thereby making a mockery of devolution.

Mr Gould said:

I should like to protest on behalf of Hon. Members on this side of the Committee, and, I suspect, of Conservative Members as well, at the way that the Government Front Bench have handled the debate. We have spent two and a half hours trying to extract information from the Minister that he could have given us in short order. He did not tell us, either because he did not know what the proposal represented, or because he did not want to tell us and was unable to provide an answer that was politically satisfactory to him. We have finally extracted from him that in the event of a dispute, the joint committee will have no power to resolve it . . . If the dispute remains unresolved, the Secretary of State for the Environment will solve it. That is an accurate statement of the position. It is worth recording why the Minister ducked and weaved for such a long time before acknowledging the position. It reveals that the structure created by the Government provides that there will be no effective conservation body able to make national decisions. The only person able to make such decisions will be the Secretary of State for the Environment — there is, therefore, no meaningful measure of devolution.[7]

The actual interpretation of how the relevant sections (ss.131–3) of the Environmental Protection Act will operate in practice has still not been satisfactorily explained.

However, it was not only the *powers* of the joint committee which caused considerable controversey. Its *remit* was equally illogical. While the Government was happy to integrate nature and countryside functions in Scotland and Wales, arguing that this would 'allow a more comprehensive approach to pursuing the special inheritances of wildlife and natural beauty in those two countries' the Joint Committee

[7] House of Commons Hansard, Environmental Protection Bill, Standing Committee H, 13 March 1990.

was to have a remit limited solely to nature conservation. When the representatives of the new Scottish and Welsh agencies attended meetings of the Joint Committee they would be expected to leave behind all notions of integration for the purposes of that committee.

Recognizing the vulnerability of its position on this issue, the Government accepted the Carver Committee's recommendations that the chairman of the Countryside Commission for England should at least be given a place on the Joint Committee 'to set nature conservation in its wider countryside context'. However, there was to be no widening of the remit to include countryside matters, and therefore no actual context through which to air or discuss his concerns.

Landscape and Countryside Conservation

The preoccupation with the 'science base' of the NCC at UK level had the undeniable effect of securing the significant Government concession of the establishment of the Joint Committee, but it distorted the debate considerably when it came to discussion of landscape, countryside conservation and public enjoyment issues.

Because there was no apparent 'scientific' dimension to these functions within the structures of the existing Countryside Commissions, the Government rejected the inclusion of their concerns within the Joint Committee. National *policy* considerations affecting nature conservation were, if indirectly, to be tackled by the Joint Committee; but the same was not to happen in relation to strategic policy-making in the field of countryside and public enjoyment.

The Government further emphasized its insistence on a limited remit for the Joint Committee by renaming it, at Committee stage in the House of Lords, the Joint *Nature Conservation* Committee (JNCC). As far as the Government was concerned, the reforms changed none of the functions of the old NCC and Countryside Commissions, merely redistributed them; and in so doing limited the strategic or national considerations to the minimum possible.

The different arrangements in the various countries and the precise nature of the Joint Committee created a situation where conceding a merger of the NCC and CC in England and/or of nature and countryside conservation on the Joint Committee became virtually impossible for the Government: it would have created significant imbalances on the Joint Committee.

As drafted, the Joint Committee was to deal solely with nature conservation. NCC England was to be represented on the Committee by two members. If NCC(E) was merged with CC(E) the nature conservation lobby, and the Earl of Cranbrook (chairman-designate of

NCC(E)) would have been unhappy at effectively losing one representative on the Joint Committee: the merged body would still only be represented on the Joint Committee by two members, in line with Scotland and Wales.

If nature and countryside functions were merged on the Joint Committee but not in England, CC(E) would expect equal representation, i.e. two members on the Joint Committee. There would then be four English members and only two each from Scotland and Wales. The Government had backed itself into an administrative and political corner from which it could not easily escape.

Merger, either in England or on the Joint Committee, or both, would have created a very sizeable English lobby with a degree of power and influence which the Government might not wish to see. It would hardly have satisfied the nationalist lobby in Scotland and Wales who were already suspicious of the powers of the Joint Committee. In short, any merger of functions in England or on the Joint Committee would require a fundamental rethink of the *raison d'être* of the Joint Committee.

A Missed Opportunity

The missed opportunity for achieving *improvements* to the delivery of conservation in the UK — an aim apparently shared by the Government — was a fact repeatedly stressed by the voluntary conservation movement. Instead of taking the quangos forward as a whole, the Government's proposals for reform were partial, and reinforced pre-existing inadequacies and inconsistencies in the structure of the conservation agencies.

These historical inadequacies were particularly evident in two areas: first, the exclusion of Northern Ireland from both the former and new systems (although the Government agreed in response to the Carver Committee to give Northern Ireland an observer's seat on the JNCC); and second, the lack of a GB or UK perspective for countryside functions, given the separate establishment of a Countryside Commission for Scotland in 1968.

There was a real opportunity, through the full integration of both Northern Ireland interests and countryside and nature conservation functions in England and on the JNCC to remedy both defects of the previous system.

In particular, it was argued that a UK dimension for countryside functions was needed to:

provide advice to Government on designations which affect or may affect all three/four countries (such as National Parks) both in a national and international context;

identify research and other needs which are of significance to more than one country;

establish common standards and protocols which are relevant to the needs of all the country agencies, for example on designation and management;

represent the agencies in international forums with countryside and recreation interests.

Thus, it was argued, as strong a case exists for an overview of countryside matters throughout Great Britain, and indeed the United Kingdom, as there is for nature conservation. There are common problems that require common, or similar, solutions.

The Government's acceptance of the arguments in relation to nature conservation reflects both the extent to which the 'scientific' argument hijacked the wider debate; and the absence of a GB or UK perspective in the previous composition and structure of the countryside agencies.

Moreover, future events seem likely to emphasize more strongly the need for such integration at JNCC level. For instance, in its Environment White Paper (September 1990)[8] the Government refers to its intention to review the landscape designations in Scotland, with the possibility of establishing National Parks (or similar designations), as proposed by the Countryside Commission for Scotland's report, *The Mountain Areas of Scotland*. There is considerable experience of National Parks in England and in Wales, and it would clearly be sensible if there was an opportunity to consider National Parks (or their equivalents) throughout the United Kingdom and to establish and maintain common countryside standards and criteria in each country. The JNCC would seem to be the most appropriate — indeed is the only — body able to do so.

Funding and Resources

The real costs of restructuring were finally acknowledged by the Government on the last day of the House of Lords Report stage (17 October 1990), when it confirmed that an additional £10 million was required to pay for the reorganization alone. The Government also confirmed that it would be making a generous extra allowance to the NCC, including additional staff posts, to enhance the level of conservation and other work which could be undertaken by the new agencies.

This announcement provoked considerable anger among members of the House of Lords, who had not been given prior notice of the announcement despite the Government's assurance that copies of the

---

[8] *This Common Inheritance — Britain's Environmental Strategy*, UK Government White Paper, Cm. 1200, HMSO, September 1990.

relevant financial reports had been placed in the House of Lords library the previous week. The House was even suspended while the facts were clarified, an event which has happened only three times since 1949.

The current allocation of funds for 1991/2 is undoubtedly more generous than previous years:-

NCC (England)	£32.4 million (includes £2.23 million for JNCC): 724 staff
Countryside Council for Wales	£14.55 million (includes £0.55 million for JNCC): 225 staff
NCC (Scotland)	£19 million (includes £1.18 million for JNCC): 385 staff
Countryside Commission (England)	£30.277 million: 200 staff (in post)
JNCC	£3.96 million: 51 staff (allocated and seconded from other agencies)

This adds up to £96.227 million, as compared with £70.106 million before reorganization: £44.82 million for the whole of the NCC (GB) and £25.286 million for the CC (E&W) in the financial year 1990/1.

The new allocation is, however, spread around three countries and five organizations, and although staffing figures indicate that there will be an increase in total staff of about 50 per cent, many of these will be involved in performing administrative and other tasks that will now have to be undertaken in triplicate, and in servicing the JNCC.

Moreover, there are staffing problems and inconsistencies that have yet to be resolved. For example, the differences in culture between the two organizations must be overcome in a positive manner: building on the strengths of (the much larger) NCC staff's practical and scientific expertise as well as the much smaller staffs of the Countryside Commissions, whose experience tends to be in strategic and management roles. There are also anomalies in the distribution of expertise between countries: there is, for instance, no provision for pollution work in Wales or in Scotland, although it is reasonably well provided for in England. There is currently only a quarter of a post in Wales dealing with water matters.

It seems inconceivable that the resolution of these problems will not, ultimately, require yet more resources to ensure that at both country and JNCC level the new agencies have adequate staff for the range of practical, scientific, management, liaison and policy tasks that face them.

The White Paper and Future Prospects

Chris Patten's White Paper exercise sat ill at odds with Part VII of the Environmental Protection Bill. A review of environmental policy across the spectrum of Government activity was bound to raise matters of institutional significance which would be pre-empted by the reorganization proposals simultaneously being authorized by Parliament.

In the event, as in so many areas of policy, the White Paper did not measure up to expectations. It simply repeated the Government's justification for reorganization, and did not address either the opportunity or the challenge posed by more fundamental institutional reform.

It did, however, equivocate over the possibility of a merger of NCC and CC functions in England in the light of experience in Scotland and Wales; and Baroness Blatch, speaking in the House of Lords a fortnight or so later elaborated further, saying:

> The Government's recent Environment White Paper on the Environment made it clear that Ministers have not closed the door on merger of the NCC and the Countryside Commission in England in the longer term. We will review this and other options when the new agencies have had a chance to settle down. If the Government does eventually opt for a merger, then further legislation would be needed, and I am sure that this would have to deal with the role of the Joint Committee.[9]

It was the closest the Government had come to an admission that its proposals were incomplete and inconsistent, and in need of further reform to work effectively and coherently.

It does, therefore, seem likely that within a matter of years these reforms will be made: to merge the NCC and CC in England and to extend the JNCC's remit to countryside and public enjoyment matters, although the latter is likely to need complete reconsideration for the reasons already discussed. This would undoubtedly be a considerable improvement on the current proposals, but will it meet the anxieties of those bodies who opposed the principle of free-standing country bodies?

Already, it seems clear that some at least of their anxieties were well-founded. The Natural Heritage (Scotland) Bill was introduced into the House of Lords in the autumn of 1990 to effect the merger of the NCC Scotland and the Countryside Commission for Scotland. During Committee Stage, amendments to allow landowners to appeal against conservation designations (other than SSSIs) in Scotland — passed 65 to 45 in favour — and to require Scottish Natural Heritage to review all SSSIs every five years and allow appeal against continued designation — passed 44 to 33 in favour — although contrary to the Government line, tend to bear out the fears of conservationists about the strength of

---

[9] House of Lords Hansard, col. 894, 17 October 1990, intervention made by Lady Blatch.

the landowners' lobby in Scotland and their desire to see the NCC operating differently there.

One cannot help reflecting that if the Government's primary motive in reforming the conservation agencies had been in order to make conservation more effective and to advance the cause of conservation throughout the UK, it would both have looked at other options, and would have been prepared to consult on them. Other models exist: for example, the National Rivers Authority (NRA) is a single body covering both England and Wales and decides much policy at that level, but devolves considerable management powers and responsibilities to regional boards and committees. The existence of such federal models — one of which the NCC was itself considering at the time reorganization was announced — illustrate that devolution of many responsibilities can be achieved without causing either disintegration or loss of national policy impetus or expertise. Because the Government proposed devolution — apparently for its own sake — first, and then had to claw back under pressure some strategic functions for the JNCC, the prospects for a coherent national and international dimension to conservation policy in the UK look less promising than they should have been at a time when the UK's effective participation in the global environment crisis is urgently needed.

Observers now wait to see whether, and to what extent, the conservation agencies are now able to move the conservation agenda forward. The extent to which these reforms represent a setback or the new agencies can in fact operate more effectively than their predecessors is a vital question. Whatever the outcome, there are many important issues which have yet to be adequately resolved.

5

The Enforcement of Conservation Legislation: protecting Sites of Special Scientific Interest

DAVID WITHRINGTON AND WYN JONES

Introduction

Since 1949, the Nature Conservancy and its successor bodies have identified areas of land or water containing plants, animals, geological features or landforms of special interest. Some 5,600 Sites of Special Scientific Interest (SSSIs) exist today, covering 8 per cent of the land surface of the United Kingdom. This means that conservation management can be extended beyond the limited number of reserves that can be purchased by public and private bodies. The system is much admired by conservation agencies abroad, not least because the sites are selected by a national conservation body rather than being allocated as not required for agriculture or industry. However, this does lead to conflicts with other land uses.

SSSIs were given increased protection under the provisions of the Wildlife and Countryside Act 1981. This essay assesses the measures available for protection of SSSIs and describes the experience of the Nature Conservancy Council in enforcing the legislation between 1981 and 1991.

Evolution of the Legislation

The report[1] of the Wildlife Conservation Special Committee, chaired by Julian Huxley, was presented to Parliament in July 1947. It recommended the establishment of statutory National Nature Reserves, to be managed by a national Biological Service; Local Nature Reserves, to be run by local authorities; and lists of special sites of

[1] Ministry of Town and Country Planning, *Conservation of Nature in England and Wales* (Report of the Wild Life Conservation Special Committee), Cmd. 7122, HMSO, 1947.

biological or other scientific importance, to be made available to local authorities and private owners.

The recommendations of this committee were the genesis of the Nature Conservancy and the sites for which it was made responsible under the National Parks and Access to the Countryside Act 1949. Section 23 of that Act gave the Nature Conservancy a duty to notify to the local planning authority 'any area of land, not being land for the time being managed as a nature reserve . . . of special interest by reason of its flora, fauna, or geological or physiographical features' (SSSIs). The local planning authority was required, in turn, to consult the Nature Conservancy where development was proposed within such an area (Town and Country Planning General Development Order 1950, article 9 (9)).

The emphasis in terms of management of habitats for wildlife was placed on National Nature Reserves (NNRs). Section 16 of the 1949 Act empowered the Nature Conservancy to enter into management agreements, where expedient in the national interest; section 17 gave powers of compulsory acquisition; and section 19 enabled the Nature Conservancy to make by-laws on NNRs. This situation continued for almost twenty years, until powers to enter into management agreements with owners and occupiers of SSSIs were given to the Nature Conservancy in section 15 of the Countryside Act 1968. It should be noted, however, that the Nature Conservancy still had no formal relationship with owners and occupiers of SSSIs, many of whom carried out operations in ignorance of the fact that their land had been notified to the local planning authority.

In the event, very few management agreements were negotiated. By 1975 there were only nine, covering 236 ha. By 1981, this had risen to seventy agreements covering 2,577 ha at a total cost of £39,000. (Since compensation agreements were introduced in the 1981 Act, the number has increased to nearly 1,800 at an annual cost of some £7 million.)

The adverse effects of drainage and river engineering on wildlife habitats were recognized in the extension of the Nature Conservancy's duty to notify SSSIs to river authorities in England and Wales (section 102 of the Water Resources Act 1963). In 1968 the Nature Conservancy pointed out that 'the limited safeguards afforded by law to the scientific interest of notified sites exclude any protection against forestry and agriculture, which can be just as devastating as building or road-making'.[2]

In 1973 the Nature Conservancy Council was founded by Act of Parliament. Most of the research staff were transferred to the Institute of Terrestrial Ecology. A greater emphasis was placed on protecting sites and species, and many more SSSIs were notified. In 1980 regional

[2] *The Nature Conservancy Progress 1964–1968*, Nature Conservancy, 1968.

staff of the NCC visited a random sample of 399 of the nearly 3,000 biological SSSIs. Significant damage to 13 per cent of sites was noted — with agriculture accounting for over half of the area damaged.[3]

This survey was instrumental in the argument for greater protection for SSSIs during the passage of the Wildlife and Countryside Bill through Parliament in 1981. The so-called 'voluntary principle' — whereby owners, occupiers and bodies who could influence the management of sites were made aware of their importance to nature conservation by the NCC and could decide whether or not to carry out damaging operations — remained the basis for site protection. However, it was backed up by three important additions in Part II of the Wildlife and Countryside Act: the NCC was to be consulted when any damaging operations were proposed on SSSIs; compensation payments were made available on a 'profit-forgone' basis; and orders could be made by the Secretary of State on nationally important sites.

SSSIs and other designations

The 1981 Act also removed the distinction between SSSIs and National Nature Reserves. All NNRs had to be notified as SSSIs. Indeed the SSSI legislation was to form the basic protection for designations made by the UK Government. Before 1981 only National Nature Reserves were designated under the Ramsar Convention on Wetlands of International Importance. Now the basic requirement is for sites to be notified as SSSIs. The same applies to Special Protection Areas designated under Article 4 of the European Council Directive on the Conservation of Wild Birds. This is the reason why the UK has not yet designated any 'international' sites in coastal waters, as the SSSI notification only extends to low-water mark.

The selection of SSSIs is entirely a matter for the Nature Conservancy Council, which published Guidelines for Selection of Biological SSSIs in 1989. Most SSSIs are notified because they are representative of a particular type of habitat — e.g. ancient woodland, hay meadow or chalk downland — whose special interest depends on the continuation of traditional management practices. The aim of the NCC is, therefore, not only to prevent damaging operations from taking place, but also to ensure sympathetic management of the land.

The SSSI Renotification Programme

Section 28 of the Wildlife and Countryside Act 1981 requires the NCC to notify owners and occupiers and the Secretary of State, as well as the local planning authority. The notification comprises a statement of the special interest, a boundary map and a list of operations which appear

[3] Seventh Report, Nature Conservancy Council, 1982.

to the NCC to be likely to damage the flora, fauna, geological or physiographical features for which the site was selected.

The NCC had to embark upon a major programme of renotifying 4,000 sites which had previously been notified to local planning authorities. SSSIs had assumed a greater importance under the law, and great attention had to be paid to the boundaries, which in many cases meant resurvey of the site. A good deal of 'legwork' was needed to try to identify some 30,000 owners and occupiers across Great Britain. The NCC also decided to notify new sites, which had been identified during the course of regional and national surveys, and to denotify some 575 existing SSSIs whose interest had declined. By the end of 1990, the NCC had renotified or denotified 97 per cent of existing SSSIs and notified over 2,000 new sites.

The NCC was required by the 1981 Act to give owners and occupiers three months to make representations or objections on proposed SSSI notifications. It was soon found that this consultation period was abused by owners or occupiers. There were cases where farmers ploughed up flower meadows, so that the land was no longer of special interest. This loophole was closed in the Wildlife and Countryside (Amendment) Act 1985. The notification of SSSIs is now followed (rather than preceded) by a consultation period, and the NCC must confirm the notification within nine months.

Criminal Offence on SSSIs

Section 28 of the 1981 Act, made it an offence for an owner or occupier of an SSSI, without a reasonable excuse (which includes planning permission and emergencies), to carry out (or cause or permit to be carried out) any operation specified in the site notification unless certain conditions are met: notice of a proposal to carry out an operation must have been given to the NCC in writing; the operation must have been carried out with the written consent of the NCC or in accordance with the terms of a management agreement with the NCC; or four months (originally three months) must have expired from the giving of written notice.

In England and Wales proceedings are taken by the NCC, though another person could institute proceedings with the consent of the Director of Public Prosecutions. In Scotland proceedings are taken by the Procurator Fiscal.

Nature Conservation Orders

The effect of orders made by the Secretary of State under section 29 of the 1981 Act, is to extend the period of notice of damaging operations on SSSIs from four months to some sixteen months. Where the NCC has not been able to negotiate a management agreement and considers that an owner or occupier may carry out damaging operations when the four months have expired, it has applied to the Department of the Environment, Welsh Office or Scottish Office for a so-called Nature Conservation Order to be placed on the land. Before the 1985 Amendment Act, Nature Conservation Orders were also requested to protect sites known to be under threat in the three-month pre-notification period.

The Secretary of State may make an order on land which he considers to be of special interest, to ensure the survival in the United Kingdom of any kind of animal or plant or to comply with an international obligation (e.g. to protect Special Protection Areas designated under the European Council Directive on the Conservation of Wild Birds). More generally he can make an order to protect any land which he considers to be of special interest and of national importance. All orders made so far have been in the latter category. The NCC must be consulted by the Secretary of State before he makes an order and, in practice, has requested all the orders to date. After the order has been made, Departments have looked to the NCC (in England and Wales) to institute proceedings where there has been a breach of section 29.

Up to December 1990, forty-one Nature Conservation Orders were made under the 1981 Act (see Table 5.1). That the provisions of section 29 are not available to protect all SSSIs became clear after the public inquiry into the West Mersea Meadow (Essex) Nature Conservation Order 1985. This small meadow of less than one acre was subject to planning applications for residential development. An NCC survey in May 1985 showed that the flora included some 15,000 green winged orchids *Orchis morio*, the uncommon adder's tongue fern *Ophioglossum vulgatum*, and the dragon's teeth *Tetragonolobus maritimus*, a possible colonist from central Europe. The NCC discussed the importance of the site with the owners and its intention to notify it as an SSSI. Within a week the owners had the site sprayed with herbicide, despite attempts by Friends of the Earth to prevent it. The NCC requested the Secretary of State to make a Nature Conservation Order; this was done two days later.

At the inquiry, the objectors sought to show that the site was not of national importance, despite the NCC's contention that all SSSIs were of national importance. It transpired that the NCC's national expert on grassland flora had not visited the site or been asked to comment on its importance before the decision to notify it as an SSSI. On the evidence of the occurrence of this habitat elsewhere and the characteristics of the site, including its small size, against NCC's own criteria, the Inspector found that it was not of national importance. The

Table 5.1   *Nature Conservation Orders made by the Secretary of State under section 29 of the Wildlife and Countryside Act 1981*

Year	Name of Site	County/Region
1981	*Sandford Heath	Dorset
	Baddesley Common	Hampshire
1983	*Tealham and Tadham Moors	Somerset
	*Waltham Chase Meadows	Hampshire
	Annesley Woodhouse Quarry	Nottinghamshire
1984	*Carstairs Kames	Strathclyde
	West Westray	Orkney
	Llyn Mawr	Powys
	Cadair Idris	Gwynedd
	*Carnkief Pond	Cornwall
	*Uddens Heath	Dorset
	Walton Moss	Cumbria
	Horse Field	North Yorkshire
1985	*Upton Heath	Dorset
	Leek Moors	Staffordshire
	West Mersea Meadow	Essex
	*Tealham and Tadham Moors	Somerset
	Hencott Pool	Shropshire
	*Coedydd a Chorsydd Aberteifi	Dyfed
1986	Chesil and the Fleet	Dorset
	Loch of Strathbeg	Grampian
1987	*River Spey and Insh Marshes	Highland
	*East Devon Pebblebed Heaths	Devon
	*North Fetlar	Shetland
	*Westhay Moor	Somerset
	*Loch of Strathbeg	Grampian
1989	*Barn Meadows	Worcestershire
	*Exe Estuary	Devon
	*Woolcombe Fen	Dorset
	*River Hull Headwaters	Humberside
	*Culbin Foreshore	Highland
	*Barking Woods	Suffolk
	*Kinneil Lagoon	Central
	*Upton Heath	Dorset
1990	*Grove Farm	Somerset
	*Gwenfro and Rhos y Gad	Anglesey
	*Black Loch (Abdie)	Fife
	*Loch Obisary	Western Isles
	*Drimnin to Killundine Woods	Highland
	*Helmdon Disused Railway	Northampton
	*Leek Moors	Staffordshire

* Order in force as at 31 December 1990

Secretary of State upheld the Inspector's conclusion and revoked the order.

Thereafter, the Secretary of State has refused some of NCC's requests for orders or requested further information on aspects of national importance. The NCC has been more rigorous in screening requests from its regions for order applications. At the same time, it has pressed the Government, without success, to ask Parliament to amend section 29 so that it can be used to protect all SSSIs.

Nature Conservation Orders have been generally effective in getting owners and occupiers to negotiate management agreements with the NCC. In only one case, on the Somerset Levels (see below), has the NCC resorted to making a compulsory purchase order — which is an option referred to in section 29(7).

Injunctions

During the period of uncertainty after the West Mersea Meadow inquiry, other legal mechanisms for the protection of SSSIs were explored. Injunctions have proved successful on the small number of occasions they have been sought in England and Wales. The NCC has not sought the use of the Scottish equivalent, interdict.

The first injunction obtained by the NCC was in 1985 to prevent damage to part of Cadair Idris SSSI in Gwynedd from agricultural operations. Although a Nature Conservation Order was made by the Secretary of State, the owner did not accept that farming operations could be controlled by the Wildlife and Countryside Act. A judge granted the NCC an interim injunction, which was confirmed at a High Court hearing. Further injunctions have been obtained to forestall damage or prevent it from continuing at SSSIs in Gwynedd (Cors Erddreiniog, Craig y Benlog, and Cutiau), on the Somerset Levels, at Barking Woods in Suffolk and the Swale in Kent. At Rainham Marshes in Essex, the NCC obtained an interlocutory injunction in 1989 to prevent damaging operations, which were continuing although summonses had been laid by the NCC under section 28. The owners then agreed to negotiate and to carry out some habitat restoration. As a consequence the injunction was not renewed. A few months later damaging operations were recommenced, and the NCC then sought and obtained an indefinite prohibitive injunction. In some of these cases, it is not clear that the NCC should have been applying directly for orders to restrain owners and occupiers. However, judges have apparently been sympathetic to NCC's argument that, without injunctions, destruction of the nature conservation interest would ensue.

SSSI Loss and Damage

The NCC has published statistics on loss and damage to SSSIs in its annual reports since 1983. The number of sites affected each year is running at about 5 per cent of the total. This represents a significant improvement over the 13 per cent found in the 1980 sample survey referred to earlier. However, the post-1981 Act statistics are not the result of systematic monitoring, and it is likely that the actual incidence of damage is somewhat higher.

The question to be asked is: why have there only been one or two prosecutions a year, when over 250 SSSIs a year are being reported as damaged? Part of the answer is given in NCC's annual report for 1989–90: 'Cases of intentional damage by owners and occupiers of SSSI land are relatively few, and the great majority of reported incidents are the result of past activities and decisions or are caused by persons, such as commoners or the general public, who are . . . not bound by the legal provisions concerning SSSIs'.[4] (It should be noted that commoners are now treated as occupiers following a statement by Ministers in response to proposed amendments to the Environmental Protection Bill — House of Lords, 17 October 1990.) Under section 28 it is a reasonable excuse if an operation has been granted planning permission. Although not numerous by comparison with agricultural activities, these developments represent the most serious cases of damage (21 ha of six SSSIs lost in 1989–90). Perhaps less than half of reported incidents of damage to SSSIs constitute breaches of section 28. Nevertheless, a total of only twelve prosecutions since the 1981 Act (see Table 5.2) is less than one would expect, a comparable rate to that achieved by the National Rivers Authority[5] on incidents of pollution from farm waste would be about four prosecutions a year.

The NCC as a Prosecuting Authority

Section 28 came into force on 30 November 1981, making the NCC a prosecuting authority for the first time. As we shall see, the process of adjustment from a body with few powers to one responsible for enforcement has been a difficult one for the NCC.

It seems that no particular consideration was given to the policy which the NCC should adopt on taking prosecutions, for instance, defining what was in the public interest. It was probably felt that solicitors would advise in each case. Decisions on whether to prosecute were delegated to NCC's country HQs. A note to regions in England in

[4] *Sixteenth Report*, Nature Conservancy Council, 1990.
[5] National Rivers Authority and Ministry of Agriculture, Fisheries and Food, *Water Pollution from Farm Waste 1989 (England and Wales)*, National Rivers Authority, 1990.

June 1984 suggested that they use local solicitors. The first prosecution under section 18 was heard at Loughborough Magistrates Court on 31 October 1984. The owner pleaded guilty to permitting lime to be spread on wet acidic grassland at Ulverscroft Valley SSSI. A fine of £200 was imposed. The NCC was represented by a Nottingham solicitor, Tom Huggon, who was known to have experience in wildlife prosecutions.

More detailed procedural guidance was issued to NCC staff in Wales in 1985, influenced, no doubt, by the fact that one of the staff most closely involved is an ex-policeman. It again stated that a local solicitor would be appointed for each case.

Regional staff in the front line

The NCC does not have any in-house legal expertise or prosecution unit. This means that in each prosecution the county officer (Assistant Regional Officer) is responsible for gathering evidence and witnesses. After the Ulverscroft Valley case, the NCC wished to secure future management of the site through an agreement. The owner was willing to discuss this, provided that it did not involve meeting the county officer again. Obviously, the conduct of a prosecution can make the day-to-day relationship of NCC's county officers with the local farming community very difficult and, in some cases, impossible.

Problems have arisen in taking cases to court when NCC's county officer has failed to caution defendants or to date documentary evidence. This highlights the need for a professional approach. The Treasury Solicitor commented to the NCC in 1988:

> The problems encountered . . . are typical of the difficulties which arise when officers who may be well versed in their own specialisation are required to move outside that specialisation in order to enforce the law. Parliament has made breaches of the Wildlife and Countyside Act offences punishable by the Criminal Law, and it is therefore necessary for any officers enforcing that Act to adopt the same approach as with a police officer investigating an allegation of crime.[6]

It was not only county officers but also those in HQ who found it difficult to deal with NCC's 'policeman' role. Staff in some English regions were under instruction for a considerable period not to deliver cautions to potential defendants. The collection of evidence and preparation of the case needs to be done efficiently (summonses must be laid within six months of the offence) and observing the rules of criminal evidence. In order to instil a more professional approach, two

[6] Letter from the Treasury Solicitor of 26 May 1988 to D. K. J. Withrington, Head — Sites, Freshwater and Legislation Branch, Nature Conservancy Council.

training courses were organized for NCC staff — one in England in 1987 and a second in Scotland in 1988. These benefited greatly from contributions by the police, Treasury Solicitor's staff, the Crown Office and Scottish Office Solicitors, the Royal Society for the Protection of Birds, which has its own enforcement unit, and many others with expertise in the law. However, less than thirty NCC staff received this training, and it is by no means certain that they personally will ever be involved in a prosecution.

Of the twelve prosecutions brought by the NCC since the 1981 Act came into force (see Table 5.2), three county officers have been responsible for more than one case, with the result that only nine county officers have taken SSSI cases to court. It may be concluded that the understandable reluctance of NCC county officers to get involved in legal proceedings is one of the main reasons why so few prosecutions have been taken.

The initial prosecutions

It has been mentioned that the first prosecution, on Ulverscroft Valley, went smoothly. The second one, in Wales, proved to be somewhat of a nightmare for the NCC. At first sight, it may have seemed a straightforward case when the county officer saw the owner ploughing up meadows at Gweunydd Yr Afon Fach SSSI: a total of 8 ha was damaged. However, the defence raised a number of technical points after the first hearing at Lampeter Magistrates Court. At the second hearing, on 12 March 1985, magistrates dismissed the case and awarded costs of £250 to the farmer. Unusually, they issued a written ruling in which they stated that the original notification of the SSSI under section 28 was invalid, because the NCC had invited the owner to 'comment' on the proposed notification rather than make 'representations or objections'. Another point raised by the defence was that the NCC had not served notification on all the owners, as the farmer's wife was a part-owner — a fact not known to the NCC.

The NCC imposed an immediate moratorium on SSSI notifications and sought advice from the Treasury Counsel on its notification practice. One of the most crucial questions was who should be classified as an 'occupier' of an SSSI, as there is no definition in relation to section 28 (but see High Court judgement of 24 May 1991 reported below).

A third prosecution was already under way and was heard at Kington Magistrates Court, Hereford, on 4 April 1985. A farmer had caused the 1.5 ha Broadstone Meadow SSSI — a noted site for autumn crocus — to be ploughed and planted with swedes. Magistrates decided that he had no case to answer and awarded costs of £1,437 against the NCC. The defendant had employed counsel. NCC's solicitor advised

Table 5.2 *Prosecutions brought by the Nature Conservancy Council under section 28 of the Wildlife and Countryside Act 1981*

Date	Name of SSSI	County	Nature of operation(s)	Outcome
31 October 1984	Ulverscroft Valley	Leicestershire	Spreading lime	Guilty verdict. Fine £200 with £50 costs.
12 March 1985	Gweunydd Yr Afon Fach	Dyfed	Ploughing 8 ha	Case dismissed. NCC paid £250 costs.
4 April 1985	Broadstone Meadow	Hereford and Worcester	Ploughing 1.5 ha	Case dismissed. NCC paid £1,437 costs.
6 October 1987	Chesil Beach	Dorset	Extraction of sand and shingle	Guilty verdict. Fine £1,500 with £1,000 costs.
4 January 1988	Hurn Common	Dorset	Ploughing 7 ha of heathland	Guilty verdict. Fine £800 with £800 costs.
4 March 1988	Westhay Moor	Somerset	Application of herbicide	Guilty verdict. Fine £250 with £500 costs. Unsuccessful appeal to Crown Court, 18 July 1988.
5 May 1988	Tealham and Tadham Moors	Somerset	Application of herbicide	Case dismissed.
17 October 1988	East Devon Pebblebed Heaths	Devon	Grazing and stock feeding	Guilty verdict. Fine £300 with £100 costs.
30 September 1988	Swithland Woods	Leicestershire	Extraction of slate, construction of paths, use of vehicles	Guilty verdict. Fine £1,000 with £1,262 costs.
9 January 1990	Alverstone Marshes	Isle of Wight	Drainage operations	Guilty verdict. Fine £6,000 with £2,326 costs. Conviction quashed by High Court and costs awarded against NCC.
11 April 1990	Cors Llyferin	Gwynedd	Extension of golf course	Guilty verdict. Fine £800 with £750 costs.
3 September 1990	Cwm Gwynllyn	Powys	Drainage operations	Guilty verdict. Conditional discharge with £150 costs.

that the case had been lost because the NCC was unable to prove that the owner had been served with the notification. The defence also contended that the owner's admission to the offence was not admissible in evidence because of NCC's failure to caution.

Closing a loophole

After the NCC moved its headquarters from London to Peterborough at the end of 1984 a small section was established to deal *inter alia* with SSSI policies and procedures. Staff had been in contact with David Clark MP over his 1985 Amendment Bill. He very readily agreed to promote another bill to provide the NCC with service of notice procedures equivalent to those applying to documents served under the Town and Country Planning Acts. This bill passed through both Houses in only four weeks and became the Wildlife and Countryside (Service of Notices) Act on 25 July 1985.

Revision of NCC's notification procedures

Progress with renotification of SSSIs was the main performance indicator in the Corporate Plan on which NCC's annual grant-in-aid from Government is based. It was therefore imperative that the moratorium should be lifted as quickly as possible. The HQ section drafted new standard notification letters (it appeared that at least three different versions had been in use previously). These were included in eighty-four pages of instructions on notification procedures issued to NCC staff in August 1985. These have generally stood the test of time.

Provision of legal advice

The HQ section also arranged with the Treasury Solicitor in 1985 for the provision of a legal advice service to the NCC. Various options were considered, but it was decided that the Treasury Solicitor had expertise across a very wide range of the law, with particular authority in relation to the interpretation of statutes. In addition, the Treasury Solicitor already provided a conveyancing service for all NCC's management agreements and land purchases.

Arrangements were also made for one of the Treasury Solicitor's litigation sections to deal with NCC's representation at public inquiries and another to handle NCC's prosecution work. A local solicitor, who may be suggested by the NCC or nominated by the Treasury Solicitor, is instructed by the Treasury Solicitor to prepare each case and present it in court. This system has the advantage that the Treasury Solicitor's litigation section builds up experience of section 28 prosecutions which can be passed on to the solicitors presenting subsequent cases.

One solicitor at the Treasury Solicitor's office is assigned to NCC's advisory work. Queries are channelled through one HQ section at the NCC. This enables expertise to be built up by those involved. The NCC now carries out its decision-making and operations as a statutory body very much on the basis of legal advice provided by the Treasury Solicitor. Counsel's opinion is sought where the issue is in any doubt.

It is not clear what arrangements will be made by NCC's successor bodies, but it may be appropriate to record here the authors' thanks to all the solicitors and Counsel who have advised the NCC and shown so much interest in nature conservation.

Subsequent prosecutions

In the two years after 1985 the NCC contemplated a number of prosecutions. Most were not pursued because of lack of evidence. In some cases Crown immunity was involved. A case in Nottinghamshire involved the felling of over 150 trees, but the defendant died before it came to court.

Eventually a fourth prosecution was undertaken. This involved the removal of large quantities of sand and shingle from Chesil Beach SSSI by the owner, destroying part of a classic landform. The case was heard by Bridport magistrates on 6 October 1987. Video evidence was presented by an employee of Dorset County Council who had been observing the damaging operations with NCC staff. After the case, the County Council obtained an injunction against the owner removing any more material from the beach.

In 1988 five prosecutions were brought (see Table 5.2). The NCC was successful in all of these except one. On 5 May 1988, Burnham-on-Sea magistrates acquitted the owner of land at Tealham and Tadham Moors SSSI of permitting herbicide to be sprayed on a field because she had a reasonable excuse under section 28(7) of the 1981 Act. She had received a notification letter from the NCC containing the sentence, 'you will only need to consult NCC if you wish to change your farming practice or wish to carry out one of the other listed operations'. The owner contended that it was her normal farming practice to spray herbicide on her fields.

A similar case was heard by Glastonbury magistrates on 4 March 1988. A farmer on nearby Westhay Moor SSSI was convicted of spraying herbicide without giving notice to the NCC, and fined £250 with £500 costs. He appealed on the grounds of having a reasonable excuse for not giving notice because he was following normal farming practice. The case was heard in the Crown Court sitting in Wells on 18 July. Although a similarly worded notification letter had been sent, NCC's barrister was able to show that the farmer owned other SSSI land on which he had given notice of similar operations for which the

NCC had refused consent. The Recorder held that the list of operations notified by the NCC quite clearly included the spraying of herbicide.

The Somerset Levels saga

It was not only these last two cases that involved farmers in the Somerset Levels. It is perhaps worth noting that the conciliatory tone of the NCC's notification letter was intended to soften the impact of notification. This was a management decision, after the NCC's Chairman and Regional Officer were burnt in effigy by local farmers in 1983 together with letters informing them of proposed SSSI notifications on the Levels. This episode and the appointment of an NCC project officer for the Levels with an ADAS background were described in some detail by Lowe and others in 1986.[7]

The longest-running legal proceedings in which the NCC has been involved on SSSIs also concern a farmer on the Somerset Levels, Mr Mervyn Sweet. He gave notice to the NCC in October 1984 that he intended to carry out ploughing of meadows prior to possible peat extraction on land at Tealham and Tadham Moors. On NCC's advice, the Secretary of State made an order under section 29 of the 1981 Act on 8 July 1985, after negotiations had broken down. Mr Sweet was reported in the press as saying that he intended to level one field despite the order. The NCC obtained a High Court injunction restraining him. He objected to the order, but it was upheld after a public inquiry and is still in force.

Mr Sweet also owns meadow land on Westhay Moor SSSI; he gave notice to the NCC in February 1987 of his intention to extract peat and sell turves. Because the removal of peat would need planning permission, which he had not obtained, the NCC did not offer compensation at a level which satisfied Mr Sweet. An order was made on the land under section 29 on 17 June 1987. Mr Sweet objected and gave notice of further operations, including growing arable crops and using a strip of land for light aircraft. The NCC refused consent and offered a management agreement, thus extending the protection under the order. A Local Inquiry was held into the Westhay Moor (Somerset) Nature Conservation Order on 10 and 11 November 1987. The Secretary of State accepted the Inspector's recommendation that the order remain in force.

Mr Sweet appealed to the High Court against the order on the grounds that the Secretary of State was *ultra vires* in including in the order land which by itself was not of national importance and matters which were not 'operations' within the meaning of section 29(3). The

---

[7] P. Lowe, G. Cox, M. MacEwen, T. O'Riordan and M. Winter, *Countryside Conflicts — the Politics of Farming, Forestry and Conservation*, Gower, 1986.

case was heard by Mr Justice Schiemann in the Queen's Bench Division on 24 January 1989.[8]

This is probably the first judicial decision dealing with section 29. Mr Justice Schiemann found that the order land, comprising three meadows and associated ditches covering 7.5 ha, constituted a single environment and that the Secretary of State was entitled to draw the boundaries of the order site where he had done and to find that it was of national importance by reason of its flora, fauna etc. (as required by section 29(2)). It was not disputed that, had 3 ha of the site been put forward as of national importance in their own right (rather than as part of a larger unit), they might not qualify. As to the objector's contention that the order specified things which were activities rather than 'operations' (all that is allowed under section 29(3)), Mr Justice Schiemann considered that the word does not have a very precise meaning and could cover the matters specified in the schedule to the order — including grazing, application of fertilizer, release of any animal, plant or seed, and storage of materials.

In February 1989 the NCC served a compulsory purchase order on Mr Sweet for the land, under section 17 of the National Parks and Access to the Countryside Act 1949 — the first time it had used this power in order to prevent damage to an SSSI. An Inquiry was held into the order on 10 October. The Inspector found that the NCC had exhausted all its statutory powers and had made great efforts to conclude a management agreement (a necessary precursor to compulsory purchase under section 17).

Meanwhile NCC's county officer had gained access to the order land on Westhay Moor, with a written authorization under section 51 of the 1981 Act and accompanied by two police officers. He found evidence of a breach of section 29(3), and the NCC prosecuted Mr Sweet in August 1989 at Wells Crown Court. During the case Mr Sweet gave an undertaking that he would sign a management agreement and the NCC withdrew the charges.

In March 1990, the Secretary of State confirmed the compulsory purchase order. Mr Sweet sought an injunction against the NCC on the grounds that the order had been improperly made, because he had signed a management agreement. He applied for judicial review, and the case was heard in the High Court on 1 February 1991 by Mr Justice Browne. He made a 'Tomlin' order by consent of both parties under which Mr Sweet signed an agreement over all his landholdings in the SSSI (7.5 ha). A further development in this saga is that criminal

---

[8] J. D. C. Harte, 'The scope of protection resulting from the designation of SSSIs', *Journal of Environmental Law*, 1(2) (1989), 245–52; G. Kirkwood and M. Purdue, 'Sweet v. Secretary of State for the Environment and the Nature Conservancy Council', *Journal of Planning and Environmental Law*, (December 1989), 927–34.

proceedings were instituted against Mr Sweet alleging assault on staff of the NCC and of the Treasury Solicitor's office. He was found guilty by Burnham-on-Sea magistrates on 13 June 1991, fined £250 and ordered to pay £525 compensation.

Record fine but conviction quashed by High Court

The last prosecution in England brought by the Nature Conservancy Council was against Southern Water Authority for drainage operations at Alverstone Marshes SSSI on the Isle of Wight. The work was carried out in January 1989 and the case was heard nearly a year later by Newport magistrates. The damage to the site was still obvious when magistrates undertook a site visit. They imposed a record fine of £6,000 (£750 on each of eight counts).

Although Southern Water Authority no longer exists (its drainage functions were taken over by the National Rivers Authority in September 1989), the residuary body appealed on a case stated to the High Court. A judgment was given on 24 May 1991 by Lord Justice Watkins and Mr Justice Owen. The conviction was quashed and costs were awarded against the NCC. The magistrates had found that Southern Water Authority were occupiers of the SSSI land because they undertook works over a continuous period of about four weeks which physically prevented others from enjoying the full use of that land: the operations carried out were akin to treating the land as if it were one's own. The judges found that the word 'occupier' in section 28 is referable only to a person who has some kind of interest in the land as, for example, a tenant or licensee who occupies it for such purposes as dwelling upon it or farming upon it. A different interpretation would mean that anyone brought on to the land by an owner or occupier to perform work would be an occupier and subject to the Act, which would be absurd. This meant that the Southern Water Authority were not technically occupiers when they damaged the SSSI and could not be prosecuted under section 28. The judges did, however, state that the Southern Water Authority ought either to have consulted the NCC before carrying out operations which resulted in such obviously devastating damage to the SSSI or ensured that the owners of the land had conformed to section 28 with full knowledge of what the Water Authority intended to do.

It should be noted that drainage authorities have a duty to consult the NCC and to further conservation under the Water Act 1989. Such a duty would be subject to judicial review proceedings. This may be a more effective means for the NCC of dealing with such cases in the future.

Last prosecutions

The NCC's last two prosecutions were in Wales. On 11 April 1990 at Pwllheli Magistrates Court, Abersoch Golf Club pleaded guilty to extending their course by spreading soil over an area of Cors Llyferin SSSI containing the rare moss *Scopelophila cataractae*. The club was fined £800.

In September 1990 a farmer from near Rhayader was found guilty at the local Magistrates Court for deepening the outflow stream of a natural lake lying within Cwmgwynllyn SSSI. The lowering of the water levels could damage the fragile zone between the lake and the adjacent bog land. The farmer was given a conditional discharge for twelve months and required to pay £150 towards the NCC's legal costs. It is evident that the court had little sympathy for the NCC's case.

Progress in Scotland

To date there have been no prosecutions under section 28 in Scotland. In August 1984 the NCC reported to the police that a tenant farmer on Aberlady Bay SSSI, East Lothian, had damaged 5 ha of dune grassland by application of weedkiller. The farmer was charged by the police, who submitted a report to the Procurator Fiscal. On 24 September the Procurator Fiscal informed the NCC that he had decided to take no proceedings on grounds of insufficiency of evidence. The NCC later learned that the key point was lack of proof of receipt of notification by the occupier of the SSSI. This occurred before the Service of Notices Act in 1985.

In another case in 1988 summonses were laid by the Stonehaven Procurator Fiscal, but the case was later abandoned on advice of the Crown Office. The Glenshee Chairlift Company had used piste machines on Caenlochan SSSI without giving notice to the NCC. NCC's local officer provided evidence to the Procurator Fiscal including photographs of the pisting operations. The Chairlift Company pleaded not guilty and submitted papers relating to planning permissions. The full reasons for the decision to abandon the complaint were not given to the NCC, who would probably have pursued the case had it been able to instruct its own solicitor.

Three other cases have not been taken by Procurators Fiscal. One of these was also a breach of planning law, when sand dune material was removed from Sheigra-Oldshoremore SSSI in Sutherland. The Dornoch Procurator Fiscal decided in June 1988 that, as the planning authority did not intend to institute proceedings but was seeking to arrange voluntary restoration, it would not be proper to take proceedings under the Wildlife and Countryside Act. Until there is a successful prosecution, uncertainties will surround the enforceability of the SSSI legislation in Scotland.

Conclusions

Parliament has determined that a breach of section 28 is a criminal offence, but it is for the courts to determine how the legislation should be interpreted and to impose appropriate penalties. The fines imposed indicate that magistrates, in general, are taking breaches of the Wildlife and Countryside Act seriously.

Prosecutions have served to demonstrate weaknesses in the legislation which brought about two amending Acts in 1985. It will be interesting to see whether there are further changes in the legislation or different procedures in relation to SSSIs as a result of decisions by the courts.

This essay has examined the role of an enforcement body, and we have seen that the NCC has had an eventful time and perhaps not yet come to terms with its enforcement role.

On 1 April 1991 the NCC was dissolved and replaced by three new agencies in England, Scotland and Wales (see Chapter 4). The new agencies will be expected to ensure that enforcement is carried out fairly and consistently so that the legislation does not fall into disrepute.

6

Land Development: the role of planning law

J. D. C. HARTE*

The Changing Context

Planning law in England and Wales is currently based on the Town and Country Planning Act 1990. This is a consolidating Act which still essentially follows the national framework for land use planning which was laid down in 1947.[1] The Act controls development in the form of new buildings and other operations and also restricts changes of use by prohibiting them unless they have been given planning consent by a local authority or by central government.[2] Since 1970 this has meant the Department of the Environment (DoE).

Agriculture and forestry have always been treated as a special case. Their interests have been ensured by leaving them largely to the control of the Ministry of Agriculture, Fisheries and Food (MAFF), which in the case of forestry operates largely through the Forestry Commission. Unlike the DoE their main concern has traditionally been simply with productivity. The use of land for agriculture and forestry is not treated as development.[3] This means that planning permission is not needed for major changes in agricultural practice such as ploughing up grassland or large afforestation schemes. In addition the primary legislation in successive Town and Country Planning Acts has delegated power to the Minister or Secretary of State responsible for

* I am most grateful to Professor Michael Purdue for a number of valuable comments on a first draft for this essay. I hope that I have adequately taken them into account in the final version.

[1] The major consolidating Act for planning law prior to 1990 was the Town and Country Planning Act 1971. For a study of developments between 1947 and 1971 see Neal Alison Roberts, *The Reform of Planning Law*, Bowering, 1976.

[2] Town and Country Planning Act 1990, Part III, see especially s.55 for the definition of 'development'.

[3] Ibid., s.55(2)(e).

planning to relax the requirements for obtaining planning permission. Thus blanket planning permission has been given by General Development Orders for certain farm buildings and other operations.[4]

The new climate

The system of development control has served a valuable purpose in safeguarding the agricultural industry and in providing at least some protection for the rural landscape. However, rapid changes in agricultural practice have themselves now altered that landscape dramatically, in some areas beyond recognition. Miles of hedgerow have been removed so as to form large fields for efficient ploughing and harvesting. There has been a trend towards larger farms, and at the same time farmers have often specialized in more limited ranges of crops on individual farms. These changes have come at a time when the public are enjoying more leisure and transport to get into the countryside, so that change and especially a reduced variety in the landscape are more obvious. There is a heightened interest in the environment generally, including concern about pollution to which farming contributes, and there is constant pressure for increased freedom of access to open country for recreational use. Not surprisingly, there are demands for increased planning restrictions in the countryside.[5]

The influence of the European Community

The pressure for greater use of planning law in the countryside has been sustained by the growing influence of the European Community. Although the Community began as an essentially economic organization, by the time that the United Kingdom became a member state, significant moves had been made to produce policies designed to protect the environment.[6] The Single European Act Treaty of 1986 has expressly recognized the environment for its own sake as a major concern of the Community.[7]

A significant intervention by the European Community into the planning law of member states has been made by a directive of 1987

[4] Town and Country Planning General Development Order 1988, SI 1988 No.1813, part 6.

[5] See e.g. Marion Shoard, *This Land is Our Land*, Paladin, 1988.

[6] Following the accession to the EEC by the UK by the European Communities Act 1972, see Environmental Action Programmes: 1973 (OJ C 112); 1977 (OJ C 139); 1983 (OJ C 46); 1987 (OJ C 328).

[7] See especially new Title VII added to the EEC Treaty. For comment see Nigel Haigh, *EEC Environmental Policy and Britain*, 2nd revised edition, Longman, 1989, and Stanley P. Johnson and Guy Cornelle, *The Environmental Policy of the European Communities*, Graham and Trotter, 1989.

which requires environmental impact assessment in respect of proposed new development where this is likely to have a significant effect on the environment.[8] The directive assumes that member states will have their own systems for regulating development and requires that in deciding whether to grant permission, and on what terms, the relevant supervisory bodies should be provided with full information about the consequences of the scheme for the environment and of steps to be taken to minimize harm.

The Environmental Assessment Directive contains two annexes, one specifying forms of development where impact assessment is to be mandatory, the other listing development where assessment should be called for by the relevant public body overseeing development if it appears that significant environmental damage is likely. The second annex includes large-scale agricultural, and particularly forestry, schemes. The British Government has complied with the directive by means of a number of Statutory Instruments.[9] The most important of these is the Town and Country Planning (Assessment of Environmental Effects) Regulations 1988. This provides for environmental assessment as part of the process for obtaining planning consent for most types of development envisaged by the directive. It incorporates much of the directive, especially its annexes, word for word. However, since farming and forestry are not treated as development in British law they are left out of the schedule which corresponds to Annex II.

Changing government policy

Although the British Government has not complied with the directive on environmental impact assessment by bringing agriculture and farming within the definition of development requiring planning permission, assessment for agricultural schemes is imposed in other circumstances, notably on applications for grants for afforestation and

[8] Directive 85/337 on 'The Assessment of the Effects of Certain Public and Private Projects on the Environment' (OJ L 175, 5.7.8).

[9] Particularly Town and Country Planning (Environmental Effects) Regulations 1988, SI No. 1199. See too: Environmental Assessment (Afforestation) Regulations 1988, SI 1988 No. 1207; Land Drainage Improvement Works (Assessment of Environmental Effects) Regulations 1988, SI 1988 No.1217; Environmental Assessment (Salmon Fishing in Marine Waters) Regulations 1988, SI 1988 No.1218; Highways (Assessment of Environmental Effects) Regulations 1988, SI 1988 No.1241; Harbour Works (Assessment of Environmental Effects) Regulations 1988, SI 1988 No.1336; Electricity and Pipe-line Works (Assessment of Environmental Effects) Regulations 1989, SI 1989 No.167; Harbour Works (Assessment of Environmental Effects) (No.2) Regulations 1989, SI 1989 No.424; Town and Country Planning (Environmental Effects) (Amendment) Regulations 1990, SI 1990 No.367; Electricity and Pipe-line Works (Assessment of Environmental Effects) Regulations 1990, SI 1990 No.442.

woodland planting.[10] More generally, the Government has moved in the direction of greater regulation in the countryside. For example, the special problem of pollution arising from agricultural use of fertilizer is recognized in the provision for Nitrate Sensitive Areas under the Water Act 1989, where farmers are to be paid grants for reduced application of fertilizer.[11]

The main contribution to the countryside of the Government's much vaunted Environmental Protection Act 1990 was the reordering of the Nature Conservancy Council, an agency with functions covering the whole of the United Kingdom, and the Countryside Commission, which had related functions especially in National Parks for England and Wales. These were dismembered into four bodies. Thus there are now separate Nature Conservancy Councils for England and Scotland. The Countryside Commission is concerned with England alone and a Countryside Council for Wales deals with the functions in the Principality originally divided between the Countryside Commission and the Nature Conservancy Council.[12] The reorganization was bitterly opposed by conservation interests on the ground that protection would be much less effective if it was no longer promoted by a single island-wide body. In fact the changes appear to have been intended to soothe nationalist sensibilities by allowing more local control of the rural environment, rather than as a device to weaken possible opposition to Government policies. The Government did take account of criticisms but it did so by adding a Joint Committee to co-ordinate nature conservancy functions, and so further complicated matters.

Another provision of the Environmental Protection Act relating specifically to the countryside is section 152, which envisages regulations to outlaw the burning of crop residues, particularly straw and stubble. Meanwhile, the Government's 1990 white paper on the environment, *This Common Inheritance*, has further stressed the importance of protecting the general character of the countryside as well as airing other major environmental issues, particularly the need for more effective pollution control.[13] Significantly, the white paper's proposals for the countryside concentrate on ways to extend the various voluntary regimes which have already been established for encouraging land management with a strong emphasis on con-servation.

Some earnest of the Government's intentions to carry through new ideas for conservation is apparent in the bill which recently reached the

[10] Environmental Assessment (Afforestation) Regulations 1988, SI 1988 No.1207.
[11] Water Act 1989, s.112; and see Ch. 3 above.
[12] Environmental Protection Act 1990, Part VII and Schedules 6–11; and see Ch. 4 above.
[13] 1990, Cm. 1200.

statute-book as the Planning and Compensation Act 1991. This contains a number of significant provisions for the countryside, such as including the siting of fish tanks in water at fish farms within the statutory definition of engineering operations which require planning consent. The new Act should also ensure that the regulation of mineral development and waste disposal more effectively covers reclamation of deposits of mineral spoil and waste tips.

The place of planning law in the countryside

Although it may take a long time, the process has begun of transforming the law so as to provide much more coherent protection for the environment. However the form this transformation will take is far from clear. In particular it is difficult to predict how far planning law, as opposed to a range of special controls, will be extended to regulate agricultural land use. The titles of successive British Town and Country Planning Acts have explicitly recognized a basic distinction between Town and Country Planning. The planning system has held sway in urban areas, directing new development in accordance with policies worked out between central and local government, particularly through development plans. To a large extent areas have been earmarked for particular types of new development on social and economic criteria. Aesthetics and improved quality of the townscape seem to be given little attention except where Conservation Areas or individual buildings listed by the Department of the Environment have been identified as of particular aesthetic or historic interest.[14] Even listing has been forcefully criticized as a frequently unnecessary interference with the developer's idea of the march of progress.[15] However in the countryside aesthetics and public amenity tend to be regarded as much more relevant planning considerations.

Planning law may be used in positive ways to channel new development to where planners want it, but the system is essentially a negative one which works by forbidding new development unless it has been licensed by planning consent. In the countryside the planning system is even more negative. In urban areas there is a presumption in favour of new development unless it can be shown that it will damage interests of acknowledged importance.[16] In the countryside the same basic presumption applies, but central and local government policy is

[14] Planning (Listed Buildings and Conservation Areas) Act 1990.

[15] See contrasting views in Journal of Planning Law Occasional Papers, *A Future for Old Buildings*, and *Making the Most of our Heritage*, Sweet and Maxwell, 1977 and 1989, especially Richard G. Saxon 'Architecture and Design as Material Considerations', JPL Occasional Papers No.17, 1989.

[16] See DoE Circular 22/80, *Development Control — Policy and Practice*, paras 18–21 and DoE Circular 31/85, *Aesthetic Control*.

so framed that most building, and indeed other forms of development, will be presumed to damage the quality of open countryside or of existing settlements.[17]

Britain was late in developing a system of administrative law, but the judges are now rapidly making up for lost time.[18] As a major area of modern administrative law, planning law has a different feel from many traditional fields. The distinctive character of English administrative law is that it is based on legislation, with much detail filled in through Statutory Instruments which can relatively easily be amended without the need to take up Parliamentary time. Decisions applying the legislation, such as whether to give permission for a proposed development, are left to administrators. These administrators are required to interpret the law and to determine relevant facts, but they are then left with wide discretion which is very difficult to challenge. Although there may be an appeal to the courts or an application for judicial review, the judges are concerned only with erroneous interpretations of law or procedural impropriety. They cannot use their discretion in a different way to remake an administrative decision. Thus a judge cannot grant planning permission for a particular proposal where it was improperly refused by a local planning authority and by the Secretary of State or one of his inspectors. The judge can do no more than send the case back to the administrators to decide again.

Although the role of the judiciary is restricted, they have had substantial scope for moulding the legal framework within which planning and other administrative decisions are made. Notably they have laid down what considerations are or are not material in deciding whether to grant planning consent or in imposing conditions.[19] Thus the judges have laid down rules which allow listed buildings to be sacrificed and other policies against development to be overridden if this enables planning gain, for example if it finances the maintenance of other listed buildings or the conservation or improvement of public amenity in other ways.[20]

Indeed the courts may be prepared to go further and to quash administrative decisions on the grounds that they are unreasonable.

[17] See DoE Circular 22/80, *Development Control — Policy and Practice*, paras 15–18; DoE Circular 14/84, *Green Belts*; Planning Policy and Guidance Notes 2; *Green Belts*, 1988; DoE Circular 17/86. The Town and Country Planning (Agricultural and Forestry Development in National Parks etc.) Order 1986.

[18] See e.g. Anthony Bradley, 'Judicial Review: the Need for Legislative Intervention', *New Law Journal* (1991), 339.

[19] See e.g. Michael Purdue, 'Material Considerations: an Ever-Expanding Concept', JPL (1989), 156.

[20] *Brighton BC v Secretary of State for the Environment and St Aubyn's School Trust Ltd* [1979] JPL 173. Also see *R. v. Westminster City Council ex parte Monahan* [1990] 1 QB 87.

Thus in *R. v. South Herefordshire District Council ex parte Felton* a decision granting permission for a large potato store on a farm was quashed on the ground that it was absurd. The permission had been granted on the basis that the store would not affect the site of Bollitree Castle, a nearby listed building, but although the store would not be visible from the castle it would clearly affect the view of the castle from elsewhere.[21]

Judges are reluctant to enter into the relative aesthetic merits of a proposal.[22] Nevertheless as such considerations become increasingly controversial there may be growing pressure even here for clearer guidance from the courts. Such pressure may be particularly significant as the role of planning in the countryside changes. For example one result of the current decline in farming may be applications for planning consent for large new country houses set in miniature estates.[23] Such applications raise a variety of social and amenity issues. Policy guidance and individual decisions are likely to be controversial and could well come before the courts.

A major gap in planning law has been the lack of any statutory right of appeal against a grant of planning consent which is opposed by local amenity groups or other interested parties. Only a disappointed developer has a right of appeal to the Secretary of State.[24] However an improper grant of planning consent may be challenged directly in the High Court by an application for judicial review. Here the courts have shown a tendency to recognize the standing of a widening range of bodies such as amenity groups. This trend received a setback when Schiemann J. refused to recognize the standing of a trust company set up by a group of distinguished actors and archaeologists to challenge the refusal by Mr Nicholas Ridley as Secretary of State to schedule as an ancient monument the site of the Rose Theatre at Southwark.[25] The judge stressed that the group did not have any proprietary interest in the site and they could not create standing by incorporating themselves

[21] [1990] JPL 515. The principle that administrative decisions may be quashed if they are unreasonable to the point of absurdity is based on *Associated Provincial Picture Houses* v *Wednesbury Corpn* [1948] 1 KB 223.

[22] See *Winchester City Council* v. *Secretary of State for the Environment* [1976] 36 P&CR 455 and *Lord Luke of Pavenham* v. *Minister of Housing and Local Government* [1969] 1 QB 172, but see also *Re St Stephen Walbrook* [1987] Fam 146 and discussion in J. D. C. Harte, *Doctrine, Conservation and Aesthetic Judgement in the Court of Ecclesiastical Causes Reserved, Ecc LJ*, 1 (1, 2) (1987–8), 22.

[23] Michael A. B. Boddington, 'Agriculture and the Rural Economy: Times of Change', in *Making the Most of Our Heritage*, JPL Occasional Papers No. 15, Sweet and Maxwell, 1989.

[24] Town and Country Planning Act 1990, s.78, but cf. appeals to the High Court in respect of decisions by the Secretary of State, s.288.

[25] *R. v. Secretary of State for the Environment ex parte Rose Theatre Trust Co. Ltd.* [1990] 1 QB 504.

could be particularly valuable would be in establishing a more satisfactory framework for resolving the expectations of amenity groups, of the public generally and of those particularly affected by specific proposals.[31]

Agriculture as a land use

The basis for the exclusion of agriculture and forestry from development control is now section 55(1)(e) of the Town and Country Planning Act 1990, which provides that development for the purposes of planning control excludes 'the use of any land for the purposes of agriculture or forestry (including afforestation) and the use for any of those purposes of any building occupied together with land so used'. This means that farmers are free to change from one crop or agricultural activity to another. For example arable land may be made over to grazing, or downland or water meadow ploughed up for crops. Equally land may be freely brought into agricultural use even though it was previously derelict or used for some quite different purpose such as industrial storage.[32] Unlike certain activities which require planning consent, agriculture may be freely carried out at a greatly increased level of intensity.

Under section 336 of the Town and Country Planning Act 1990,

'Agriculture' includes horticulture, fruit growing, seed growing, dairy farming, the breeding and keeping of livestock (including any creature kept for the production of food, wool, skins or fur, or for the purpose of its use in the farming of land), the use of land as grazing land, meadow land, ozier land, market gardens and nursery grounds, and the use of land for woodlands where that is ancillary to the farming of land for other agricultural purposes . . .

By contrast, section 109 of the Agriculture Act 1947 contains an almost identical definition but refers simply to 'livestock breeding and keeping', without any qualification or inclusion of 'any creature kept for the production of food, wool, skins or fur, or for the purpose of its use in the farming of land'. Even the restricted definition under the planning legislation includes activities which may be very different from traditional British farming. One example is rearing foxes for their fur.[33] However recreational activities involving animals have tended to require planning consent. In particular, the use of land for breeding horses other than heavy horses for use in farming, operating a riding

ss.82–9.
[31] Patrick McAuslan, *The Ideologies of Planning Law*, Pergamon, 1980.
[32] *McKellan* v. *Minister of Housing and Local Government* (1966) 198 EG 683.
[33] *North Warwickshire Borough Council* v. *Secretary of State for the Environment* [1984] JPL 434.

school or training horses for racing would all require planning consent.[34] On the other hand the use of land for grazing horses of any sort or indeed for grazing rare species which may then be taken elsewhere for display to the public is within the planning law definition of agriculture.[35]

The general principles of planning law mean that there is limited scope for farmers to diversify without the need for planning permission. It is permissible to introduce new uses which are ancillary to the principal use of a piece of land so that a farm shop selling produce exclusively from the farm does not need to be approved by the planning authorities. However if more than a minimal range of extra items from outside sources is offered for sale, permission is needed. A classic example was when a farmer added to his stock oranges and lemons which he had not grown on his farm.[36] If a new building is put up for use as a farm or indeed if an automatic vending machine for farm produce is installed in the open, planning permission may be required.[37]

The approved planning use or uses of any piece of land are restricted within the boundaries of a planning unit. For example a farmer who has obtained extra income by using part of his land for a non-agricultural purpose such as summer camping may not be able to extend this activity to a larger part of the farm without obtaining planning consent. Nor can private householders buy chunks of land to incorporate into their gardens without planning consent. Even though use as a garden may look very like an agricultural use it will have become ancillary to a domestic use. By contrast, provided they are self-contained, there would not seem to be any restriction on dividing up land into tiny areas for intensive cultivation, as allotments or as paddocks for grazing one or two horses.[38]

It would doubtless be impractical and excessively bureaucratic to use the planning system to control many of the changes in agriculture which strike the casual visitor most forcefully. For example it would seem quite out of touch with reality to suggest that a local planning authority should have to be asked for permission to plant a crop of rape on the grounds that its brilliant yellow would significantly change the appearance of the countryside. On the other hand more long-term

[34] *Belmont Farm Ltd.* v. *Minister of Housing and Local Government* (1962) 13 P&CR 417 and see *Warnock* v. *Secretary of State for the Environment* [1980] JPL 590.

[35] *Sykes* v. *Secretary of State for the Environment* [1981] JPL 285.

[36] *Williams* v. *Minister of Housing and Local Government* (1967) 65 LGR 495; and see Ch. 1 above.

[37] See generally here A. J. Scrase 'Agriculture — 1980s Industry and 1947 Definition' [1988] JPL 447.

[38] *Crowborough Parish Council* v. *Secretary of State for the Environment* [1981] JPL 281.

changes, such as ploughing pasture or afforestation, could more realistically be included within a definition of development requiring planning consent as a change of use.[39] Major changes are likely to be associated with amalgamation or subdivision of land holdings. Where boundary changes involve attaching agricultural land to some other activity, permission is now likely to be required.[40] In continental Europe much more control is often exercised over regrouping of agricultural land units, in the interests of agricultural efficiency, and it may be that greater control would be desirable in the United Kingdom with a view to maximizing the public amenity of the landscape.[41]

Agricultural building and other operations

A common complaint about damage to the appearance of the countryside by farmers is that an agricultural building has been sited without any regard to its relationship with the landscape. This has been possible because of the extensive freedom for agricultural buildings and other operational forms of development which are now contained in Schedule II, part 6 of the Town and Country Planning General Development Order 1988.[42] Similar concessions are made for forestry in part 7.

Part 6, Class A permits 'The carrying out on agricultural land comprised in an agricultural unit of – (a) works for the erection, extension or alteration of a building, or (b) any excavation or engineering operations, reasonably necessary for the purposes of agriculture within that unit'. However the provision only applies where agriculture is being practised as a trade or business, and it may be difficult to distinguish between a hobby which is to some extent made to pay for itself and one which is run on sufficiently commercial lines to amount to a business.[43] It may also be difficult to identify whether the concession applies to buildings used for multi-purpose farm businesses, as where byres are erected for rare animals which the public pay to look at. The concession is specifically not granted for erecting, extending or altering dwelling houses or buildings, structures or works not designed for the purposes of agriculture.

[39] However see alternative approach of hedgerow management agreements in the Planning and Compensation Bill 1991.

[40] *Sampson's Executors* v. *Nottinghamshire County Council* [1949] 2 KB 439 and *Asghar* v. *Secretary of State for the Environment and Harrogate Borough Council* [1988] JPL 189.

[41] See here Directive 85/337 on 'The Assessment of the Effects of Certain Public and Private Projects on the Environment' (OJ L 175, 5.7.8), Annex II 1.(a), not incorporated in Town and Country Planning (Environmental Effects) Regulations 1988, SI No.1199, Sched.2.

[42] Town and Country Planning General Development Order 1988, SI 198 No.1813.

[43] *Custom and Excise Commissioners* v. *Lord Fisher* [1981] 2 All ER 147.

There are detailed exceptions where planning permission will be required, notably building on small sites of less than 0.4 ha. In identifying the size of a site it cannot be added in with other physically separate land, and the ground covered by any domestic or non-agricultural building is excluded. Thus a farmer cannot buy a small piece of land some distance from the remainder of his holding, perhaps in a village, and put up farm buildings there without planning consent.[44]

On the other hand if a farm is made up of a number of distinct pieces of land, a building may be put up for the use of the agricultural holding as a whole on any one piece which is of at least 0.4 ha. Curiously it would seem that permission would be needed to convert an existing building on a separate piece of land for use for the farm as a whole, perhaps to store grain or other crops, because the normal rule in planning law would apply that permission is needed for any new use which is not merely ancillary to any existing principal use on the same planning unit.[45]

Buildings within 3 km of an aerodrome are restricted to 3m and there is a general height limit of 12 m. Development under the Order must be at least 25 m from the metalled portion of any trunk or classified road. Any works associated with the accommodation of livestock or the storage of slurry or sewage sludge are permitted only if they are carried on further than 400 m from any inhabitable building which is not itself part of an agricultural unit.

The ground area to be covered by any new building or other structure must generally not exceed 465 sq. m. However any number of buildings up to this size may be built provided they are at least 90 m apart. Also, after a two-year interval, a further building up to the same size may be added to any which has already been constructed. There is therefore much scope for piecemeal intensive building on farms.

The Government issued a consultation paper in October 1990 on Planning Controls over Agricultural Buildings in England and Wales, in which it proposed empowering local planning authorities to require details of any new agricultural buildings to be submitted to them for approval and an increase in the size of agricultural units entitled to the special concessions in the General Development Order. However, though agricultural buildings may be subjected to greater control, there seems to be no serious prospect at present of them being subjected

[44] Cf. previously to the present General Development Order *Hancock* v. *Secretary of State for the Environment* [1979] JPL 360; in the Court of Appeal *sub nom. Tyack* v. *Secretary of State for the Environment; Hancock* v. *Secretary of State for the Environment* [1988] EGCS 98, and in the House of Lords, *Times,* 8 December 1989.

[45] *Fuller* v. *Secretary of State for the Environment* [1987] JPL 854, and see *G. Percy Trentham* v. *Gloucestershire County Council* [1966] 1 All ER 701.

to anything like the same restrictions as other building in the countryside.

The significance of the freedom of agriculture and forestry from development control

The rather detailed discussion above illustrates that whereas changes of agricultural use are essentially outside development control, what amounts to an agricultural use can be a complex question. Whether or not operational development on farms requires planning consent can also be far from straightforward.

Forestry raises special considerations. Trees are subject to their own code of protection by means of Tree Preservation Orders.[46] However in the countryside, a parallel system of control is exercised by the Forestry Commission under the Forestry Act 1967. Where the Commission grants a felling licence in respect of a tree which is subject to a tree preservation order this obviates the need for consent from the local planning authority. Significantly however, the commercial approach of the Commission is much more geared to sound management. It allows for progressive replanting, by contrast with the more static approach of many local planning authorities, where trees are protected from felling even though they have grown far too large for their setting and there are inadequate powers to ensure that replacements are planted in good time so that they can take over from the original tree when it is felled.

Farming and forestry can make very large-scale alterations to the landscape without restriction. Those who argue that this freedom should be retained point to the manner in which the countryside has evolved through very different phases in the past. The popular image of cosy picturesque fields was very much a creation of the enclosure movement which reached its peak in the eighteenth century and was as controversial in its day as the more recent reversion to very large fields. It is argued that there is objectively no reason why the British countryside should be stuck in the eighteenth century. On the other hand it is clear that there are major public interests today in handling the form of the landscape specifically so that it allows for maximum enjoyment by the ordinary member of the public. Attention must also be paid to the ordinary country dweller who is more likely than not to have no direct connection with the agricultural industry. In addition it makes economic sense to consider the overseas tourist who can contribute to invisible import earnings by paying for the appeal of a distinctive British countryside.

In the case of agriculture and forestry a whole sector of the economy was left in a privileged position. Not only has it largely been free of

[46] Town and Country Planning Act 1990, ss.197–214.

development control; it has also been spared the payment of rates on agricultural land.[47] Within this sector no one form of farming has been able to benefit over others by obtaining planning permission, but it is difficult to tell how much this has determined the appearance of the countryside, because farming practice has been at least as greatly affected by policies in grants and subsidies, particularly under the European Common Agricultural Policy.[48] It is also difficult to conclude whether the relative freedom of agriculture from planning control and the corresponding restriction on other activities in the countryside has on balance helped to further the ends of conservation or hampered them. However there must be a real danger that changing the balance by imposing new restrictions on farming may actually hasten its decline. This may lead to more pressure to fill the resulting vacuum with new forms of development. Those who wanted more controls over farming may well regard such quite different forms of development as even more alien.

Unfortunately development control, like all restrictive law, can do little more than control serious abuses. It is ineffective in stimulating new and creative change in the countryside or elsewhere. There are plenty of instances of small-scale insensitive development by farmers as by other land users, where the negative controls have failed and which could still occur even if the General Development Order were tightened up. A common example is provided by caravans or derelict vehicles or other temporary structures which may be particularly unsightly in place of more permanent farm buildings. Introducing such a structure is not development if it is not sufficiently permanent to constitute a building and provided it is used for agricultural purposes.[49]

In general the law is rarely used to enforce positive care of land use. This is illustrated by the distinction drawn by the courts between restrictive covenants which may run with land and positive ones which generally can not. A landowner who sells part of his estate may bind his purchaser's successors not to uproot the hedgerows but he cannot ensure their long-term maintenance. Planning law could not easily be extended to require farmers to care positively for their land and to keep it in good heart even if this were desirable. However, more positive regimes can be set up to achieve these ends by means of management agreements. Development control can at least prevent deterioration being speeded up through the demolishing of buildings or taking off their roofs, as has often happened in the past, for example to avoid the

[47] The Uniform Business Rates introduced along with the Community Charge in 1988 do not provide for any tax on agricultural land, Local Government Finance Act 1988, Sched.5, para.1.

[48] See Snyder, note 28 above.

[49] *Wealden District Council* v. *Secretary of State for the Environment and Colin Day* [1983] JPL 234.

payment of rates. It is now established that the demolition of a building is in itself likely to amount to development requiring planning consent, although this had long been thought not to be the case.[50]

Planning Control over Activities which compete with Agriculture

Planning control over non-agricultural activity in the countryside is generally strict. However in ordinary rural areas the emphasis is mainly on protecting highly productive land. The amenity value of land will normally be taken into account in development plans, but existing plans were generally prepared whilst the overriding concern was the protection of land for growing food. Until existing plans are consistently reviewed with a new emphasis on public amenity there would seem to be a risk that land which could be conserved for amenity reasons will be sacrificed unnecessarily for new building.

Protection of productive agricultural land

The standard method of protecting rural land from development consists in requiring local planning authorities to consult with MAFF before granting planning consent for development. This requirement is currently contained in Article 18 of the General Development Order 1988. Since 1987 it applies where, in the opinion of the local planning authority, development, not for agricultural purposes and not in accordance with a development plan, would involve a loss of over 20 ha of grades 1, 2 or 3a agricultural land which is for the time being used, or was last used, for agricultural purposes. The requirement also applies to smaller areas in circumstances in which the development is likely to lead to a further loss of agricultural land amounting cumulatively to 20 ha or more. Previously consultation was required where only 10 ha of any agricultural land was at risk. The grading of agricultural land is explained in Annex B to DoE Circular 16/1987, 'Development involving agricultural land', although the five grades were modified in 1989. In particular the three categories in the middle grade, 3, were reduced from three to two.

In the past the assumption appears to have been that consultation with MAFF before allowing building on agricultural land would not only safeguard food supplies but would conserve the sort of rural landscape sought by the public. This assumption is now outdated, partly because consultation has become less common and partly because farming is under great stress, so that it no longer guarantees the variety of landscapes which it used to. Moreover there are growing demands for change in the countryside and these demands have widely differing objectives. Fundamentally the MAFF grading of land has

[50] *Cambridge City Council* v. *Secretary of State for the Environment* [1991] JPL 428.

little to do with amenity. Grades 1 and 2, excellent and very good-quality land, some 17 per cent of the total, and grade 3, a further 50 per cent, are all deemed worthy of special protection because of their productivity for a wide variety of crops. Grades 4 and 5 are poor or very poor from an agricultural point of view but could be of high scenic value. MAFF may be concerned to protect poorer land in areas where the higher-grade land does not exist or is very scarce, especially on the hills and uplands. Here development may be unlikely anyway. Elsewhere, however, it may do relatively little harm to amenity to build on high-quality agricultural land. It may do considerable harm to build on land which is of poor quality from an agricultural point of view.

The framework for regulating non-agricultural development in the countryside

The pattern for regulating non-agricultural development in the countryside is significantly different from that in towns. Not only is the predominant place of agriculture represented by MAFF but also there are special arrangements for controlling other activities which are more prominent in rural than in urban areas. Thus watercourses and large areas of water, including lakes and reservoirs, are now regulated by the National Rivers Authority. Since the water industry was privatized under the Water Act 1989, regulation has been in separate hands from the management and development of water resources, and this could mean that public amenity will be given greater prominence in the development of water resources. However, the National Rivers Authority's primary concern is with the purity of water. Like the Authority, the commercial water companies which actually administer the industry are under a statutory responsibility to take amenity into account in carrying out their functions. However, and more significantly, they also have good commercial reasons for maximizing the recreational value of rivers and lakes provided the cost of dealing with contamination is kept in mind.[51]

By contrast, other statutory undertakers which make great impact on the countryside have no real interest in amenity. Most notable is the recently privatized electricity industry. Pylons for power lines are perhaps the single most devastating form of intrusion into the rural landscape. These are followed closely by major new road schemes, which at present are generally the responsibility of the Department of Transport, although there is likely to be new scope for private involvement in the construction of fast toll roads such as that proposed up the east side of England. Statutory undertakers and other large-

[51] See William Howarth, *Water Pollution Law*, Shaw and Sons, 1988 and *The Law of Aquaculture*, Fishing News Books, 1990; John Bates, '*Water and Drainage Law*' (loose leaf), Sweet and Maxwell, 1990.

scale developers in the public sector, such as the Department of Transport, are in various respects independent of the normal planning system. They are generally obliged to allow public debate before introducing new schemes, and are expected to take account of their environmental impact. However visual deterioration of the landscape is notoriously difficult to value in accountancy terms so as to set against other factors. Also individual schemes tend to be introduced piecemeal, so that visual damage may be duplicated.

Another major form of development which occurs in the countryside is mineral abstraction. This is very much linked with waste disposal in filling up the excavated holes. To some extent mineral abstraction may permanently reduce the quality of a landscape and it is likely to disrupt local property rights for considerable periods. However, mineral development is peculiar in that eventually the land will be reclaimed, and in some circumstances the resulting landscape may be of more interest than what was there in the first place. Disused gravel pits may be admirable nature reserves, particularly for birdlife, or provide for new rural industries such as fish farming.[52] Larger expanses of water such as those left by brick clay extraction may provide new recreational opportunities. Historically the Norfolk and Suffolk Broads, perhaps the outstanding British area for inland water recreation, were created by ancient peat workings.

Major efforts are now made to ensure that where abstraction is allowed the land will satisfactorily be reclaimed afterwards. Thus the Town and Country Planning (Minerals) Act 1981 introduced complex provisions for aftercare conditions on the granting of planning consent for mineral abstraction. The emphasis in selecting sites for quarries and other mineral abstraction is likely to be on their commercial attractiveness to mineral operators. However there is scope for this sort of development actually to be led by environmental considerations. Thus silica sand is a particularly valuable commercial material, especially for glass making, and is not generally available like ordinary building sand. Department of the Environment Circular 24/85 lays down Guidelines for the Provision of Silica Sand in England and Wales. This circular specifically recognizes that in some cases 'extraction may offer opportunities to create new habitats for wildlife or bring other benefits'.[53] The Guidelines indicate that choice of location for new workings should take account of environmental enhancement.[54]

Generally, county councils rather than district councils exercise development control over mineral abstraction. Land in the countryside which has been used for this purpose is likely to be returned to

[52] See DoE Mineral Planning Guidance Notes, especially MPG 1 of January 1988.
[53] Para.5.2.
[54] Para.7.2(a)(iv).

agricultural or other rural use. Building is relatively unlikely because of the problems of subsidence. It may be that if new planning controls were to be extended to agriculture they could appropriately be linked to existing expertise in rural planning concerned with mineral control. However, government proposals for a move to unitary local authorities throughout the country seem to rule out the possibility of complementary planning functions exercised by two tiers of planning authority in the countryside, one concerned with more urban activities and the other with those which are more specifically rural.

Buildings in the countryside

Buildings in agricultural areas pose special problems. Purely agricultural buildings enjoy substantial concessions under the General Development Order. However, farm buildings, including recent and unsightly ones, may become redundant. If interesting farm buildings are demolished or allowed to decay the landscape may lose part of its character. Government policy favours the retention of existing structures and encourages new uses to be found for them, but it discourages new non-agricultural building. On the other hand there is much pressure for development on green-field sites, particularly for new houses with the attraction of a country setting. Where new houses are permitted or where they already exist they are protected from unpleasant new farming activities. Thus the General Development Order provides that building or other works need specific planning consent if it is 'for the accommodation of livestock or for the storage of slurry or sewage sludge' and is to be sited within 400 m of a protected building, that is a dwelling outside the farm.[55]

The concession in the General Development Order permitting new agricultural buildings requires these to be 'designed' for agricultural use. This can be used as a basis for forbidding the erection of multi-purpose buildings, such as sheds or hangars which would be out of keeping with traditional farm buildings in the area.[56] On the other hand a farmer will not be allowed to erect a building on the pretext that it is a pigsty or some other agricultural building if his real motive is to use it as a house.[57]

The 'erection, extension or alteration' of dwellings on agricultural land is not permitted development. However part of the legacy of agriculture's special position in countryside planning is that new

[55] General Development Order 1988, SI 1988 No.1813, Part 6 Class A.1.(b) and (j), A.3(2) and D.

[56] *Belmont* v. *Secretary of State for the Environment* [1962] 13 P&CR 417.

[57] *Harding* v. *Secretary of State for the Environment* [1984] JPL 503 and *Green* v. *Secretary of State for the Environment* [1985] JPL 323.

housing may be allowed for agricultural workers where other development would not. New dwellings may be permitted even in open country subject to conditions restricting their use to those involved in agriculture.[58] Such conditions can give rise to difficulties of interpretation. For example a standard requirement is that a house should be occupied only by a person whose present or last occupation was in agriculture. This would not allow the house to be bought by parents of a farmworker who had retired from a city job or by a mechanic working at the village garage. Conditions are likely to stipulate that the occupant must work or have worked locally, but it is often difficult to impose a satisfactory definition of what is local for the purpose.

The value of agricultural residence conditions is more in preserving housing stocks for a dwindling group of farm workers than in protecting the countryside from intrusive building. If a farmer obtains permission for a new farm worker's cottage and shortly afterwards shows that he no longer needs it for that purpose, he will have a strong case for the removal of any condition restricting its use. However, it may be that he would have been prepared to commission a building of more distinction if he had been given unfettered planning consent in the first place. Indeed where a farmer does need to build new accommodation it may be that a planning authority could benefit the amenity of the area by encouraging him to put up several dwellings to a high standard, which would be profitable to him and provide planning gain by ensuring that the necessary agricultural dwelling was of a high quality.[59]

Department of the Environment Circular 22/80 on 'Development Control: Policy and Practice' makes clear that generally

> the bulk of future development must take place both by rebuilding within existing towns and by expanding the towns within the limits of employment of local community capacity, e.g. infrastructure and social facilities. In considering proposals for development which involve the expansion of an existing town, regard should first be had to the amount of suitable cleared but undeveloped land within the town.[60]

The circular stresses that 'Expansion of a town into the countryside is objectionable on planning grounds if it creates ribbons or isolated pockets of development, or reverses accepted planning policies for separating villages from towns . . .' In villages, infilling of sites is said to be acceptable, and modest expansion may be permitted where villages

[58] *Fawcett Properties* v. *Bucks County Council* [1961] AC 636; *Alderson* v. *Secretary of State for the Environment* [1984] JPL 429; *Tyack* v. *Secretary of State for the Environment* [1988] EGCS 98.

[59] See here *R.* v. *Westminster City Council ex parte Monahan* [1990] 1 QB 87.

[60] DoE circular 22/80 on 'Development Control: Policy and Practice', para. 16.

have not 'reached the limit of their natural growth'. However this begs the question of what is the natural size of a village and suggests a policy of cramming modern buildings into any available sites. The sites are likely to be prominent, and the buildings may well be of inappropriate materials as local planning authorities are told generally not to concern themselves with the niceties of aesthetics such as the colour of bricks.[61]

Circular 22/80 specifically recognizes that development which would otherwise be unsuitable may be permitted if 'there is an exceptional need to make land available for housing'. Taken together, therefore, government policies may result in small villages left inviolate but unviable as living communities, whilst larger ones risk being saturated with insensitive development. In pursuit of social aims, government policy can specifically encourage building on a site which will damage the amenity of a village. Thus it was expressly stated by Mr Nicholas Ridley during his tenure as Secretary of State that needs for low-cost housing could be an important material consideration in releasing 'small sites within or adjoining existing villages which would not otherwise be allocated for housing'. By contrast, *This Common Inheritance* does stress that some aspects of aesthetics are valid planning considerations, notably location in relation to other properties, bulk and overall relationship to the surroundings. The white paper goes so far as to encourage new villages and larger settlements because they should offer opportunities for high-quality design.[62]

Special Planning Regimes in the Countryside

General government planning policy in respect of development in the countryside still seems primarily to be concerned with the preservation of productive agricultural land and with preventing existing settlements from spreading. However a variety of special regimes are explicitly concerned with conserving natural resources such as rare species and the quality of the landscape and with enhancing public enjoyment of the countryside. These regimes range from National Parks, with a variety of functions covering wide areas, and other large areas which are designated mainly as planning tools for restricting future development, that is, Areas of Outstanding Natural Beauty, and Green Belts, to smaller areas which are subject to more substantial protection, such as Sites of Special Scientific Interest. In villages, as in larger urban areas, special protection may be provided by the creation of Conservation Areas or by the listing of individual buildings. Other smaller areas may be identified essentially for public recreation, such as

[61] See ibid. para. 19 and also PPG 1, para. 27; also ministerial statement reported at [1990] JPL 335.

[62] See R. H. Hutton 'Local Needs Policy Initiatives in Rural Areas: Missing the Target?' JPL (1991), 303.

Country Parks which may be set up by local authorities under the Countryside Act 1968.[63]

The special regimes in the countryside can be criticized on the ground that they do not offer adequate protection even for particularly valuable or sensitive areas, and also on the ground that they distract attention from ordinary areas which are therefore left more vulnerable. However they offer a range of possible ways for furthering the aims of conservation in the countryside and for allowing its adaptation to changing needs. They emphasize the distinctive nature of countryside as opposed to town planning law, and in particular they rely on a co-operative approach with landowners, which depends upon a close relationship between public law regulation and land management arrangements devised through the evolution of private land law.[64]

National Parks and Areas of Outstanding Natural Beauty

National Parks have been designated by the Countryside Commission, under section 4 of the National Parks and Access to the Countryside Act 1949, as

> extensive tracts of country in England and Wales as to which it appears to the Commission that by reason of – (a) their natural beauty and (b) the opportunities they afford for open-air recreation, having regard both to their character and their position in relation to centres of population, it is especially desirable that . . . necessary measures shall be taken . . . for the purpose of preserving and enhancing [their natural beauty and] for the purpose of promoting their enjoyment by the public.

There are nine National Parks, along with the Norfolk and Suffolk Broads which operate under similar arrangements.[65] The possible creation of more has been given some encouragement in *This Common Inheritance*. Their qualities are safeguarded by more stringent planning supervision than usual, partly through exceptions to the General Development Order. Thus cladding is not permitted with stone, artificial stone, timber, plastic or tiles. The permitted size for an extension is smaller than normal and roof alterations require express approval.[66] The local planning authority may require submission of detailed proposals for choice of site and design of farm buildings for its

[63] Countryside Act 1968, ss.6–8.

[64] Cf D. R. Denman, *The Place of Property*, Geographical Publications, 1978.

[65] Norfolk and Suffolk Broads Act 1988 and Town and Country Planning Act 1990, s.5.

[66] Town and Country Planning General Development Order 1988, SI 1988 No.1813, Class A.2(2).

approval. There are also special arrangements for the preparation of plans and the exercise of planning control.[67]

Areas of Outstanding Natural Beauty (AONBs) have been designated by the Countryside Commission, under section 87 of the National Parks and Access to the Countryside Act 1949, as areas outside National Parks which appeared to the Commission 'to be of such outstanding natural beauty' that it is desirable for the relevant provisions of the Act to apply. Government policy in these areas is primarily the conservation of natural beauty. Recreation is not an objective in designating an area, although, once designated, an area should be used to meet the demand for recreation so far as that is consistent with conservation and the needs of other users, amongst whom those in agriculture and forestry are emphasized.[68]

The same qualifications on planning permission given by the General Development Order apply in AONBs as in National Parks. Otherwise the effect of designation is mainly to ensure that there is consultation with the Countryside Commission or the Countryside Council for Wales before development plans are prepared and before development is authorized. Because AONBs cross local authority boundaries there are practical problems in ensuring co-operation in their protection between local authorities. There may be a danger if one authority allows development in its part of an AONB assuming that there will be 'enough left' in the neighbouring district.

In general it is regarded as inconsistent with the aims of designation to permit the siting of major industrial and commercial development in AONBs.[69] Only proven national interest and lack of alternative sites are recognized as justifying any exception. However as each individual case must be determined on its merits it would seem that other exceptions may be allowed in practice, provided environmental effects of any proposal are taken into account as a major consideration. As so often in the planning system, provided those granting planning permission for new development clearly acknowledge the damage which such development will cause to public amenity, they may in practice give it little weight when faced with attractive arguments put forward by a developer. Quarrying and road building are specifically recognized as forms of development where AONBs are likely to be sacrificed. Although general policies do not favour building houses in the countryside there does not seem to be a particular commitment to exclude new housing from AONBs.

[67] Town and Country Planning Act 1990, s.4.

[68] Policy Statement by Secretary of State for the Environment 29 July 1982, HC Deb. Vol. 28, cols. 707-10, set out in the *Encyclopedia of Planning Law and Practice*.

[69] Ibid.

Green Belts

The special regimes where pressure for development in the countryside is generally most intense are Green Belts. These may be regarded as essentially tools of town rather than country planning since their main object is to protect urban areas from overdevelopment. Green Belts are creations of planning authority policy rather than general legislation. Major conurbations are now protected by Green Belts designated in development plans. General government policy on these regimes has been set out by the Department of the Environment in circulars and in planning guidance notes.[70]

The original purpose of a Green Belt was to check further growth of built-up areas, to prevent neighbouring towns from merging into one another or to preserve the special character of a town.[71] In addition it is now stressed that Green Belts are important on the one hand in safeguarding the countryside from further encroachment and on the other in stimulating urban regeneration.[72] To achieve these aims its is envisaged that Green Belts should be several miles wide. They are expected to be long-term, and therefore it is advised that they should not include land on which there may be particularly intense pressure for new development. Granting of piecemeal planning consent could weaken the protection of the whole.

There is a presumption against the construction of any new building or any material change of use of an existing building in a Green Belt 'for purposes other than agriculture, sport, cemeteries, institutions standing in extensive grounds or other uses appropriate to a rural area'. Existing towns and villages should not be expanded although 'a strictly limited amount of "infilling" or "rounding off" may be permitted'. However in accordance with the overriding discretion given to planning authorities, permission may always be granted in 'very special circumstances'.

Even in towns and villages within a Green Belt, new building for commercial or industrial purposes is discouraged, 'since this, if allowed, would lead to a demand for more labour, which in turn would create a need for the development of additional land for housing'. On the other hand in recent statements made in Parliament it has been stressed that redundant buildings in Green Belts as much as elsewhere in the countryside may be used for individual residences and may even be appropriate for 'encouraging new types of employment and enterprise'.[73] New uses are particularly encouraged for buildings of

[70] See note 17 above.
[71] Circular 42/55.
[72] PPG 2, 1988.
[73] 30 April 1986 (Hansard, HC Vol. 96, col. 414) now included in PPG 2, 1988, para. 16.

attractive appearance which are likely to last for a substantial period if properly maintained. There is a shift in emphasis which reflects the decline in farming and the need to diversify the rural economy. However, there may also be an indication of a more open attitude to development which positively enhances the appearance of the countryside.

The effect of Green Belt policies was considered by the Court of Appeal in *Pehrsson* v. *Secretary of State for the Environment and the Council of the Royal Borough of Windsor and Maidenhead.*[74] The Court quashed a decision in which planning permission had been refused to turn a cricket pavilion in the Berkshire Green Belt into a staff residence for a country house. The judges agreed that the policy in favour of finding new uses for redundant buildings in the countryside applied to all buildings in Green Belts as well as elsewhere, and to various sorts of building, not just agricultural ones. It also appears from this case that in a Green Belt the normal presumption in favour of development does not apply unless the development was one of those categories listed as appropriate, because, except in those categories, development would by definition cause demonstrable harm to interests of acknowledged importance. Permission could only then be given in very special circumstances.

More recent case law suggests that once good reasons have been raised for making an exception, for example because a proposed new factory would be of considerable social benefit, the planning authorities must refuse permission only if they clearly demonstrate the basis on which they are satisfied that the damage to the Green Belt would outweigh the advantages. In such circumstances the fact that harm to the Green Belt would be minimal would itself seem to be capable of being part of the special circumstances justifying an exception to the normal presumption against development.[75]

In *Pehrsson* the judges did not resolve the extent to which the presumption against new development may be applied more rigorously against new building as opposed to the change of use of an existing building which is not redundant. The case illustrates the uncertainty of what is a suitable use for a rural area. There is ever-increasing pressure for new uses of agricultural land both by farmers who want to diversify their businesses and by developers keen to take up surplus land. There are likely to be frequent claims that certain types of development are inherently suitable in the countryside, including a Green Belt, even though they are nothing to do with agriculture or one of the other categories at present encouraged by government policy. The planning

[74] *Pehrsson* v. *Secretary of State for the Environment and the Council of the Royal Borough of Windsor and Maidenhead* [1990] JPL 764.
[75] *Vision Engineering Ltd* v. *Secretary of State for the Environment and Guildford Borough Council*, as yet unreported.

guidance notes themselves beg the question of the status of country houses with miniature estates and whether they are the sort of institution standing in extensive grounds which it is intended to encourage.

Management regimes

The purposes of various sorts of regime may differ significantly and can be in conflict with one another. In particular, encouraging public access may threaten conservation. Thus the notification of Sites of Special Scientific Interest under sections 28 or 29 of the Wildlife and Countryside Act 1981 is intended to protect rare species and their habitats. Notification prohibits the carrying out on the land of operations specified in the notice, within a limited period during which the relevant Nature Conservancy authority or the Secretary of State may negotiate a management agreement or in certain cases compulsorily purchase the land. However notifying say a slope where orchids grow may prove of little value if there is a network of public footpaths over it. Ironically, the same Act which governs the creation of SSSIs provides for Definitive Maps of rights of way. If a right of way is marked on the map this guarantees rights of public access even if it will clearly harm the SSSI. Such conflicts may become apparent where steps are taken to notify a new site and the local authority then has to decide whether a right of way should be stopped up or diverted.[76]

What can be particularly startling is that notification of an SSSI may give very little protection from a planning point of view. Two recent cases concerned with SSSIs have demonstrated both their strengths and their weaknesses. In *Sweet* v. *Secretary of State* an area of marshland on the Somerset Levels was notified as an SSSI.[77] Schiemann J. dismissed a challenge to the notification by the owner of the land. The judge made clear that an SSSI may include land which does not itself contain species worthy of protection but which is part of a single unit which needs to be treated as a whole so as to safeguard species. The judge also made clear that a very wide range of operations may be banned during the waiting period, such as cutting grass or grazing, and not merely substantial works which would amount to operational development under the Town and Country Planning Act.

However in *R.* v. *Poole Borough Council ex parte Beebee and others* the same judge demonstrated that notification may have limited practical value.[78] He rejected an application for judicial review sought

---

[76] For relevant powers see Highways Act 1980, ss.116–18; cf. Town and Country Planning Act 1990, ss.247–61. For discussion of public access rights see Tim Bonyhady, *The Law of the Countryside*, Professional Books, 1987 Part 2.

[77] *Journal of Environmental Law*, 1 (1989), 245; and see Ch. 5 above.

[78] See note 26 above.

by the British Herpetological Society, the specialist conservation body
concerned with reptiles, which was supported by the World Wildlife
Fund, and which objected to a grant to itself by Poole Borough
Council of planning permission for housing development on an SSSI
on Canford Heath containing some of the last remaining sand lizards
and slow-worms in Britain. Even though the local planning authority
had mistakenly thought that the site was still only provisional it had
been aware of its conservation importance and had been entitled to
subordinate this to its views of the housing needs in the area. The
importance of the site for nature conservation was clearly a material
consideration for planning purposes but not one which provided any
significant protection against housing development on the edge of a
town.

Although this planning decision was subsequently called in and
overturned by the Secretary of State, the limited value of notification of
SSSIs faced with a planning application has been underlined by a
Department of the Environment consultation paper issued in March
1991. This indicates that more planning applications affecting SSSIs
will be called in in future but expressly rejects creating a presumption
against development on such sites as there is in Green Belts.

Another regime which depends on creating management agreements
is designation of Environmentally Sensitive Areas (ESAs), under
section 18 of the Agriculture Act 1986. These allow the Minister of
Agriculture to enter into management agreements with farmers in the
area and pay them to manage their land in such a way as to further
conservation. There is no restriction on farmers who have not entered
into such an agreement in an ESA even during a waiting period, as
there is in the case of SSSIs. On the other hand farmers may not be
tempted to threaten damage to land in an ESA unless they are paid, as
they might with an SSSI. However land in an ESA is just as likely to be
as vulnerable as an SSSI when planning permission is sought to
develop it. Its status will be a material consideration to weigh against
arguments in favour of a grant of planning permission for new housing
or other development. However there is no guarantee that much
weight will necessarily be attached to that status.

Where the aim is to allow the public to enjoy something which is
fragile and in need of protection, an area may be made a Nature
Reserve. Such reserves may be set up under the National Parks and
Access to the Countryside Act 1949

for the purpose – (a) of providing, under suitable conditions and control,
special opportunities for the study of, and research into, matters relating to
the flora and fauna of Great Britain and the physical conditions in which
they live, and for the study of geological and physiographical features of

special interest in the area, or (b) of preserving flora, fauna or geological and physiographical features of special interest in the area.

Nature Reserves in private hands depend on management agreements made with a Nature Conservancy Council or a local authority.[79]

At least where a public management agreement can be set up, the land should be protected, even if the local planning authority would prefer it to be built on or otherwise developed. Private arrangements may also be made to protect land from development by means of restrictive covenants. Such a covenant may be given extra force if it is made with the National Trust.[80] Generally where a landowner creates covenants over his land so as to preserve it for public enjoyment, a future owner of the land can be prevented from developing despite the blessing of the local planning authority's consent. However there are powers for the Lands Tribunal to modify or quash such covenants even where the National Trust is a party, and those powers to some extent allow local planning policy to override private restrictive covenants.[81]

The Positive Contribution of Planning Law to the Future British Countryside

It does seem that the system of development control will be tightened up so as to regulate farming more strictly. On the other hand the major changes which will continue to occur in rural society may call for new patterns of control over development in the countryside generally. Two matters may prove of particular significance in shaping such patterns. First, changes in the organization of local government are bound to be important in determining who will exercise control in future. Second, the tradition of co-operative schemes for managing farming, rather than the essentially negative system of development control, could help the emergence of a more innovative and sensitive system of rural planning. In any event the Planning and Compensation Act 1991 now requires that all local authority development plans upon which development control is based should specifically include policies in respect of the conservation of the natural beauty and amenity of the land and the improvement of the physical environment. It has become increasingly common for statutes to require ministers to have account of such matters in exercising various duties in the countryside but such duties would normally be very difficult to enforce through any court action. The duty to include such policies in statutory plans may

[79] National Parks and Access to the Countryside Act 1949, s.21 and also ss.17, 18 and 103; Wildlife and Countryside Act 1981, s.35.
[80] National Trust Act 1937, s.8.
[81] *Gee* v. *National Trust* [1966] 1 WLR 170.

provide more effective opportunities for amenity groups to insist on more tangible policies for ensuring conservation.

The location of control

At present, planning functions are largely exercised by district councils although counties have played a major role in policy-making through the creation of Structure Plans. These generalized statements of policy for future development still provide the framework for determining the shape of development in the countryside, the detail being filled in by Local Plans which are produced by district councils particularly in respect of existing centres of population. Counties do also exercise specific planning functions for highways and for controlling mineral abstraction.[82] However, the Government has made clear that a further reorganization of local government is imminent, and it appears that there will be a move to unitary authorities in the countryside as there already are in London and the six other densely populated metropolitan areas.

The pattern of new rural authorities seems likely to vary considerably from one place to another, sometimes based on existing districts and sometimes on counties. The form taken by reorganization is likely to be crucial for the future exercise of planning law in the countryside. The transfer of development control to larger and more powerful authorities than the present districts would offer opportunities for more creative and positive planning in the countryside. It could equally lead to more bureaucracy and less variety.

Farming and forestry are still largely regulated in terms of economic productivity by MAFF and by statutory agencies such as the Forestry Commission, but today these are not solely concerned with productivity of farms and woodlands. They are charged with duties to take account of environmental and amenity interests. In the past MAFF's main role in the planning system has been to ensure that new building in the countryside is kept off high-grade agricultural land. Now its tradition of encouraging production may fit it to the new positive role of devising and supervising management agreements designed for more effective conservation and more imaginative innovation. Set- aside polices for agricultural land and new grant systems to encourage the diversification of farm businesses give MAFF an increasing opportunity to shape the future of the countryside in a manner to contrast with urban planning regimes. It may even offer an alternative to local authorities and the DoE for operating a

---

[82] Highways Act 1980, s.1, General Development Order 1988, SI 1988 No. 1813, and Town and Country Planning Act 1990, s.1(4).

comprehensive system of planning control in respect of new development in the countryside generally.

The scope for a positive countryside planning system

Crucial for the quality of the rural landscape is the maintenance of diversity and the encouragement of positive improvement. Planning tends to be used as a negative tool restricting new development. This may be partly because of underlying assumptions about private property rights. These tend either to be treated as sacrosanct, so that restrictions on what a landowner may do with his own property are minimized, or they are regarded as antisocial obstructions to using land in the general public interest. By contrast, in the countryside, efforts have been made to develop more constructive voluntary regimes which can channel private initiative into both preservation and enhancement of the landscape and into the provision of facilities for public enjoyment of the rural environment.

The more positive contribution of general planning law includes the use of planning conditions and statutory planning agreements to achieve planning gain.[83] Under the Town and Country Planning Acts developers have been able to agree with local authorities to impose restrictions on their land or to provide particular facilities such as open spaces for recreational purposes. Such arrangements have generally been made in conjunction with a grant of planning consent to a developer for some new scheme. They have allowed more substantial benefits to be obtained for the community than could be imposed by planning conditions. The Planning and Compensation Act 1991 includes provisions to improve and extend such arrangements, particularly enabling more positive obligations to run with land. There would seem to be considerable opportunities for using these new land obligations to support a wide-ranging system of management in the countryside to further conservation, not merely as a supplement to development control.

The system for land use planning in the countryside has tended to leave much to the initiative of private landowners. This may sometimes produce better, sometimes worse, results, than a more compulsory system. However, a variety of regimes may have better prospects for maintaining diversity and for allowing creative new developments than any single uniform regime. Whatever system emerges, a major subject for debate is bound to be the contribution which is allowed to the public in the formulation of policy and in the creation of new regimes for controlling land use. A scheme which effectively draws on the co-operation and the good will of landowners may tend to exclude public participation.

[83] Under what is now Town and Country Planning Act 1990, s.106.

The rural infrastructure

This essay has been concerned mainly with public law regimes, especially development control, which are available to protect and to enhance the amenity of the countryside. A major contribution to the future of the countryside could be a more effective system of proactive planning for long-term infrastructure needs. Especially with the shift of statutory undertakers' obligations to private organizations, there is a clear need for centralized regulatory and planning authorities to oversee the services they provide. The reorganization of water resources provides a model in certain respects for the infrastructure generally. For example, anticipating long-term major needs for roads, power lines and water mains could enable dual-purpose corridor routes to be identified much longer in advance and could enable preparations to be made by tree planting and other landscaping work so as to minimize disruption when it occurs. If the structure of local authorities is changed, particularly if county councils are abolished, it may become increasingly difficult to maintain the distinction between town and country. Altogether, a new system of long-term and flexible planning for the siting of major infrastructure systems in the country-side seems particularly apposite at the moment when traditional farming patterns and the landscapes which they created may be on the verge of extinction.

7

Land Management Agreements and Agricultural Practice: towards an integrated legal framework for conservation law

CHRISTOPHER P. RODGERS

Introduction

The principal means by which legally enforceable controls have been introduced on agricultural land use has, to date, been the conclusion of land management agreements with owners and occupiers of farmland in areas designated as worthy of special protection. The introduction of legislative control, via enabling legislation providing for designations of areas for protection, has to some extent proceeded on an *ad hoc* basis. One consequence of this is that, for instance, the detailed interaction of conservation legislation with the rights and duties of an occupier under the Agricultural Holdings legislation, or under any other contractual arrangement by which he holds the land (for instance, a share farming arrangement), is not provided for. This chapter examines some of the problems caused by the implementation of conservation policy through management agreements, and the practical workability of the current legislative framework for conservation law.

Provision for Designation and Protection of Special Areas

Land can be designated as worthy of special protection under a variety of statutory designation measures. Some, but by no means all, of the statutory designations have the effect of making management agreements available to owners and occupiers with farmland within the designated area. Other contributions in this volume examine several of the extant legislative designating measures e.g. the Wildlife and Countryside Act 1981 in relation to sites of special scientific interest, and the Water Act 1989 in relation to Nitrate Sensitive Areas.[1] It is therefore not proposed to review the enabling legislation in detail here. Before considering the specific problems arising from management agreements concluded under the various statutes, however, it might be helpful to review the operation of the various designations and the scope for the conclusion of management agreements thereunder.

The following sites can be designated for special protection:

Sites of Special Scientific Interest. The Nature Conservancy Council (and its successors)[2] has power under section 28 of the Wildlife and Countryside Act 1981 to designate an area a 'Site of Special Scientific Interest' and notify it to the local planning authority as such. The designation must specify the flora/fauna or other features of the site by reason of which it is of special interest, and any agricultural operations likely to damage the site.[3] The broad effect of designation is to make it a criminal offence to carry out the prescribed operations without the NCC's consent or pursuant to a management agreement. Proposed operations must be notified in advance to the NCC, who then have four months in which to offer a management agreement. After the expiry of this period the operation can be carried out without criminal penalty, unless the NCC has requested the Secretary of State to make a nature conservation order under section 29 of the 1981 Act. If this is done, the period during which operations cannot be carried out is extended to twelve months in order to enable the NCC to conclude a management agreement or, ultimately, consider using its compulsory purchase powers to acquire the site.

Environmentally Sensitive Areas. These are designated by Statutory Instrument under powers contained in section 18 of the Agriculture Act 1986. The 1986 Act implements in domestic law the requirements of Title V of Council Regulation (EEC) No.797 of 1985 on the improvement of agricultural structures. The terms of proposed management agreements in an Environmentally Sensitive Area are laid down in the designation orders themselves, of which fourteen have been made to date.[4] These in most cases seek to impose *positive*

---

[1] See Chapters 3 and 5 above.

[2] i.e. the Nature Conservancy Council for England, the Nature Conservancy Council for Scotland and the Countryside Council for Wales. These bodies assume the NCC's conservation designation functions under the Environmental Protection Act 1990, s.128 and Sch.9, paras 4 and 11.

[3] Wildlife and Countryside Act 1981, s.28(4).

[4] The following designation orders have been made under s.18 of the 1986 Act in relation to England and Wales: South Downs (SI 1986 No. 2249), West Fenwith (SI 1986 No. 2252), Somerset Levels (SI 1986 No. 2552), Pennine Dales (SI 1986 No. 2253), the Broads (SI 1986 No. 2254), Cambrian Mountains (SI 1986 No. 2257 and SI 1987 No. 2026), Lleyn Peninsula (SI 1987 No. 2027), Breckland (SI 1987 No. 2029), North Peak (SI 1987 No. 2030), Shropshire Borders (SI 1987 No. 2031), South Downs Extension (SI 1987 No. 2032), Suffolk River Valleys (SI 1987 No. 2033), Test Valley (SI

obligations on participants in the ESA scheme to adopt traditional and non-intensive farming methods, e.g. by restricting the use of herbicides and pesticides, and reducing stocking levels to prevent overgrazing.

National Parks. These are designated under the National Parks and Access to the Countryside Act 1949 by the Countryside Commission. The conservation functions of designation are in this instance pursued largely through the medium of planning control, and not management agreements, e.g. special requirements as to notification and approval of the siting and design of agricultural buildings apply.

Areas of Outstanding Natural Beauty. These are also designated under the 1949 Act. Control of environmental policy is conducted largely through planning control and not by the use of management agreements, and local authorities have power to make by-laws in designated AONBs.[5]

Nature Reserves. These are designated under powers in the 1949 Act, which also gives the Nature Conservancy Councils power to enter into management agreements with owners and occupiers of land in the designated site. Where no satisfactory agreement can be concluded to protect the site, the NCC enjoys powers of compulsory purchase to acquire the land concerned.[6]

Limestone Pavements. The Wildlife and Countryside Act 1981 [7] makes special provision for the designation of areas including limestone pavements by means of a 'limestone pavement order'. Designation is by the Secretary of State or local planning authorities, acting with advice from the NCC or Countryside Commission. The protection afforded to limestone pavements is more rigorous than that afforded (for instance) to Sites of Special Scientific Interest. It is a criminal offence to disturb a designated site, e.g. by carrying out agricultural operations, unless planning permission has been obtained.[8]

Nitrate Sensitive Areas. These are designated by the Minister of Agriculture under the terms of the Water Act 1989, with the intention of preventing or controlling the entry of nitrates from farming operations into controlled waters and water supplies.[9] The Minister has power to enter into voluntary management agreements within a NSA area. The designation mechanism is applied more flexibly by the 1989 Act than in previous countryside legislation. The Minister is given powers to impose requirements, restrictions and prohibitions on

1987 No. 2034). Further designations relate exclusively to land in Scotland. See Ch. 9, p. 210 ff. below.

    [5] National Parks and Access to the Countryside Act 1949, s.90.
    [6] See ibid. ss.17 and 18.
    [7] Wildlife and Countryside Act 1981, s.34.
    [8] Ibid. s.34(4).
    [9] Water Act 1989, s.112.

agricultural practices when designating an area, and to pay compensation to affected owners and agricultural occupiers.[10] These designation provisions mark a significant development in conservation law, in that they provide for positive obligations as to land management to be compulsorily applied where the Minister considers this necessary, either with or without compensation. Hitherto, positive obligations as to land management have only been applied under voluntarily concluded management agreements, e.g. in Environmentally Sensitive Areas. Ten 'pilot' NSAs have been designated using the voluntary model, and providing for management agreements with affected landowners and agriculturalists.[11] The special problems of Nitrate Sensitive Area designations are separately considered elsewhere in this volume.

Water Protection Zones. The Water Act 1989 also makes provision[12] for the designation of 'water protection zones' in which the Secretary of State can impose restrictions (but not positive obligations) as to agricultural practices with a view to preventing the entry of pollutants into water supplies. This designation mechanism has not, at the time of writing, been exercised.

Management Agreements: Availability and Scope

Management agreements remain the primary mechanism hitherto employed to control environmentally damaging agricultural practices. The legislation providing for the designation and protection of special areas (above) makes provision for different classes of management agreement in different areas, and in some cases prescribes the terms on which agreements can be offered and concluded.

Availability of management agreements

Nature Reserves. The National Parks and Access to the Countryside Act 1949[13] gives the NCC power to enter into an agreement to secure the management of land as a nature reserve, where they consider it would be in the national interest that it should be so managed. An agreement can be made with 'every owner, lessee or occupier' of agricultural land and can impose such conditions as seem expedient on the exercise of rights over the land by the other party to the management agreement. The agreement is thus intended to limit the exercise of legal rights (of use or otherwise) over the land by the contracting party.

Sites of Special Scientific Interest. Power to enter into management agreements where land is included in a notified SSSI is conferred on the

[10] See ibid. s.112(4).
[11] See the Nitrate Sensitive Areas (Designation) Order 1990, SI 1990 No. 1013. See further Chapter 3 above.
[12] Water Act 1989, s.111.
[13] National Parks and Access to the Countryside Act 1949, s.16.

NCC by s.15 of the Countryside Act 1968. As a result of amendments introduced by the Environmental Protection Act 1990, the NCC can also offer a management agreement to the occupier of land adjacent to a designated SSSI where this is, for instance, necessary to protect the site itself.[14] It has now been held, in *Sweet* v. *Secretary of State and Nature Conservancy Council*,[15] that a designation under the 1981 Act can include land which forms a 'single environment' with a site considered of special interest or importance, with the consequence that a management agreement may be available to restrict agricultural operations on land adjacent or near the site of primary interest, but which forms part of a single wildlife habitat with it. Where the site is within a nature reserve, power for the NCC to conclude management agreements is also conferred by s.16 of the 1949 Act (above). The NCC will commonly offer a management agreement where the owner or occupier has notified his intention to carry out agricultural operations prohibited by the SSSI designation order. If a management agreement cannot be concluded to protect a site designated under s.28 of the 1981 Act, the only recourse open to the NCC is currently to seek the imposition of a nature conservation order. Ultimately, if an agreement cannot be concluded following the making of a nature conservation order, damaging agricultural operations can only be prevented by the NCC invoking its powers of compulsory purchase.[16]

Refusal of capital grant. Where an application is made for a capital grant (for instance to finance agricultural improvements,[17] but is refused on conservation grounds after objections by the NCC or local authorities, the objecting bodies can in some circumstances be compelled to offer a management agreement.

By virtue of s.32 of the Wildlife and Countryside Act 1981, when considering an application for capital grant to finance operations on land notified as an SSSI, the Minister must exercise his functions so as to further the conservation of the flora, fauna, or geological/physiographical features by reason of which the land is of special interest. Furthermore if the NCC object to the making of a grant, the Minister cannot make one without first considering the terms of the NCC's objection. Similar provision is made in respect of applications for capital grants to carry out operations on land within a national park. Where, in consequence of an objection by the NCC (or in the case of land in a national park by the relevant planning authorities), the application is refused, the NCC (or authority if appropriate) must, within three months of receiving notice of refusal, offer to enter into a

---

[14] Environmental Protection Act 1990, Sch.9 para. 4, amending Countryside Act 1968, s.15.

[15] [1989] JPL 927. And see Ch. 5, p. 112 ff. above.

[16] i.e. under s.16 National Parks and Access to the Countryside Act 1949.

[17] e.g. under a grant scheme established under the Agriculture Act 1970, s.29.

management agreement with the applicant. This must include restrictions on the carrying out of the operations in respect of which grant was refused.[18]

Environmentally Sensitive Areas. In the case of a designated ESA the Agriculture Act 1986[19] confers on the Minister power to enter into a management agreement with 'any person having an interest in agricultural land' wholly or partly within the ESA area. This can make provision for payments by the Minister to secure the management of the land in accordance with the agreement. The terms of individual management agreements will be specified in the relevant designation order. The latter must specify the requirements as to agricultural practices, methods and operations, and the installation or use of equipment, which must be included in management agreements, and the period for which agreements are to run (for instance five years, as is commonly the case). Management agreements concluded under s.18 will commonly impose restrictions as to the application of herbicides, pesticides and certain fertilizers, and provide for maximum stocking levels to prevent over grazing. The prescriptions naturally vary according to the area of the country concerned and the predominant form of agriculture (livestock farming, arable etc.) current in the locality.

There is no residual power to compel the Minister to offer an agreement, as exists under the 1981 Act if capital grant is refused in an SSSI or National Park. The Environmentally Sensitive Areas scheme therefore operates on strictly voluntary principles.

General powers. Section 39 of the Wildlife and Countryside Act 1981 confers a general power to enter into management agreements upon county and local planning authorities. This can be exercised by the latter for the purpose of conserving or enhancing the natural beauty or amenity of land which is both in the countryside and within their area, or for promoting its enjoyment by the public. An agreement under s.39 can be entered into with any person 'having an interest in the land' concerned (e.g. a tenant or freehold owner) and can be made irrespective of whether the land is in a designated SSSI or any other area given protection by statutory designation (above). The use of this power is actively encouraged by central government, although it is, of course, subject to the financial constraints within which local government operates.[20] A management agreement under s.39 can impose restrictions in respect to the method of cultivating the land, its use for agricultural purposes or the exercise of rights over the land, and

---

[18] Wildlife and Countryside Act 1981, ss.32(2) and 41.
[19] Agriculture Act 1986, s.18(3)
[20] See DoE Circular No.27 of 1987, paras 39 and 40.

may also impose positive obligations to carry out works or agricultural or forestry operations.[21]

Nitrate Sensitive Areas. The terms on which management agreements are available in the designated NSAs are prescribed in considerable detail in the Nitrate Sensitive Areas (Designation) Order 1990.[22] This provides for participation at two levels in the NSA scheme. Farmers and landowners can opt for either a 'basic scheme agreement', or a 'premium scheme agreement' with enhanced levels of grant.[23] The terms on which both basic and premium scheme agreements may be entered into are prescribed in detail in Schedules 1 and 2 to the designation order. The principal objective of basic scheme agreements is to impose restrictions on the use of nitrates on arable crops. Where a premium scheme agreement is offered, a participating farmer will be obliged to cease arable production altogether and establish a grassland sward by 1 October next following. He will, further, be obliged to opt for one of four alternative modes of management, and to comply with the detailed obligations appropriate thereto laid down in the 1990 Order. The latter enables a farmer to opt for conversion to unfertilized and ungrazed grassland, to grassland with grazing (with or without limited application of fertilizers), or for conversion of arable land to grassland with woodland.[24] Premium scheme agreements also impose more extensive positive obligations as to land management on the participating farmer or landowner.[25]

Objectives: restricting damage or improving agricultural practice?

It will be immediately apparent that the voluntary principle in conservation management is not universally, or consistently, applied. A coherent and integrated conservation policy necessitates the selective use of compulsory measures to enforce environmental control in appropriate circumstances. These can be applied through the use of criminal sanctions, through planning law or through civil liability (for instance for breach of contract where a management agreement is disregarded). Regrettably, no coherent policy towards the use of compulsory measures is apparent in the existing countryside legislation. Similarly, the various statutory measures adopt different approaches to the use of management agreements — some seek to improve agricultural practices by imposing positive obligations as to

[21] Wildlife and Countryside Act 1981, s.39(2).
[22] SI 1990 No. 1013 and SI 1990 No. 1187.
[23] SI 1990 No. 1013, regs.2 and 7, Scheds.1 and 2.
[24] Detailed conditions to be observed by participating farmers are laid down for each of the options in Sched.2 of the designation order.
[25] e.g. to increase the area of grassland on the holding to at least the area of grassland at 31 July 1989 and to cut grass and remove the cuttings from the land (Sched.2 ibid. para.2 and Option A(ii)).

management and conservation, on the one hand, while others seek solely to *restrict* otherwise damaging operations. When considering the sanctions currently available to enforce conservation measures, a distinction must be drawn between the use of compulsion to encourage the conclusion of a satisfactory management agreement, and its use in enforcing compliance with the terms of an agreement, once concluded.

The principal measures used to encourage the conclusion of satisfactory management agreements are compulsory purchase orders and criminal sanctions. Where land is in a notified SSSI, the carrying out of proscribed agricultural operations will be a criminal offence unless planning permission has been obtained or they constitute an 'emergency' operation.[26] The criminal sanction only applies, however, where the operation is carried out within four months of its having been notified to the NCC.[27] After this, if the owner refuses to conclude an agreement he may carry out the proposed operations without penalty. The only recourse available to the NCC is to seek a nature conservation order to protect the site. This will have the effect of extending the bar on operations to give further time to conclude an agreement. The NCC can use its residual power compulsorily to purchase a site only where it is satisfied that it is unable to conclude a reasonable agreement to protect it.[28] The procedures in the Wildlife and Countryside Act 1981 are open to the objection, of course, that if conduct is considered sufficiently damaging to constitute an offence under the 1981 Act, it should be such irrespective of *when* it occurs. Moreover, once a management agreement has been concluded, criminal penalties cease to be available to enforce compliance with its terms. Compulsory purchase orders are also available where land is within a designated nature reserve, but (similarly) can only be used by the NCC where they are satisifed that a satisfactory management agreement cannot be concluded.[29] Compulsory purchase powers are not available to reinforce conservation objectives in designated Environmentally Sensitive Areas, Nitrate Sensitive Areas or Areas of Outstanding Natural Beauty. Compulsory purchase is a selective remedy for the enforcement of conservation policy — where large tracts of land are involved (as in designated ESAs) it would clearly be impractical, and expensive, to enforce conservation measures in this way. The criminal law would also, to some extent, be an inappropriate tool to enforce the positive obligations as to cultivation and farming methods prescribed in the Environmentally Sensitive and Nitrate Sensitive Areas designation orders. Designations under the Wildlife and Countryside Act 1981 and National Parks and Access to the

[26] Wildlife and Countryside Act 1981, s.28(7).
[27] Ibid. s.28(6).
[28] See National Parks and Access to the Countryside Act 1949, s.16.
[29] Ibid.

Countryside Act 1949 (Nature Reserves), on the other hand are intended primarily to *prohibit* damaging operations. The prohibitions in an SSSI designation can more properly, therefore, be made the subject of criminal penalties.

A variety of sanctions are currently used to enforce the terms of a management agreement once concluded. This, also, is an area which might benefit from reappraisal and the formulation of a more integrated approach. The remedies available to enforce management agreements under the various designations include the following:

Civil Remedies. Where a management agreement relates to an SSSI the agreement will invariably include a provision providing for the repayment of a proportionate part of any lump sum paid, in the event of the agreement being breached by the landowner or occupier.[30] If annual periodic payments are payable under the agreement, the latter will provide for payment to cease following breach. Department of the Environment guidelines make it clear, however, that the terms included in agreements should not go beyond this and provide a financial penalty for breach of a management agreement.[31] Moreover, once an agreement has been concluded, the civil remedy is all that is available, in the short term, to protect a site — the criminal sanctions in s.28(5) of the Wildlife and Countryside Act 1981 cease to apply four months after notification of intended agricultural operations. Where an agreement is concluded in a designated Environmentally Sensitive Area, the civil penalties for breach are, likewise, the primary remedy available to enforce compliance with the conservation objectives of the agreement. The various Environmentally Sensitive Area designation orders provide that an agreement must include a term by which the Minister can, following breach of the agreement's terms, give the farmer notice terminating the agreement, and thereupon recover as a civil debt the whole of the payments made under the agreement or such proportion as the Minister may specify.[32] In so far as an agreement can provide for reimbursement of the whole of any monies paid, the civil remedy is more in the nature of a penalty than that applicable under SSSI management agreements, and of commensurably greater deterrent effect. The Nitrate Sensitive Areas designation order, likewise, provides that any management agreement concluded under its terms *must* include a term providing for the reimbursement of all monies paid under the agreement in the event of the breach of all or any of its terms.[33]

---

[30] See generally DoE Circular No.4 of 1983 ('Wildlife and Countryside Act 1981 — Financial Guidelines for Management Agreements').

[31] Ibid. para.43(a) and (b).

[32] See e.g. SI 1986 No. 2026 reg.5 (Cambrian Mountains), SI 1987 No. 2031 reg.5 (Shropshire Borders), SI 1987 No. 2033 reg.5 (Suffolk River Valleys).

[33] SI 1990 No. 1013, reg.8.

Compulsory Purchase. Compulsory purchase remains a residual remedy where land is within an SSSI or nature reserve. Existing conservation legislation fails to confer specific compulsory purchase powers upon the Ministry where breach of a management agreement occurs in an ESA or NSA however. Where land is within a nature reserve, the NCC can only exercise compulsory purchase powers if a management agreement is being breached in such a way as to prevent or impair the satisfactory management of the land as a nature reserve. The NCC must give the defaulting party notice to remedy the breach within a reasonable time.[34] Dispute as to whether there is sufficient breach to trigger the compulsory purchase provisions is referable to arbitration.[35]

Restorative action. An order requiring restorative action to remedy damage is available only where a nature conservation order has been made in an SSSI, and in any event only where an owner or occupier has been convicted of a criminal offence under the 1981 Act. Where a management agreement has already been concluded the statutory bar on operations, backed by criminal sanctions, will only endure for three months following notification of the proposed operations to the NCC. In the last resort compulsory purchase will be the only effective remedy to prevent damage to a protected site. Nevertheless, the use of restoration orders merits consideration as an alternative to civil remedies and compulsory purchase in enforcing management agreements. The extension of the concept to apply to management agreements concluded in ESAs, NSAs and other protected sites, as a measure of last resort, would reinforce existing civil remedies for breach, and provide a more effective framework of protection for the various designated conservation sites.

Residual compulsory powers. The Water Act 1989 is unique in providing for mandatory directions to be prescribed, by order, if the voluntary approach to conservation via management agreements fails. Although the current NSA designations proceed along strictly voluntary lines, the 1989 Act[36] provides that the Minister may impose such 'requirements, restrictions or prohibitions' as seem appropriate in a Nitrate Sensitve Area, either with or without compensation. The flexible legal regime put in place by the 1989 Act provides a useful model which would, if extended to cover other designated conservation areas (SSSIs, ESAs etc.), provide residual powers of enforcement of a more effective nature than, for instance, compulsory purchase — which latter is, at best, a highly selective remedy incapable of widespread application. It would also not do violence to the voluntary principle in

[34] National Parks and Access to the Countryside Act 1949, ss.17 and 18.
[35] Ibid.
[36] Water Act 1989, s.112(4).

conservation management, being a measure of last resort. It should be added that the 1989 Act also makes provision for *positive* duties as to management to be imposed, and not simply restrictions (as is the case in, for instance SSSI designation orders). Positive obligations can currently be applied under ESA or SSSI management agreements, but only where these have been freely negotiated with farmers and landowners. A further weakness of the approach adopted by the SSSI designation provisions, in imposing *restrictions* on otherwise damaging actions, is that it is heavily dependent on the NCC being aware of potentially harmful agricultural operations. Most agricultural operations do not require planning permission, or are given deemed permission by Part 6 and Sched.2 to the General Development Order,[37] and the NCC will often not have ready access to development proposals. The proposed extension of planning control on the siting and appearance of agricultural buildings would, it is suggested, have the incidental benefit of improving the SSSI designation provisions by giving local planning authorities and the NCC prior notice of a wider range of potentially harmful operations.

Parties to a Management Agreement

A common theme of the various designating measures is that they empower the NCC, Minister, or local authority (whichever applies) to enter into management agreements with any person having an 'interest' in the land to which the agreement relates.[38] The classes of potential participant are therefore defined by reference to the categories of estate and interest in land recognized by law. Although not clearly expressed, a management agreement could presumably be concluded with a person holding an *equitable* estate or interest (for instance an equitable mortgagee), and not simply the holder of a legal estate or interest in the land. The only restriction would appear to be that the offeree have an 'interest' or estate in the land recognized within the terms of the Law of Property Act 1925.[39]

The failure of the various conservation measures to define, specifically and clearly, which classes of agricultural occupier are entitled to participate in management agreements can cause difficulty in practice. An agreement can clearly be concluded in most cases with a tenant occupying land within a designated area, or any other person

[37] i.e. the Town and Country Planning General Development Order 1988, SI 1988 No. 1813.

[38] See the wording of s.15 Countryside Act 1968 (SSSIs), s.18(3) Agriculture Act 1986 (ESAs) and s.39(1) Wildlife and Countryside Act 1981.

[39] As to which see ss.1 and 205(1) Law of Property Act 1925. See also above Chapter 5 (p. 105) for discussion of the litigation in *NCC* v. *Southern Water Authority* (1991), in which this point was taken.

having a sufficient legal interest to be able to guarantee performance of the prescriptions in the proposed management agreement. The landlord and tenant relationship gives rise to special problems, some of which are addressed below. It should be noted also, however, that it is increasingly common for land to be occupied for agricultural purposes under a variety of arrangements, many of which do not create an 'interest' in land. A share farmer occupying under a joint venture arrangement will have control of the farming of a holding, but would not possess a sufficient interest to enable him to conclude a management agreement. Share farming contracts normally provide for exclusive possession to remain in the landowner, with the result that the 'sharer' will not have a recognized 'interest' in the land. He will, however, have contractual rights and duties *vis-à-vis* the landowner under the terms of the share farming contract. Although the landowner would be entitled to conclude a management agreement, therefore, its performance may put him in breach of his contractual obligations under the share farming arrangement — indeed it may be outside his power to carry out the terms of a proposed management agreement at all, especially if the share farming arrangement contractually vests substantial control of husbandry and cultivation in the 'sharer'. The ability of the parties to a joint venture to participate in management agreements will ultimately depend, therefore, upon the terms of the joint venture contract. *Semble* occupiers holding as graziers, under management contracts or as employees, will also have an insufficient interest in the land to be able to conclude management agreements. Such occupiers will, in any event, lack both the long-term security of occupation, and exclusivity of use, necessary to be able to guarantee performance of the terms of a management agreement. Graziers exercising rights of common may be able to guarantee management in accordance with a proposed management agreement if all registered commoners act in concert, and unanimously. Commons give rise to special problems of land management, however, and these are separately considered in this volume.[40]

Landlord and Tenant: Some Problems

Special problems can arise where a management agreement is sought in a designated site with a tenant, or someone occupying under some lesser form of interest (for instance a licence) caught by the Agricultural Holdings Act 1986. Two separate issues will commonly arise: (1) the impact of the obligations which would be imposed under a proposed management agreement on the tenant's existing contractual obligations to his landlord, and (2) the need for the participation of the

[40] See Chapter 8 below p. 165 ff.

landlord's interest in a management agreement to secure the long-term protection of the site, and the manner in which this participation can be secured.

Regrettably, much of the extant conservation legislation does not make provision for these problems at all. In some cases provision *is* made for the special problems caused by the landlord and tenant relationship, but without any consistent or coherent policy being immediately apparent. This is an omission of some importance. The landlord/tenant system has been in decline for many years. Nevertheless the last thorough survey of land tenure in the UK, conducted by the Northfield Committee in the late 1970s,[41] found that the overall area of land subject to tenancy had fallen by 1978 to around 43 per cent of total agricultural land. Because of the development of forms of tenancy not at arms length, the true proportion of let land was, they felt, probably somewhere between 35 and 40 per cent. Given the residual importance of the tenanted sector, it follows that legislative policy towards the management of tenanted land needs to be clearly formulated. The failure of current legislation to address the impact of conservation obligations on the rights and duties of landlord and tenant *inter se* must, additionally, create practical problems in the implementation of an integrated conservation management policy.

Participation in management agreements — requirements

The various conservation measures make different provision as to the formal requirements to be satisfied by a tenant wishing to enter into management agreements. Some (for instance the Water Act 1989) make the landlord's written consent a precondition to a management agreement being concluded. Some, such as the Environmentally Sensitive Areas provisions,[42] require written notice to be given to a landlord prior to the conclusion of an agreement. Yet other legislative measures make no provision whatever for the landlord/tenant relationship — this is the case, for instance with the SSSI provisions in the Wildlife and Countryside Act 1981. There would appear to be no coherent policy reason for the different treatment of management agreements entered into in the various designated conservation areas.

Where land is within a nature reserve, the National Parks and Access to the Countryside Act 1949 expressly envisages the conclusion of management agreements with 'every owner, lessee or occupier' of agricultural land affected.[43] The manner in which the participation of a tenant is to be secured is not, however, specified. An agreement made

[41] See the Report of the Committee of Inquiry into the Acquisition and Occupancy of Agricultural Land (1979), Cmnd. 7599.

[42] Agriculture Act 1986, s.18(6).

[43] National Parks and Access to the Countryside Act 1949, s.16.

under the 1949 Act can impose such conditions as seem expedient on the exercise of *rights* over the land by an owner or other occupier. Management agreements are therefore intended to limit the exercise of legal rights, of both exploitation and user, which are vested in the occupier. As a tenant's legal rights over the land will be limited by the terms of his tenancy agreement and the Agricultural Holdings Act, it follows that the landlord's interest will commonly have to be included in a complementary management agreement if the long-term protection of the designated site is to be preserved. This would appear to be the case, even though the 1949 Act does not require the landlord's consent to a tenant entering an agreement with the NCC, neither does it require formal notification of entry to the landlord.

Where a management agreement is concluded in respect of an SSSI, or by a local authority under s.39 of the 1981 Act, there is no obligation on a tenant to notify the owner. For similar reasons, however, the concurrence of the owner will be necessary to secure the long-term performance of the terms of the management agreement. Indeed, the policy of the NCC in such cases has been to seek a complementary management agreement with the owner, or to include his interest in the principal agreement. A landlord entering into a complementary agreement will normally receive only a nominal consideration for doing so, his rights otherwise being adequately secured by the Agricultural Holdings Acts.[44] Where an agreement is offered under the 1981 Act in respect of an SSSI, or following a refusal of capital grant on conservation grounds, Ministerial guidance indicates that the NCC should require that a tenant give a written assurance that his landlord has been informed

> of the proposed agricultural operation which has led to the offer of a management agreement under the terms of the 1981 Act;
> that the offer of a management agreement is likely to be accepted by the tenant;
> and
> of the area and location of land to be included within the proposed management agreement.[45]

Although the only requirement is to notify the landlord, it should be appreciated that if the proposed works which led to the offer of an agreement constituted improvements within the meaning of the Agricultural Holdings Act 1986, the landlord's consent to their execution will have been required. Most such improvements will fall within Sched.7 Part II of the 1986 Act, viz. they will be improvements to which the landlord's consent will be necessary if a claim for

[44] See DoE Circular No.4/1983, para. 8.
[45] Ibid. para.7.

compensation is to be made on the later termination of the tenancy, or to which (in default of consent) the tenant can apply for the consent of an agricultural land tribunal.[46] Improvements within this category include the erection of buildings, construction of silos and other facilities, reclamation of waste land, removal of obstructions to cultivation, land drainage work and the erection of fencing. The landlord's consent to the execution of improvements can be given either unconditionally or upon such terms as to compensation *or otherwise* as may be agreed.[47] There would appear to be no reason, therefore, why a landlord should not grant consent subject to his agreed participation in grant monies payable under any subsequent management agreement — even though this is not envisaged in the ministerial guidance on management agreements.[48] If, on the other hand, an application for tribunal consent to improvements is made, the tribunal will consider the agricultural merits of the application, exclusive of conservation considerations. If the landlord has consented to improvements this will not, furthermore, necessarily provide a tenant with a defence to any claim for breach of tenancy arising out of the performance of a subsequently concluded management agreement. Neither will the consent of an agricultural land tribunal. The tenant has the option, furthermore, of executing the improvements without consent, and forgoing a later claim for compensation in respect thereof. The policy underlying the compensation provisions in the 1986 Act is to encourage long-term improvements aimed at increasing agricultural efficiency, irrespective of conservation considerations. There must be a case, therefore, for amendment of the tenancy legislation to entitle a tribunal or landlord to refuse consent to improvements on conservation-related grounds. This would relieve the NCC of the need to offer a management agreement if the likelihood of landlord or tenant carrying out proposed improvements in the longer term is called into question. The need to offer a management agreement could also be removed were the NCC to be given a right to refer proposed improvements to an agricultural land tribunal, for adjudication as to their agricultural and/or conservation merits. At the very least, it must be said that the policy underlying the 1986 Act, in encouraging improvements on agricultural grounds, sits uneasily with that of the Wildlife and Countryside Act 1981, and other conservation measures.

Ministerial guidance indicates that the NCC should seek to secure the long-term protection of SSSIs by including the landlord's interest

[46] Agricultural Holdings Act 1986, s.67.

[47] Ibid. s.67(2).

[48] 'Normally there should be no need to make more than a nominal payment . . . as the landlord's interests will be secured by the Agricultural Holdings legislation' (DoE Circular No.4/1983, Appendix para.8).

in the principal agreement, or otherwise concluding a complementary agreement with him. A landlord entering into a complementary arrangement will normally be entitled to a nominal payment only, to secure his agreement, as his rights will otherwise be secured by the Agricultural Holdings Acts.[49] If the landlord intends to take the land in hand at the end of the tenancy, he should be obliged by the terms of the management agreement to give at least six months' notice to the NCC of his wish to terminate the agreement.[50]

The policy of the NCC in these circumstances is to seek a complementary agreement with the landlord, or to include his interest within the principal management agreement, *and* to include in that agreement an undertaking by the landlord not to serve notice to remedy breaches of tenancy on the tenant, contrary to the intentions of the management agreement.[51]

Where land is in a designated Environmentally Sensitive Area, the Agriculture Act 1986 provides[52] that the Minister cannot enter into a management agreement with a tenant unless the latter has certified that he has notified the owner of his intention to make an agreement. In practice, however, the consent of the landowner may be required to secure the long-term performance of the prescriptions contained in the ESA designation orders. In the first place, although a management agreement will bind successors in title of the offeree, where the latter is a tenant it will not bind the owner or a subsequent tenant, none of whom derive title from the offeree tenant. Similarly, some of the prescriptions in the proposed management agreement, such as reducing stocking levels, may give rise to a breach of the Rules of Good Husbandry (below). Further, some of the prescriptions may be outside the tenant's power to perform at all, e.g. conditions as to maintenance and retention of broadleaved trees, which will commonly be reserved to the landlord under the terms of an agricultural lease. The terms on which the landlord's participation should be secured, and the manner in which this should be done, are not prescribed in the 1986 Act. Neither are they the subject of formal ministerial guidance (cf. management agreements in SSSIs, which are the subject of a ministerial circular). Similar considerations to those arising in SSSIs will, however, be relevant.

In sharp contrast to the above, where land is within a Nitrate Sensitive Area, a tenant can enter into a management agreement only with the written consent of the landlord.[53] As with ESA and SSSI

---

[49] Ibid, i.e., presumably, by the provisions in the Agricultural Holdings Act 1986 Sched.2 as to rent review.

[50] Ibid. Appendix para.9.

[51] See *Sites of Special Scientific Interest*, Nature Conservancy Council, 1988, p.13.

[52] See Agriculture Act 1986, s.18(6).

[53] See s.112(2)(b) Water Act 1989.

management agreements, an agreement in a Nitrate Sensitive Area will bind successors in title of the offeree, and not (where the latter is a tenant) the freehold owner taking the land in hand at a later stage, or a subsequent tenant.[54] The rationale for requiring the landlord's consent here, but not (for instance) in an ESA or SSSI, is not immediately apparent. The Nitrate Sensitive Areas (Designation) Order 1990[55] further provides that a tenant who has written consent may enter into a management agreement even if he has other land in the designated area held of a different landlord, which latter has not given his consent to participation in the scheme. The 1990 Order also envisages the Minister entering into an agreement with both landlord and tenant, even though the land is not occupied by the landlord (or his agent) for agricultural purposes. The landlord's consent is presumably required in this instance because the adoption by the tenant of one of the options for participation in the NSA scheme[56] would, in the longer term, substantially affect the character of the holding and its profitability as a farming enterprise. For similar reasons, for instance, a landlord's consent is required where a tenant with an arable holding wishes to participate in the set-aside scheme for arable land.[57] Whatever the merits, the detailed treatment of the landlord/tenant relationship in the Nitrate Sensitive Areas Order has the merit of avoiding many of the problems (of both a legal and practical nature) to which the participation of tenant farmers in conservation agreements can give rise. Some of these issues are dealt with below.

Good husbandry vs. conservation management — a conflict of policy?

In the absence of a landlord's concurrence, the interaction of a management agreement with a tenant's contractual obligations under his tenancy can be problematic. The performance of a management agreement can also conflict with a tenant's obligations and statutory rights under the Agricultural Holdings Act 1986.

The policy underlying the statutory code of rights in the 1986 Act is to encourage efficient farming by making a tenant's rights to security of tenure and succession, and a range of other matters, dependent upon his observance of recognized standards of husbandry and management. The applicable standards are laid down in the 'Rules of Good Husbandry', a statutory code of guidance found in s.11 of the Agriculture Act 1947. Although not enforceable *per se*, they can be enforced indirectly, by possession proceedings, where a tenant is failing

[54] This is the effect of the provision in s.112(4) Water Act 1989.

[55] SI 1990 No. 1013, reg.5(3).

[56] This is particularly so where a premium scheme agreement is concluded, with the more extensive obligations applicable thereto under Sched.2 to the designation order.

[57] Set-Aside Regulations 1988, SI 1988 No. 1352, reg.6.

to farm in accordance with the standards there laid down. The Agricultural Holdings Act 1986[58] entitles the landlord to make an application to the agricultural land tribunal for a Certificate of Bad Husbandry if the tenant is failing to fulfil his duty to farm in accordance with the Rules of Good Husbandry. If granted, a certificate enables the landlord to serve notice to quit, provided he does so within six months of the certificate being granted.[59] In many cases, the tenancy agreement will itself incorporate the Rules of Good Husbandry as a term of the tenancy. In this event the landlord can also enforce the rules by taking proceedings alleging a failure to remedy breaches of the contract of tenancy.[60]

The Rules of Good Husbandry are intended to ensure a tenant adopts the most efficient mode of farming appropriate to the individual holding. They were formulated in the immediate post-war era, when encouraging efficient production was a priority of considerable importance, and when conservation objectives were of minor significance. In many senses the priorities therein contained are contradictory to the conservation objectives of more recent legislation, such as the Wildlife and Countryside Act 1981 or the Environmentally Sensitive Areas provisions. In practice their enforceability against a tenant may prove a disincentive to the latter participating in some kinds of management agreement—at least, not without the landlord's express consent, whether legally required or not. The obligations imposed by the rules will not be examined in detail here. They require, for instance, that a farmer keep pasture in good heart and fertility, that arable crops be taken in a way which maintains a good state of cultivation and fertility, and that necessary work of maintenance to buildings and equipment be carried out.

Clearly a tenant will be in breach of the rules if he reduces stocking levels or fails to maximize arable cropping, pursuant to a management agreement, in order to protect wildlife habitats. A common feature of many of the Environmentally Sensitive Areas designation orders, for instance, is that they require a farmer to refrain from ploughing, reseeding, and applying herbicides or pesticides — all of which should, arguably, be done by a farmer complying with the Rules of Good Husbandry.

The model clauses — fixed equipment

Observance of prescriptions commonly included in management agreements may also involve the tenant in breach of the 'model clauses' implied into tenancies by s.7 of the 1986 Act. These provide a statutory

---

[58] Agricultural Holdings Act 1986, Sched.3, Part 11, para.9.
[59] Ibid. Sched.3 Case C.
[60] Ibid. Sched.3 Case D.

code allocating liability for the repair and maintenance of various items of fixed equipment on a holding to either landlord or tenant. If the clauses have been expressly incorporated into the tenancy agreement, breach may give rise to a right to serve a notice to quit.[61] The clauses place a tenant under a duty, for instance, to replace fences and walls which have fallen into disrepair, unless this liability is placed by the lease on the landlord.[62] Clearly, if a management agreement includes terms which restrain a tenant from erecting new fences or walls, perhaps with the intention of preserving vernacular features of the landscape, this could conflict with the tenant's obligations under the model clauses and constitute a potential breach of tenancy. Many of the Environmentally Sensitive Areas designations, for instance, require a participating farmer to refrain from planting hedges, building new walls or erecting new fences.[63]

Conservation covenants

Problems of potential breach of tenancy are recognized in recent amendments to the Agricultural Holdings legislation itself.[64] Some protection against proceedings alleging breach of tenancy is provided, but only if the tenancy includes a suitably worded conservation covenant. When deciding whether to issue a certificate of bad husbandry, an agricultural land tribunal must disregard any practice adopted by the tenant in pursuance of a provision in the contract of tenancy (or in any other written agreement with the landlord) which indicates (in whatever terms) that its object is the furtherance of the conservation of flora and fauna, the protection of buildings or other objects of architectural, archaeological or historic interest, or the conservation and enhancement of the natural beauty of the country-side or the promotion of its enjoyment by the public. For the purpose of possession proceedings alleging either a remediable or irremediable breach of tenancy, a covenant in this form is, furthermore, to be regarded as a term of the tenancy which is not inconsistent with the tenant's duty to farm in accordance with the Rules of Good Husbandry.[65] The protection of these provisions in Schedule 3 to the 1986 Act is available, however, only where there is a suitably worded conservation covenant in the lease, or where a separate agreement is

[61] i.e. under Agricultural Holdings Act 1986, Sched.3 Case D. The breach will in most cases be a remediable breach of tenancy.

[62] The model clauses are contained in SI 1973 No. 1473. For repairing obligations of a tenant see in particular para.5 in the Schedule to the 1973 regulations.

[63] See, for instance, SI 1987 No. 2026 (Cambrian Mountains), Sched. para.1(11) and (12), SI 1987 No. 2027 (Lleyn Peninsula), Sched. paras 2, 3, 5 and 6.

[64] Introduced by Agricultural Holdings Act 1984, s.6(8).

[65] See now Agricultural Holdings Act 1986, Sched.3 Part 11, paras 9(2), 10(1)(d) and 11(2).

concluded with the landlord. The 1986 Act does not require the landlord's agreement to conservation objectives, if secured otherwise than in the lease itself, to be in writing. Clearly, where an oral agreement is alleged, there is considerable scope for uncertainty and dispute between landlord and tenant. The contents of the envisaged covenant are also somewhat vague, requiring a covenant to pursue conservation objectives (above) *in whatever terms* — clearly the scope of a loosely formulated agreement between landlord and tenant, especially if oral, could give rise to further dispute.

The Water Act 1989[66] further amended the Agricultural Holdings Act to give protection to tenant farmers entering the pilot Nitrate Sensitive Areas scheme. The 1989 amendments are more precisely drafted, and provide that where the landlord's agreement to the tenant's entering the NSA scheme has been given, nothing done pursuant to a management agreement shall be capable of constituting a breach of tenancy. This amended form of wording removes some of the uncertainty surrounding the provisions applicable to other classes of conservation agreement. The 1989 Act also provides for the contingency of mandatory obligations being imposed on the tenant under s.112, by providing that nothing done by him pursuant to obligations imposed by the 1989 Act shall constitute a breach of tenancy.

There can be little doubt that these provisions give inadequate protection to farmers proposing to enter conservation agreements. Few agricultural leases include conservation covenants of the type envisaged, and in most cases the introduction of such a protective provision will be a matter for negotiation between landlord and tenant. Where a landlord is unwilling to forgo his established rights under the 1986 Act, therefore, failure to secure a suitable conservation covenant could unnecessarily delay the conclusion of a management agreement. Although ministerial guidance on the operation of conservation agreements in SSSIs[67] indicates that a landlord should normally receive a nominal capital sum for concluding a complementary agreement forgoing his rights as to breach of tenancy etc., there is no reason (under the legislation as presently framed) why a landlord should not require a substantive consideration for offering a protective conservation covenant. There would also appear to be some uncertainty as to the scope of the conservation provisions in the 1986 Act *per se*. Where the landlord's consent to the conclusion of a management agreement is a prerequisite laid down by statute, as for instance in the case of a Nitrate Sensitive Area agreement, conservation covenants would appear irrelevant — the landlord's consent to the agreement will

---

[66] Water Act 1989, Sched.25, para.75, amending and adding to Sched.3, paras 10, 11 and 12 Agricultural Holdings Act 1986.
[67] See DoE Circular No.4/1983, Appendix para.8.

in itself provide a defence to any subsequent claim as to breach of tenancy. The granting of consent to improvements in an SSSI, however, would not be sufficient to exonerate a tenant subsequently offered a management agreement following a refusal of grant on conservation grounds. In such cases the NCC must seek a separate undertaking from the landlord not to serve statutory notices to remedy breaches of tenancy.[68] Conservation covenants will, it is suggested, be of most relevance where the landlord's participation in management agreements, through formal consent or separate provision, is not formalized by the relevant legislation or ministerial guidance. This is especially the case in, for instance, designated environmental sensitive areas. Where a covenant has been granted, of course, the participation of the landlord in complementary management agreements will be of less immediate concern. It will still be required, however, to provide for the eventuality of land being taken in hand or relet during the continuance of the agreement.

The current uncertainties surrounding the position of tenant farmers arise, of course, because existing conservation legislation makes no attempt to interfere with the established framework of rights and duties of landlord and tenant, and places no fetter on the landlord's ultimate rights (secured by the agricultural holdings legislation) to require maximization of agricultural production and profit from a holding. Where a landlord refuses to offer a conservation covenant there is currently no remedy for an aggrieved tenant wishing to conclude a management agreement — whatever the merits of his doing so or the public interest in protecting the site concerned. The Agricultural Holdings Act contains machinery enabling either landlord or tenant to request the conclusion of a written tenancy agreement, including basic leasehold conditions set out in Schedule 1 to the 1986 Act, and to require arbitration to settle the terms of a written tenancy in default of agreement. A conservation covenant is not among the Schedule 1 matters which can be reduced into writing in this way, however. Many of the difficulties arising under the current law would be avoided were Schedule 1 to the 1986 Act amended to enable a tenant to request a written agreement including a conservation covenant in suitable terms, in default of which the settling of the terms of the lease, including such a covenant, could be settled by arbitration. The landlord's position could be safeguarded by enabling an agricultural arbitrator, when making his award as to terms, to award compensation reflecting any diminution in the value of the reversionary

[68] Prescribed notices to remedy breaches of tenancy are laid down in the Agricultural Holdings (Forms of Notice to Pay Rent or to Remedy) Regulatiosn 1987, SI 1987 No. 711. These must be used by a landlord wishing to serve a subsequent notice to quit.

estate which would flow from the subsequent conclusion of management agreements. Quantifying a landlord's potential loss could be
difficult, however, unless the terms of any proposed management
agreement were known at the time of the abritration.

Rent review and estate management problems

It has already been observed that a landlord will normally expect a
nominal capital payment upon entering a complementary agreement
protecting an SSSI. The clear intention, expressed by the ministerial
circular on payments made under SSSI management agreements,[69] is
that the landlord's rights will be adequately secured by his right to
participate in grant monies paid by the NCC through review of the rent
paid for the holding concerned. Unfortunately, however, the relevance
of conservation grant payments in rent arbitrations under the
Agricultural Holdings Act 1986 is by no means clear. Moreover, the
different modes of payment available to tenant farmers under the
various conservation schemes mean, in practice, that different considerations will apply in different cases.

Where an agreement is concluded in an SSSI, the tenant will receive
annual periodic payments, calculated to reflect net profits forgone
because of the restrictions contained in the agreement.[70] The landlord
will then, according to ministerial guidance, be entitled on rent review
to recover a proportion of the payment made to the tenant as though
the management agreement did not exist and the tenant were in no way
restricted from farming in accordance with the required standards of
the Agricultural Holdings Act 1986.[71] This assumption is based, of
course, on the hypothesis that the existence of the management
agreement does not enhance the overall profitability of the farming
enterprise, payments merely replacing lost income. In practice,
whether this is so will depend on the facts of the individual case and the
restrictions on farming operations prescribed by the agreement. Where
net income *is* substantially increased, however, a further question will
arise: is the landlord entitled to participate by way of rent review in this
additional income, (generated as it is) from non-agricultural sources?
The latter problem arises more starkly where an agreement is
concluded in respect of land within an Environmentally Sensitive Area,
or in respect of land within one of the pilot Nitrate Sensitive Areas. The
Environmentally Sensitive Areas designation orders prescribe fixed
rates of payment to be made under management agreements, at a rate
per hectare of land included in the agreement eg. £30 per hectare in the

---

[69] See DoE Circular No.4/1983, para.5(xi).

[70] Ibid. para.13. The annual payments are calculated on the basis of forgone profits,
as provided for in paras 16–20 of the Circular.

[71] Ibid. para.5(xi).

Cambrian Mountains ESA, £15 per hectare in the Lleyn Peninsula ESA, rising to £30 per hectare for rough grazing subjected to additional prescriptions and £70 for hay meadow, and £10 per hectare in the North Peak ESA (rising to £20 if additional prescriptions are subscribed to).[72] Payments under the Nitrate Sensitive Areas (Designation) Order are also at a prescribed rate per hectare, with higher rates for premium scheme agreements carrying increased restrictions on agricultural operations.[73] The use of flat-rate payments may be administratively convenient, but results in practice in wildly varying net financial returns for producers entering into management agreements. The use of this technique also means that payments cannot, in many cases, be regarded as simply a replacement of lost income — indeed, where few changes in current farming practice are demanded of an individual participant, little drop in income will ensue. The majority of any grant payments will necessarily constitute enhanced profit arising from the agricultural enterprise. The degree to which payments will enhance profitability will vary from case to case. Where the prescriptions in a proposed agreement would necessitate substantial changes in farming practice, the potential loss of income may not be offset by the payments prescribed in the designation orders, and participation in a management agreement will not be financially advantageous. Fixed rates of payment quite clearly have an arbitrary effect.

Where a tenant enters the ESA or NSA schemes, in circumstances where the profitability of his enterprise will be substantially enhanced, the question will arise whether the landlord is entitled to share in this increased profitability by way of rent review. In default of agreement, rent is settled by arbitration in accordance with a statutory rent formula set out in Sched.2 to the Agricultural Holdings Act 1986. The latter directs an arbitrator to have regard, when fixing the rent, to 'all relevant factors', including in every case the terms of the tenancy, and both the productive capacity of the holding and its related earning capacity.[74] The objective of the rent formula would at first sight appear to be to link agricultural rent to the profitability of the strictly 'agricultural' enterprise carried on. The 1986 Act defines productive capacity, for instance, to mean the productive capacity of the holding and its associated fixed equipment 'on the assumption that it is in the occupation of a competent tenant practising a system of farming suitable to the holding'. Likewise, related earning capacity is defined in a manner which relates it directly to the income which a competent

---

[72] See *inter alia* SI 1987 No. 2026 (Cambrian Mountains) reg.6, SI 1987 No. 2027 (Lleyn Peninsula) reg.6, SI 1987 No. 2031 (Shropshire Borders) reg.6. Similar provision is made in the other designation orders.

[73] SI 1990 No. 1013, reg.7 and Sched.4.

[74] Agricultural Holdings Act 1986, Sched.2. para.1(1) and (2).

tenant would generate from farming the holding.[75] There can be little doubt, therefore, that enhanced profits arising from management agreement payments cannot be taken into account under either of these heads, not being income derived from agricultural activities on the holding. Although the question has yet to be judicially decided, it seems probable that grant income would come within the general clause in the rent formula, i.e. it will be 'a relevant factor' which the arbitrator will be entitled to have regard to. This clause clearly has a wide ambit, encompassing additional income from non-agricultural activities such as bed and breakfast lettings, pony trekking etc., though its ambit is not indefinite. On the one occasion when the formula has been judicially considered, albeit at first instance, it was given a wide meaning to encompass non-agricultural income.[76] Until decided authoritatively, however, the relevance of grant payments must remain a matter of uncertainty. It should also be appreciated that even if a landlord is receiving an enhanced rent as a result of management agreement payments, this in itself will not abrogate his statutory rights where breaches of tenancy are alleged, provided of course that he has not consented to the agreement, or concluded a complementary agreement under which he has agreed to forgo his right to serve notices to remedy breach of tenancy. Participation by way of rent review alone fails to resolve many of the other legal issues arising out of the performance of a management agreement.

The use of rent reviews as a medium for dealing with landlord participation also involves problems of estate management, and this may in itself obstruct the expeditious implementation of management agreements. Agricultural rent reviews normally occur on a triennial basis. A landlord or tenant cannot require arbitration of rent to take effect less than three years since the last rent review or agreed variation of rent. Moreover, to secure a statutory rent review, a landlord or tenant must give notice of at least twelve month's duration ending on a term date of the tenancy.[77] Where an agreement is concluded in an NSA the landlord's consent is required, and he will therefore have the necessary information to weigh whether a review of rent, to reflect the changed circumstances, is necessary. Where an agreement is proposed in an ESA or SSSI, however, the tenant's obligation is merely to inform his landlord of his intention to conclude an agreement. The latter has no right to detailed information as to the terms of the agreement or the payments made thereunder, and will often have insufficient material on which to base a decision as to the necessity of a rent review. Furthermore, if an agreement is concluded during the last two years of

[75] Ibid. Sched.2, para.1(2)(b).
[76] See *Enfield LBC* v. *Pott* [1990] 34 Estates Gazette 60 (county court).
[77] Agricultural Holdings Act 1986, ss.12(1) and 25.

the rent cycle for the holding concerned, the landlord will not be able to recover an increase in rent for that period. Clearly, he will wish, wherever possible, to synchronize the rent review date with the commencement of management agreements. The failure of the conservation legislation to provide for these eventualities may in practice delay the implementation of management agreements, as well as providing fertile conditions for the generation of dispute between landlord and tenant. At the very least, provision should be made for tenants entering management agreements to provide full details of the terms and rates of payment thereunder. Without this information a landlord proposing to initiate a rent review will be in difficulty when preparing gross profit budgets for the review process, and may not even be aware of the precise date on which the proposed agreement was concluded. These omissions in the more recent legislation appear the more strange, given that ministerial guidance on the operation of the SSSI designation scheme clearly envisages participation by way of rent review as the norm—presumably the same considerations are intended to apply to ESA and NSA agreements, despite a lack of official guidance.

Conclusion

There is a strong case for a review of the substantive law of nature conservation. It would have been advantageous for substantive reform to have been initiated alongside the reform of the administrative machinery of conservation accomplished in Part VII of the Environmental Protection Act 1990. Although the opportunity to do so was not taken, the need for substantive reform to improve the practical workability of existing conservation measures cannot be indefinitely delayed.

Some of the problems of implementing conservation policy in practice have been addressed in this paper. Any review of the working of the substantive law will have to consider several aspects of the operation of existing countryside legislation.

1 The effectiveness of the existing designation procedures would profit from re-examination, as would a review aimed at co-ordinating the operation and objectives of the different conservation schemes. There is a case, for instance, for the widening of the existing SSSI designation provisions to enable the NCC to enter into management agreements with persons having rights of management and use over both the designated site and adjacent land. Given the rapid expansion of conservation measures since the Wildlife and Countryside Act 1981, consideration now needs to be given to formulating a clear policy as to the sanctions to be used to enforce conservation law. If the pilot NSA scheme fails to achieve the required results, it may prove necessary to

introduce compulsory measures to improve water quality standards, as provided for in the Water Act 1989. Consideration may eventually need to be given to backing other voluntary schemes, such as the Environmentally Sensitive Areas designations, with residual compulsory powers.

2 A clear policy is required as to the basis on which payments under management agreements are to be made. At present two principles appear to be in use: one which treats payments as representative of lost income, and another (represented by the use of fixed rate payments per hectare) which seeks to reward farmers for adopting conservation obligations regardless of income. The problems this differential approach can generate, for instance when considering the legal position on rent review, have already been alluded to.[78] A wider policy issue is also at stake however, viz. the purpose and basis of farm support through conservation grant payments.

3 The practical problems of implementing the existing legislation where land is subject to tenancy, or other management arrangements of a contractual nature, have also been alluded to. The workability of the existing law would be improved, were it to be reviewed so as to cater expressly for the special legal problems arising from the landlord and tenant relationship, and for other common forms of agricultural land management, such as share farming or the exercise of rights of common.

This would necessarily involve a careful examination of the proper balance to be struck between the interests of the public in conservation, those of landowners, and those of farmers occupying and farming the land itself, under whatever tenurial arrangements. As the recent white paper, *This Common Inheritance* recognizes, countryside protection is a shared responsibility involving partnership between government, the owners and managers of land, the special countryside agencies, local authorities, and the general public who enjoy recreation in the countryside.[79] If this partnership is to work effectively it needs a more comprehensive and detailed legal framework of rights and duties than currently exists.

---

[78] Above pp.160–3. And for the implications of rent review for diversification of agricultural enterprises see Chapter 1 above at p.25–6.

[79] *This Common Inheritance*, Cm. 1200, 1990, para.7.81.

8

Common Land

JOHN AITCHISON AND GERRY GADSDEN

Introduction

The common lands of England and Wales, as they exist today, are mere fragments of a once much more extensive and widely distributed system of land tenure. However, whilst they may have declined significantly in area following inclosures and piecemeal encroachments, particularly during the first half of the nineteenth century, commons still figure prominently in contemporary debates relating to the current and future use of land in rural areas. This is because commons are highly coveted by a whole variety of land-using interests. In many upland regions commons continue to serve as grazing grounds for cattle, sheep and ponies, and as such are of vital economic importance to pastoral farming communities. The richness of wildlife on commons has long been recognized, as has their value as open spaces for recreational and sporting pursuits. In this latter context, the question of public access to common lands has been a *cause célèbre* in the long-running campaign to save commons from inclosure, and remains a particularly contentious issue. In debates relating to the use of commons, the complex and often equivocal nature of the law relating to these unique tracts of land has been of paramount importance, for it underpins and directs many of the arguments concerning alternative management opportunities.

The common lands, or commons, of England and Wales may be described generally as the last remnants of the obsolete manorial system of land tenure. The archetypal manor consisted of an area of the countryside, often coincidental with the modern parish, owned by a lord of the manor and farmed through the medium of strips of land in open fields held either on free or copyhold tenure by his tenants. In the summer tenants grazed their livestock in common on the unenclosed 'wastes of the manor'. Commons are those wastes together with the few remaining open arable fields and meadows which were also grazed in common after harvesting the crops or hay.

From the fifteenth century onwards the system broke down progressively and land became amalgamated into enclosed and separated farming units. Much of this process was undoubtedly piecemeal — the result of private enterprise — but from early in the eighteenth century was hastened by the passing of some 4,000 private inclosure Acts. In 1845 a general Inclosure Act was intended to complete the movement towards total enclosure but, in spite of the Act being responsible for the inclosure of a further 645,000 acres, by 1876 the initiative was overcome by the fear that continuation could result in the loss of all open land still available for public amenity purposes. The maintenance of open land as 'lungs' for an increasingly concentrated urban population was seen as a desirable objective. The Commons Act 1876 enacted that in future no inclosure of a common would be authorized unless it 'would be expedient, having regard as well to the health, comfort, and convenience of the inhabitants of any cities, towns, villages or populous places in or near any parish in which the land proposed to be inclosed . . . may be situate . . . as to the advantage of the persons interested in the common to which such application relates'.[1] Most inclosures are, of course, of exclusive benefit to private interests, and the Act of 1876 has effectively prevented any substantial private inclosure since the end of the nineteenth century.

The Birkenhead property legislation of 1925 effectively brought to an end the manorial system of land tenure with the abolition of copyhold. It was copyhold tenure which was the main *raison d'être* for the continued existence of manorial courts; and it was through these courts that at least some element of management of the common lands was accomplished. Unfortunately, for all practical purposes the legislation disregarded the effects the disappearance of manorial courts would have on the commons, and a period of desuetude in management and use ensued. After the Second World War, it gradually became appreciated that the common lands constituted a substantial reserve of uncommitted, and frequently underused, land where the boundaries of the land concerned and the nature of legal rights over it were becoming increasingly obscure. In 1955 a Royal Commission[2] was established to examine the position and make recommendations regarding the future use of land. After exhaustive inquiries the Commission recommended the establishment of a statutory register of the land, the rights exercisable over it and a record of persons claiming

[1] Commons Act 1876, preamble (now omitted under authority of Statute Law Revision Act 1894).

[2] *Royal Commission on Common Land 1955–8 Report*, Cmnd. 462, 1958.

ownership. So far as land use was concerned, the Commission recommended that the land be kept open, made available for use by the general public for 'air and exercise', and controlled through statutory management associations. The Commons Registration Act 1965 was passed to effect the registration proposals and it was expected, at that time, that the second-stage legislation for public access and statutory management would follow within four or five years. However, there were so many disputes involved in registration that the resolution procedures are still incomplete and are likely to continue at least until 1994.

It comes perhaps as no surprise to find that those interested in increased access to the countryside, and others eager to manage the common lands more effectively, became increasingly concerned at the lack of progress towards the second stage of legislation. In 1983 the Countryside Commission invited the major interested organizations to join a Forum to consider the extent of proposals for future legislation which would command the support of all the Forum members. The Forum reported in May 1986,[3] with most of the parties signifying assent to the proposals. The report was widely welcomed and at the 1987 general election the Conservative manifesto included an undertaking to enact legislation on the basis of its recommendations. However, it became apparent soon afterwards that support was not universal among all those to be affected. In particular, owners of moorlands used extensively for shooting were incensed at the possibility of a general right of access to the land, which they feared would interfere seriously with their established property rights. A compromise over the issue seemed impossible and a government statement in July 1990[4] made it clear that the concept of a universal right of public access to all common land had been abandoned. With new thinking and further consultation necessary, it was evident that all hopes of comprehensive legislation before the end of the 1987 Parliament had probably been abandoned. It can only be a matter of speculation as to the extent and timing of the implementation of the remaining recommendations of the Royal Commission Report, already over thirty years old.

Commons Registration

The first stage of the new deal for the common lands recommended by the Royal Commission was entry of all the land concerned, rights exercisable thereover and persons claiming to be owners, on statutory

[3] *The Report of the Common Land Forum*, Countryside Commission, CCP 215, 1986.
[4] Written Parliamentary answer to Nicholas Bennett MP by David Trippier, Minister for Environment and Countryside, 26 July 1990.

registers maintained mainly by the county councils. This was effected through the Commons Registration Act 1965, which also encompassed the registration of village greens.

Under the provisions of the Act any land and rights not registered after the end of the initial registration periods, now long since over,[5] are deemed not to be common land and not exercisable.[6] Disputes over registration of land, rights and ownership are referred to specially appointed Commons Commissioners for resolution, with a right of appeal to the High Court.[7] Where there was no objection to any entry or after a dispute has been resolved, the entries on the land and rights registers provide conclusive evidence of the matters registered.[8] The scale of disputes can be assessed from the fact that up to four Commissioners have been sitting full-time since 1972, and the work will continue for several years yet.

With the advantage of hindsight it is possible to detect many flaws in the drafting of the registration Act. This is perhaps not too surprising if it is appreciated that the main reason for requiring statutory registration was the obscurity of the nature of the land and rights concerned, that forty years had elapsed since the abolition of manorial control and, not least, that the subject had been neglected by legal academics — the most recent legal treatise was eighty-five years old.[9]

Common land

By popular assent common land is recognized as land subject to rights of common, which in turn may be defined as the rights persons may have to take some part of the produce of, or property in, the soil owned by another. The most usual right of common is that of pasturage, that is to say the right to graze animals, but others, such as the right to take turf for fuel, stone for building and even wild animals for domestic consumption are not unknown. The first category of land registrable under the Act of 1965 is land subject to rights of common. But the Act included as a second class 'waste land of a manor not subject to rights of common' thus extending the meaning of common land beyond anything previously understood by the expression.[10] As will be seen later the meaning of rights of common was also subject to some extension, which had the result of bringing in even more land which previously would not have been considered strictly as common land.

[5] The final date for any registration was 31 July 1970.
[6] Commons Registration Act 1965, s.1(2).
[7] Ibid. ss.6, 18.
[8] Ibid. s.10.
[9] J. Williams, *Rights of Common and Other Prescriptive Rights*, 1880.
[10] Commons Registration Act 1965, s.22(1).

Ignoring for the moment the various classes of land which could be registered, it might be thought a fairly simple matter to achieve registration of the correct land. But the Act contained some rather odd features. First, it was possible for 'any person' to register land.[11] Some, with a vested interest in achieving as large an area as possible for public access, responded with alacrity. At least some land was registered on the basis of appearance alone without any regard to its true legal status. No provision was made for the owners of such land to be notified, and there are many examples of registered land where the owners became aware of the registration after finality which, it will be recalled, attracts conclusive evidence of status. Secondly, there was no requirement for inspection of the land before registration, and many applications were made on the basis of Ordnance Survey maps dating from the early part of the century or even tithe maps from around 1840. It is hardly surprising that there are many registered parcels containing land enclosed and developed long ago. So difficult a problem has this proved to be that a private member's bill sought to remedy the most pernicious results. The Commons Registration (Rectification of Registers) Act 1989 now allows for the removal from the registers of domestic dwellings and/or ancillary land which has been occupied as such since 1945. Dwellings occupied only after 1945 and all other classes of misregistered land must await further legislation.

Another area of difficulty was that of interpretation of the terms used in the Act. The most striking of these has been in connection with the second head of registrable land, which is 'waste land of a manor not subject to rights of common'. In the 1925 property legislation the equivalent term used was 'manorial waste',[12] which tends towards an interpretation that the specified land is first waste and secondly of manorial origin. 'Waste land of a manor', on the other hand, had been subject to judicial interpretation in the nineteenth century when it was decided that the land must be held 'of a manor', that is to say, owned by the lord of a manor.[13] In early dispute hearings the Commissioners held that only waste land still owned by a lord of a manor was registrable. Considerable areas of waste land had, of course, come into the ownership of other persons by the second half of the twentieth century. Differences of opinion as to the correct interpretation arose among the Commissioners, and in the High Court on appeal, with the (temporary) resolution of doubts by the Court of Appeal in *Re Box Hill Common* (1978).[14] The Court held that Parliament could not have intended that land formerly part of a manor should be registered, and only land still owned by a lord of a manor was registrable. Henceforth,

[11] Ibid. s.4(2).
[12] Law of Property Act 1925, s.193.
[13] *Attorney-General* v. *Hanmer* (1858) LJ27 Ch.837 at 840 and 842.
[14] *Re Box Hill Common, Box Parish Council* v. *Lacey* [1980] Ch.109.

the Commissioners were bound to refuse registration to land which had been alienated from the manor to which it had formerly belonged. Ultimately, an appeal to the House of Lords was to reverse this decision in *Hampshire County Council* v. *Milburn* (1990).[15] By this time probably over 95 per cent of the Commissioners' decisions had been handed down on the basis of *Re Box Hill*. The result is that numerous parcels of 'manorial waste' have been refused registration, and there is now no procedure for them to become registered.

A second interpretative difficulty has arisen in connection with the lands now usually known as regulated pastures. These are not remnants of the manorial system but are a special class of land allotted (usually) by an enclosure award. Where allotments were too small to justify individual inclosure it was not unusual for them to be thrown together so that a number of persons were awarded land in undivided shares, with each share attracting the right to graze a specified number of livestock. Land held in this way on a tenancy in common is not an unusual legal phenomenon, but the combined land ownership/grazing right is found only in connection with inclosure awards. There is a common law right for regulated pastures to be partitioned, but probably only under court supervision.[16] The arrangements inherent on such land can easily be distinguished from other common land as there is no grazing by one person over the land of another, except to the extent that in grazing undivided shares it is impossible for the owner of a share to graze only his parcel of land. It is clear that Parliament intended originally that such land should be registered, but upon it being pointed out at the Committee stage of the Bill that making undivided shares in land registrable would have the effect of bringing into registration such areas as common parts of buildings the section was withdrawn and not replaced with any other wording. Registrants and Commissioners disagreed as to whether the regulated pastures were registrable, with the result that some are and some are not registered. The Common Land Forum recommended that all such land should be removed from the registers.

In conclusion it can be stated that not all land which was intended for registration has achieved that status; conversely there is a substantial number of parcels of incorrectly registered land; and there is some land of uncertain status.

An analysis of the common land registers of England and Wales, undertaken by the Rural Surveys Research Unit (RSRU) at the University College of Wales, Aberystwyth during the 1980s on behalf of the Countryside Commission, indicates that there are some 8,675 areas of registered commons and wastes. While this figure is of interest,

[15] [1990] 2 All ER 257.
[16] Cf. Law of Property Act 1925, Sch.1, Part V, paras 2, 3.

Table 8.1 *Common lands*

| | Numbers of commons | | Area of commons* | |
	with rights	without rights	with rights	without rights
England	2,478	4,572	850,386	59,300
Wales	995	630	445,356	12,241
Total	3,473	5,202	1,295,742	71,541

*Excluding village greens and exempted commons, 66,370 acres.

it needs to be emphasized that not all of these tracts of land constitute discrete, functional commons. Because of the uncontrolled manner in which land could be registered, numerous separately registered commons are simply small additions to larger blocks of common land. Conversely, many extensive areas of common have been arbitrarily subdivided into separate common land units, even though they are managed as single units. Accordingly, statistics relating to the number of registered numbers of commons have to be treated circumspectly.[17]

Table 8.1 shows that of the registered units 3,473 (40 per cent) are subject to rights of common, whilst the remainder (5,202) must be assumed to be wastes of manors not subject to rights of common. Counties with particularly large numbers of commons are Cumbria (633), North Yorkshire (552), Dyfed (552), Surrey (415), Norfolk (345), Clwyd (323) and Hereford and Worcester (310). In terms of area, commons and wastes cover approximately 1,367,250 acres, some 4 per cent of the total land area of England and Wales. These data, it should be emphasized, relate to those tracts of land currently included in the registers. If comparisons are to be made with the area estimates compiled by the Royal Commission on Common Land, then reference must also be made to the areas of village greens and the twenty-one commons exempted from the registration process.[18] These include the New Forest, Epping Forest and the Forest of Dean. Figure 8.1 shows the distribution of common land in 1989 for the pre-1974 counties of England and Wales. In broad terms it highlights the heavy concentration of commons in the upland regions of the north and west, the limited acreages occurring in the lowlands of central England, and the higher than average returns recorded for such counties as Hampshire/Isle of Wight, Sussex and Surrey in the south. Over most of the country commons claim under 5 per cent of the land area, but figures in excess

[17] J. W. Aitchison, 'Counting our Commons', *Open Space*, 22, 10, 2–4.
[18] J. W. Aitchison, 'The Commons and Wastes of England and Wales 1959–1989', *Area*, 22, 3 (1990), 272–7.

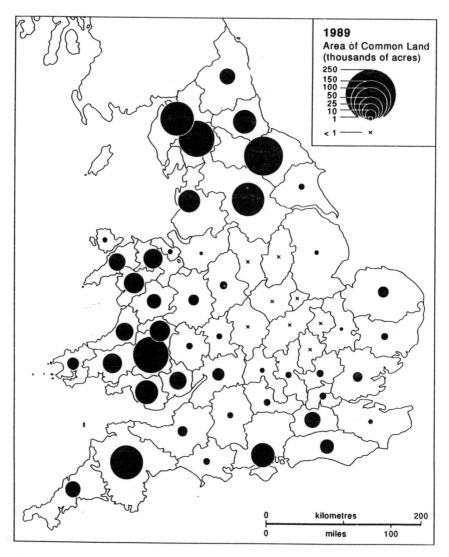

Figure 8.1.

of 10 per cent are recorded by the former counties of Breconshire (26.7 per cent), Westmorland (25.5 per cent), Radnorshire (13.7 per cent), Cumberland (11.4 per cent) and North Riding (11.2 per cent).

Rights of common

The types of land which were registrable were increased by giving an extended meaning to the term 'rights of common'. Thus, the term 'includes cattlegates or beastgates (by whatever name known) and rights of sole or several vesture of herbage or of sole or several pasture, but does not include rights held for a term of years or from year to year'.[19] The extension has created a number of uncertainties and anomalies in registration and, as with the land sections of the registers, the entries of rights on the registers are less than definitive.

A right of common is usually a right attached to land and in the case of a grazing right is *levant and couchant*, that is to say it is not quantified (except by registration under the Act)[20] but is for so many animals as can be wintered on the dominant land. It may exist as appendant, appurtenant, in gross or as a right *pur cause de vicinage*. Since registration the differences between appendant and appurtenant rights are probably no more than academic, and appurtenant, or attached, to land is now sufficient to describe such rights. Rights of common in gross are very unusual but are normal in connection with sole rights of vesture, herbage and pasture (for which see below). A right of common *pur cause de vicinage* is not a substantive right of common and is dealt with separately later. Rights of common appurtenant form by far the largest number of registered rights.

Of much less significance, but nevertheless the second major class of registrable right, is the sole or several right of pasture. In legal analysis this type of right can be distinguished from a true right of common as, unlike the situation with a true right, the owner of the soil has retained no right to graze. In other words, the owner has granted away all the rights to graze and retained none for himself. Sole rights are almost invariably quantified so that the grazing has been divided into 'stints' consisting of so many animals; for example, one stint might be the right to graze one cow or five sheep. They are almost universally held in gross, that is to say are not attached to any land. The stints frequently have local names of which the cattlegates and beastgates mentioned in the definition are common examples.

Sole vesture is a right to take all of the products of the land and sole herbage is the right to take grass by cutting as well as grazing. Neither is more than unusually encountered.

[19] Commons Registration Act 1965, s.22(1).
[20] Ibid. s.15.

Rights in gross.   Rights in gross ought to be readily identifiable from the rights sections of the registers because regulations required that rights entries should declare the land to which they were attached, if any.[21] However, it is certain that many rights in gross, particularly sole rights of pasture, have been registered as 'attached' to land. The Commons Commissioners have decided that such an entry has no more effect than a declaration that the right was used with certain land at the time of registration and does not have the effect of permanently annexing the right to the land. This, it is suggested, is a correct view as the Act did not require the registration of dominant land,[22] so that the conclusive evidence provisions in the Act do not apply to this part of the registers. The matter is of some importance as rights in gross are freely alienable without reference to land, whereas appurtenant rights are not and may not be severed from the land to which they are annexed.

Rights of vicinage.   A right of common *pur cause de vicinage* has no independent existence but is a right which a commoner on one common may have to graze over another contiguous unenclosed common. The right is inherently determinable for it may be extinguished at any time by enclosure of either of the contiguous commons. The Act provided no guidance as to whether this class of right was registrable. Many were registered and became final without objection. The Commissioners, on the other hand, have usually held them to be unregistrable. It is now impossible from the registers, and without further inquiry, to be certain whether many rights are substantive or determinable in nature.

The rights of tenants.   The definition of rights of common excludes from registration rights held for a term of years or from year to year. Thus a right of common held for a legal estate equivalent to a fee simple was registrable, whereas a right held for the legal estate of a term of years absolute was not. Both are equally exercisable rights. Some owners of commons were not unaware of the implications, obtained a surrender of the fee simple rights and regranted leasehold rights for 999 years. The result was that, as the land was not subject to registrable rights, it was not registrable as common land.

The definition did not mean that tenants could not register rights if their landlord held fee simple rights, but only that tenants of the owner of the soil of a common could not register their leasehold or tenanted rights. The reason for this is that, in strict legal theory, the owner of the soil cannot have a right of common over his own land but merely exercises a right of land ownership. This, however, is to ignore two points: first, owners (lords of the manor or their successors in title)

---

[21] Commons Registration (General) Regulations 1966, SI 1966 No.1471, reg.4(7).
[22] Commons Registration Act 1965, s.1.

exercised rights of grazing in respect of their tenanted or in hand lands *pari passu* with other tenants of the manor and are entitled to identical compensation for them in the event of inclosure or compulsory purchase; and secondly, owners' tenants or lessees with grazing rights are, and have been at least since the 1925 property legislation, just as much in possession of a legal interest over the land as a person with a freehold right.

The main purpose of the rights sections of the registers was to create a record of all rights over common land which are currently exercisable, thus providing a permanent record available to management bodies interested in the control of grazing. In cases where the owners' tenants have rights the Act has demonstrably failed in this aim, and those seeking to discover all 'commoners' should be aware that there may be unregistrable rights exercisable over the land.

It should not be thought, however, that owners of the soil of the commons, or their tenants, felt unduly inhibited by the exact wording in the Act. Tenants (and indeed many owners) ignored it and registered their 'rights'. Where such registrations came to the notice of a Commissioner he usually felt bound to refuse such an entry, but many had become final without objection. The result is that many unregistrable tenants' rights are registered while some are not.

Regulated pastures

Attention has been drawn above to lack of uniformity in registration of the land of the regulated pastures. There is also lack of accuracy in the 'rights' registered over the land. The rights, of course, are the rights of owners in undivided shares in land and not strictly rights of common. There is almost universally a correct record of these rights by reference to the ownership of the land based, usually, on an inclosure award. Examination of a sample of the registers has shown that the correct rights do not necessarily coincide with the registered rights. However, unlike the position of unregistered rights of common under the Act which cease to be exercisable upon non-registration, rights over regulated pastures can hardly be affected by the Act as they are rights of ownership and not rights of common. Thus, in the case of registered regulated pastures it is unwise to rely upon the rights registers as a true record of exercisable rights.

With these many caveats duly recognized, it is of interest to consider the information contained in the rights section of the common land registers. At the time they were last consulted (1980–3), the registers contained over 42,747 final and provisional rights entries (28,594 in England, and 14,153 in Wales). As has been noted, 60 per cent of commons were without rightholders. Of those with rights, approximately 60 per cent (2,087) had less than five rights entries; just 23 per cent (805 commons) had more than ten. These figures again need to be treated with considerable circumspection, since in addition to the inconsistencies highlighted above, there are known to be numerous instances of cross-referencing (i.e. where a right is related to more than one unit of common land) and multiple registrations of rights (i.e. where the same right is separately, but incorrectly, recorded for more than one common). The situation varies from region to region, but in general the majority of rights relate to common of pasture for sheep, and to a lesser extent cattle. Grazing for ponies also figures prominently in certain areas (e.g. Powys). Whilst some of these rights are solely for specific types of stock, in many registers they appear as convertible entries (i.e. an optional right to graze specified numbers of either sheep, cattle or ponies), or mixed (i.e. the right specifies particular combinations of sheep, cattle and ponies).[23] The fact that rights exist does not of course mean that they are exercised, either wholly or in part. It is not possible from the registers alone, therefore, to determine grazing densities on commons. However, it is evident that if all rights were exercised many commons would be grossly overstocked. Information on grazing regimes is currently being gathered by the RSRU as part of a biological inventory of common lands for English Nature and the Countryside Council for Wales.[24] This information shows that whilst the conservation value of many commons is being detrimentally affected as a result of overgrazing, many more are being degraded through understocking. As to other types of rights, it is sufficient here to note that a considerable number of entries identify the traditional rights of estovers, turbary, piscary and common in the soil.

Ownership

The Act invited registration of claims to ownership of common land. In the event of no claim being made, and following an inquiry by a Commissioner, the land is left to be vested as Parliament may determine later. Many commons have no registered owner and will no doubt eventually be vested in a local authority.[25] Currently, over 2,600 commons fall into this category. Unlike land and rights, an entry of ownership on a register does not provide conclusive evidence of the matters registered.[26]

[23] J. W. Aitchison and E. J. Hughes, 'The Common Lands of Wales', *Transactions of the Institute of British Geographers*, 13, 96–108.

[24] Thus far, fifteen regional reports have been published; these detail the biological attributes of commons over 1 ha in size.

[25] Commons Registration Act 1965, s.9; prior to any future vesting, local authorities have extensive powers to act to protect the land on behalf of the unknown owner.

[26] Ibid. s.10.

A rather odd feature for a register of public record is that when the ownership of common land becomes registered under the Land Registration Acts the entry on the commons register is removed, taking the title owner's name behind the registration curtain.[27] This is inconvenient but is of less importance than it was initially, as a search may now be made of the Land Registry title to discover the owner. The RSRU survey of the common land registers revealed that over 1,500 commons were owned (wholly or in part) by local authorities, and that a further 251 were held by the National Trust.

Amendments to the registers

Various but circumscribed amendments to the registers are possible. Most of the provisions have unfortunate peculiarities.

Rights registrations. The Act allows an amendment to the rights section of the registers when a right has been apportioned, extinguished or released.[28] It will be seen that no provision was made in the Act, or subsequent regulations,[29] for the name of the owner of a right to be amended if the whole of a right is transferred to another person. Thus the sale of a farm with rights appurtenant is not grounds for amendment and the right remains registered in the name of the original applicant. It follows that as a public record of those persons currently entitled to exercise rights the registers are now hopelessly out of date and are thoroughly misleading.

Nor was there any requirement for amendment, even where amendment is allowed. The obsolete nature of the rights registers is thereby further compounded with many farms having been sold in divided parcels with no amendment of the register. It can be almost impossible to discover all the persons with rights over an individual common without exhaustive enquiries.

A further peculiarity relates to the rights attached to dominant land owned by the owner of the soil of a common. As has been shown, these rights, and the rights of tenants of such land, are unregistrable — although legally exercisable and for other purposes ranking *pari passu* with strict rights of common. An absurd situation arises if some of this land is sold. A tenant purchaser of the freehold estate would, by operation of common law and statute, expect to continue to exercise the rights he had previously enjoyed as a tenant. The Act, however, does not allow the registration of such rights, and upon his purchase the tenant loses all rights to graze. Needless to say, the legal niceties have escaped the notice of many, who have continued to exercise the rights in exactly the way they would have done before the passing of the

[27] Ibid. s.12.
[28] Ibid. s.13(c)
[29] Common Registration (General) Regulations 1966, SI 1966 No. 1471, reg. 29(1).

Act and usually without any objection. This represents a triumph for common sense over legal confusion.

Land ceasing to be common land. The Act contains provisions which allow land to be removed from the registers if it ceases to be common land.[30] For many years the Act actually assisted the removal of common land and its conversion into ordinary freehold land. This was, of course, the complete antithesis of the Act's intention.

Before the registration Act an owner was usually in some difficulty in attempting to convert the land to his own individual use because he could not be certain that all the rights exercisable over it had ceased or been released to him. Once the Act provided that unregistered rights were unexercisable the registers provided him with a statutory list of the persons with whom he had to deal. A number of owners obtained the release of rights, if necessary severed the land from the manor, and obtained the removal of the land from the registers.

To a very marked extent this loophole in the legislation was removed as a result of the decision in *Hampshire County Council* v. *Milburn* (1990)[31] when the House of Lords decided that severance of land from a manor did not take the land outside the definition of waste land in the Act. Thus, where surrender of all rights has been obtained the land remains registrable as 'waste land of a manor not subject to rights' and cannot be removed from registration. Land may be removed now only if it can be established either that the land was not waste land of a manor at the time of registration or a registration authority can be convinced that it has ceased to be waste land by some other activity such as enclosure, occupation or cultivation.

Ownership. The regulations made under the Act make no provision for amendment to ownership registrations unless the land is sold, in which case, as we have seen, the ownership entry is removed.[32] It is not safe, therefore, to assume that ownership entries are correct, because the land may have been alienated by inheritance or otherwise than by sale, upon which events no amendment of the registers is allowed.

New land. A provision in the Act allows the registration of land which becomes common land.[33] The occasions when this will occur are likely to be few. The most likely instance is where at the time of the initial registration process the land concerned was subject only to the rights of the owner of the soil or his tenants, neither of which were registrable. If, say, one of the rented farms is sold to the sitting tenant, the purchaser is entitled to continue to exercise the grazing rights he had formerly exercised in common with other tenants. But his right is now a right of common which, under the provisions of the Act, is

[30] Commons Registration Act 1965, s.13(a).
[31] [1990] 2 All ER 257.
[32] Cf. note 27 above.
[33] Commons Registration Act 1965, s.13(b).

exercisable only if registered.[34] The right must be registered, and the land over which it is exercised becomes common land. Any other rights of common created upon subsequent sales of farms are also registrable. This, as has been shown, is in marked contrast to the position of land registered under the initial process where such further rights are unregistrable and, therefore, unexercisable.

Management

The management of common land usually requires the co-operation of all the commoners. The Act has facilitated this by providing a record of those persons with exercisable rights, subject, of course, to the limitations on accuracy already described. In addition, as has been shown, the record is not necessarily complete: for example, some leasehold and tenanted rights are not registrable, where the original rights have been divided it may not be apparent from the registers, and in some cases the rights may not be substantive but merely the lesser determinable right of common *pur cause de vicinage*. As a public record of rights exercisable over common land the registers are clearly less complete than might be desired.

A problem facing any person or body wishing to improve the management of commons is that some interference with, or restriction upon, the rights of common is usually required. If there is a substantial number of commoners then almost certainly some of the number will be unwilling to co-operate. Frequently, the commoners will be represented by an association which can take the initiative in management or negotiate with others having the same intention. The difficulty is that an association cannot bind its members unless expressly authorized by each and every one so to do. On the other hand, when owner and all commoners are in agreement there are no difficulties.

There are four enabling statutes which may be used to manage commons. The earliest is the Metropolitan Commons Act 1866, and as its name implies it is of application only in the London metropolitan area. It has not been used for a new scheme of management this century. The next is the Commons Act 1876, which allows for the establishment of a Board of Conservators with statutory powers of management. The establishment of a scheme under this Act requires a procedure akin to a private Act. It has been out of use for most of this century.

The Commons Act 1899 on the other hand is still widely used. Some 227 schemes were established in the thirty years ending in 1985. A scheme for any common may be effected by a district council adopting a model scheme prescribed in Regulations.[35] It may, however, be

[34] Ibid. s.1(2)(b).
[35] The Commons (Schemes) Regulations 1982, SI 1982 No.209.

vetoed by the owner of the soil or one third of the commoners, so that it is more usually applied where rights of common have ceased to be used or are underused. A scheme is made with a view to the expenditure of money on the drainage, levelling and improvement of the common and the making of by-laws and regulations for the prevention of nuisances and the preservation of order on the common. All schemes must allow for a right of public access and a privilege of playing games and enjoying other kinds of recreation. This type of management scheme is clearly of value on what may best be described as amenity commons.

In contradistinction, the fourth statute to be noted, the Commons Act 1908, is of value only on commons where agricultural use is still of substantial importance. The purpose of a scheme under this Act is only to effect control of entire, that is to say male and uncastrated, animals, although powers are included to appoint persons to supervise the grazing of such animals and also to raise levies on commoners to pay for the scheme.

There are, also, a number of local Acts under which specified commons or groups of commons may be managed. The latest example is the Dartmoor Commons Act 1985.

Control of Works

The Commons Acts of 1866, 1876 and 1899 bring works on commons regulated thereunder under direct control by means of regulations and supervision by Boards of Conservators or district councils. There is little likelihood of undesirable development on such commons. Some commons are similarly regulated through local Acts as, for example, are Epping Forest, the New Forest, the Malvern Hills and Wimbledon and Putney Commons. Similarly, control of works has been updated on Dartmoor through the provisions of the Dartmoor Commons Act 1985.

Most other commons rely for their protection on provisions contained in section 194 of the Law of Property Act 1925. The section is by no means of universal application. The principle of the section is that 'the erection of any building or fence, or the construction of any other work, whereby access to land to which this section applies, is prevented or impeded, shall not be lawful unless the consent of the Minister thereto is obtained'. Unfortunately, the section also defines the land to which it applies as land which at the commencement of the Act (1 January 1926) is subject to rights of common. It will be immediately apparent that not all registered common land is covered by the section. Land which is registered as waste land of a manor not subject to rights, if it was of the same status in 1926, is not covered. It also seems probable that stinted pastures subject to sole rights and not rights of common, regulated pastures subject only to the rights of owners, and common fields subject only to the rights of the owners of the strips, are not within the purview of the section.

It should also be noted that the section has application only if 'access' is prevented or impeded. The access mentioned was probably intended to mean the public right of access granted over certain 'urban' commons by section 193 of the Law of Property Act 1925. If this is so, then section 194 applies only to about one fifth of all common land. However, it is probable that a court would extend the meaning of access to cover that to which commoners are entitled. But, suppose that all the commoners agree that their access to the common is unaffected, is it possible that no consent is required? It is difficult to see, for example, how any boundary fences to a 'rural' (that is a non-urban common) are affected by the section if no commoner's access is affected.

The section is surrounded by uncertainty, and enforcement is difficult. It may be enforced only by the owner, the commoners or the county and district councils. Upon a successful application to a court there is a power, but no requirement, to make an order for removal and restoration. Courts have shown marked reluctance to order restoration when there has been any delay in taking enforcement action, presumably under the doctrine of laches. For example, where commoners had stood by without objecting and allowed a caravan club to spend £17,000 on preparatory site work, they could not afterwards claim to have the site reinstated.[36]

There can be little doubt that the section requires updating. A first step towards this was taken in the Dartmoor Commons Act 1985 when it was provided that the Commoners' Council, established under the Act, must seek consent from the Secretary of State in respect of any proposed buildings, fencing or other constructions on all finally registered commons in the Dartmoor area, whether or not access is prevented or impeded.[37]

Future Legislation

It will be recalled that the Royal Commission on Common Land, reporting in 1958,[38] recommended the establishment of registers of common land and rights, statutory management schemes and a right of public access to all common land. It was further recommended that public access and management schemes should be provided from the outset and that registration should proceed simultaneously with eight-year registration, followed by four-year objection, periods.[39] In the event it was decided to carry out the registration first and follow it with

---

[36] *Symonds* v. *Malvern Hills DC* [1978] 248 EG 238.
[37] Dartmoor Commons Act 1985, s.4(4).
[38] See note 2 above.
[39] Ibid. para.406, Timetable of Recommendations.

access and management provisions later. No doubt there were few who would have guessed that registration alone would consume the succeeding twenty-five years.

In 1977 the Department of the Environment convened an inter-departmental committee to consider future legislation.[40] The report had little noticeable effect. In 1983, following a conference sponsored by the Open Spaces Society which indicated a marked level of unanimity amongst the interested parties, the Countryside Commission sponsored the establishment of a Forum of those parties to see whether it was possible to reach a consensus over the content of further legislation. The Forum reported in 1986[41] producing a report which most of the organizations represented felt able to support. With the advantage of hindsight it is possible to say that insufficient time was taken to work out fully all the implications of the recommendations and that the Forum suffered from lack of direct representation of interested parties. There was no direct representation of practising landowning, rural sporting or commoners' interest. The report has to some extent foundered on this lack of full representation. Nevertheless the report was widely welcomed and the Conservative manifesto for the 1987 general election contained an indication that legislation would follow in the succeeding Parliament.

The main recommendations of the Forum were that the original proposals of the Royal Commission for management and a right of public access to common land should be followed. There was also a recognition that some at least of the defects in the Commons Registration Act should be rectified and the anomalies removed. The Forum was also anxious to achieve what it called 'living' registers, by which it seems to have meant registers on which all the matters noted are up to date. On the other hand, there was a determination that the registers should not be reopened to allow new registrations of land or rights and, conversely, the removal of land wrongly registered, except in the very obvious cases of land which could never be used or considered as common land.

An enhanced role was envisaged for the registration authorities, with a duty laid on them to establish a 'living record' of registers based on those which already exist.[42] Their task was to include such matters as ensuring that all dominant tenements to which rights are attached are properly identified.[43] This was backed up by the recommendation that such matters as apportionment of rights should be referred to, and approved by, an Agricultural Land Tribunal before the rights became

[40] *Common Land, Preparations for Comprehensive Legislation, Report of an Inter-Departmental Working Party 1975–1977*, Department of the Environment, 1978.
[41] See note 3 above.
[42] Ibid. App. C, para.095.
[43] Ibid. App. C, para.059.

exercisable.[44] A review of rights was recommended with the intention that the total rights registered over every common should more nearly reflect the true stock-carrying capacity of the land.[45] It is clear that a considerable amount of amendment, with consequent administrative work, was envisaged. What is not clear is whether the registration authorities would have the resources or, under the circumstances of financing through a community charge, the inclination for an enhanced role.

A comparatively short time after the report was issued, and following wide consultation with individuals and organizations, it became apparent that there was substantial opposition to an unrestricted public right of access to all common land. It came from owners of moorland used for commercial sporting purposes who feared that public access at crucial times of the year would seriously interfere with shooting interests. Observers formed the view that sustained opposition might occasion serious disruption to the legislative process — particularly in the House of Lords. The Department of the Environment must have reached a similar view, and in July 1990 the Environment Minister announced that future legislation would not provide a right of access automatically to all common land.[46] Instead management committees established under the new Act would be required to recommend to a Minister only enhanced rights of access. Thus, at a stroke, the main aim of many amenity bodies, to achieve a full right of public access to all registered common land, was defeated. It was also announced that a fresh round of consultation would take place, and this started during the last months of 1990.

At the time of writing it is possible to do no more than speculate as to the content and timing of new legislation. It does, however, seem unlikely that a comprehensive bill will come forward before a general election. It may be that there will be a short bill designed as a holding operation, merely to prevent any further removal of common land from the registers.[47]

If, as seems to have happened, the political will to enact the entirety of the Forum's recommendations has dissolved, it is possible to reconsider many of them in an entirely new light. Perhaps the most striking feature of the Forum's detailed recommendations was the emphasis laid on making the registers as accurate and current as possible. Of concern to those interested in limiting the amount of work required of registration authorities are the matters already mentioned

[44] Ibid. App. C, paras 064, 067, 068, 069, 070, 082.
[45] Ibid. App. C, para.031.
[46] See note 4 above.
[47] An amendment was introduced, and defeated, at the Committee stage of the Planning and Compensation Bill (1991) in the House of Lords to provide access to, and management of, common lands: see HL Debates, pp.618–30, 29 January 1991.

— a review of the accuracy of all dominant land associated with appurtenant rights, the recasting of the rights sections of the registers, and the requirement for a tribunal's approval of apportionment of rights. In addition, there were recommendations for the removal from registration of all rights of the tenants of the owner of the soil and the complete removal of all the regulated pastures.[48] At the same time registration authorities were expected to provide representation on the new management associations. Unfortunately, even if amended and updated in the ways required, the registers would still be of limited use because management associations would be primarily interested in persons exercising rights, and not necessarily those with a legal right to graze who never intended to do so. Thus, entirely new graziers' registers would be required, and the proposed management associations are clearly the appropriate persons to control them.

The possibility arises, therefore, of authorizing the new management associations to maintain a 'living' rights register and treat the existing registers only as a definitive land record. The existing rights registers (the current detailed accuracy of which is in many cases deplorable) could then be left just as a historical record providing no more than a root of title to rights. At a stroke such provision would reduce the registration authority's role to one of merely dealing with land changes and allowing the 'rights' matters to be controlled, perhaps as they should be, by the owners and commoners themselves. Stocking levels on individual commons could be adjusted by grazing regulation while apportionment could be left to the existing common law rules. Management associations would have every incentive to keep the graziers' registers up to date, as it is upon them that any levies will be based. The associations would, of course, have to satisfy a requirement for enhanced public access as part of any proposed management scheme.

If such an approach were to be adopted there would seem to be little point in proceeding to remove the rights of tenants of owners of the soil from the existing registers, and it might be acceptable to leave undisturbed those regulated pastures now on the registers without attempting to bring on those unregistered. It seems unlikely, anyway, that the Forum recommendation for the removal of regulated pastures would be adopted when it is realized that perhaps some 50,000–60,000 acres[49] would thereby be lost to registration. Such a scenario is a long way from the comprehensive legislation, coupled with consolidation of all the older statutes, sought by the Forum,[50] nor would it resolve

[48] See note 3 above App. C, paras 029, 032, 113; note that in the report land now referred to as regulated pastures is there called stinted pastures.

[49] The writer's estimate based on a study of the Commons Commissioners' decisions and the surveys of Rural Surveys Research Unit, Aberystwyth.

[50] See note 3 above paras 4.42–4.

many of the problems associated with the defects in the 1965 Act. But it must be doubted whether there is the political will available to provide comprehensive legislation for what is, after all, only a peripheral agricultural activity when there are so many other problems facing the industry at the present time. Perhaps, also, it is an inappropriate time to consider even greater burdens for local authorities. But limited legislation, as described, would provide increased access for the general public and allow the legally interested parties to control that access by regulations and achieve improved agricultural management.

9

Less Favoured and Environmentally Sensitive Areas: a European dimension to the rural environment

PETER WATHERN

Introduction

Membership of the European Economic Community (EC) has had a far-reaching impact upon environmental regulation in the UK. It has affected not only the way in which the UK regulates individual components of the environment, but perhaps more fundamentally, the overall policy style that the UK adopts towards the environment. With respect to the EC, the UK is often portrayed as recidivist or, at best, a reluctant European intent on resisting like some latterday Canute the waves of environmental law emanating from Brussels. 'Brugge man', however, has always been a political posture struck largely for home consumption, rather than an expression of the ideology shaping negotiations with other member states. The history of UK membership of the EC, in practice, has been little different from that of any other member state. The UK negotiation position has variously ranged from capitulation in the face of opposition, through compromise and the formation of alliances, to that of vigorous proponent and imaginative innovator.

In the field of environmental pollution, for example, the UK adopted rigid air quality standards in order to comply with the EC directive on particulates and sulphur dioxide, a quiet acquiescence that broke with a long tradition involving a 'flexible' approach to pollution regulation.[1] The UK Pesticides Safety Precaution Scheme governing the licensing and use of pesticides had to be put on mandatory basis because the existing informal procedures were in breach of the free

[1] N. Haigh, *EEC Policy and Britain*, 2nd edition, Longman, 1987.

trade provisions of the Treaty of Rome.[2] Similarly, the UK was forced to outlaw the use of hormone growth regulators in livestock farming rather than accept the political embarrassment of dual standards for food quality involving food for export having to meet higher standards than that for home consumption.[3] In the case of shellfisheries, the UK chose simply to absorb EC provisions into current UK practice.[4] With respect to the contamination of bathing beaches by faecal bacteria the UK was obliged to adopt more stringent provisions by the threat of legal action by the Commission.

The UK's seemingly comprehensive conservation legislation has had to be extended in order to give legislative compliance with the provisions of the birds directive.[5] Further, it took an EC directive on environmental assessment to force consideration of the environmental impacts of certain categories of agricultural projects and of afforestation, something that the environmental lobby failed to achieve in nearly forty years of campaigning.[6] This directive also provided a mechanism to assess the environmental impacts of salmon farms for the first time.[7] In contrast, UK waste regulation, as embodied in the Control of Pollution Act 1974 Part I, became the model for a whole series of EC directives on waste disposal.

Thus, it can be seen that environmental regulation and policy style in the UK are influenced significantly by EC membership. However, this is also a forum in which the UK is able to exert an influence. This interplay is equally evident in relation to the rural environment, especially in sparsely populated areas. By far the greatest influence of the EC upon the rural environment is through the Common Agricultural Policy (CAP). Most of the massive CAP budget goes into support for large intensive farms (the guarantee section), with relatively little to aid the small farmer.

In 1989 a mere 4.9 per cent was allotted to the guidance section which mainly benefits small farmers, even though they comprised

[2] P. Wathern and D. Baldock *Regulating the Interface between Agriculture and the Environment*, IIUG (Berlin), 1987.

[3] Ibid.

[4] P. Wathern, S. N. Young, I. W. Brown and D. A. Roberts, 'UK Interpretation and Implementation of the EEC Shellfish Directive', *Environmental Management*, 11 (1987), 7–12.

[5] Nature Conservancy Council, 'The Wildlife and Countryside Act 1981', *Nature in Wales*, 1 (1982), 24–9.

[6] P. Wathern, 'Implementing Supranational Policy: Environmental Impact Assessment in the United Kingdom', in R. V. Bartlett (ed.), *Policy Through Impact Assessment*, Greenwood Press (Westport, Connecticut), 1989, pp. 27–36.

[7] P. Wathern, 'The EIA Directive of the European Community', in P. Wathern (ed.), *Environmental Impact Assessment: Theory and Practice*. Unwin Hyman, 1988, pp. 192–209.

about 30 per cent of the total within the EC.[8] In part this maldistribution can be explained in terms of the emphasis on price support in the CAP which constitutes, in effect, a subsidy on production. It is also a reflection of the free-trade provisions of the Treaty of Rome which, in essence, demand that all producers must be treated alike with none given favoured treatment over other comparable producers. Special support can only be channelled to particular groups of farmers if they are rendered in some way 'not comparable' with the remainder. Two designations have been adopted at an EC level in order to achieve this objective with respect to special groups of farmers. These are provided for in the Less Favoured Areas (LFA) and Environmentally Sensitive Areas (ESA) programmes, which currently constitute about 1 per cent of the total agricultural budget in the UK.[9]

These programmes can be regarded, in part, as an acknowledgement of the need to balance the various demands currently placed upon the rural environment in the UK. No longer simply used for producing agricultural commodities, rural areas are also needed to provide land for growing timber, for water supply and as recreational space for an increasingly urban population. In addition, rural areas, especially the wild uplands, provide an increasingly valuable resource for wildlife and landscape conservation. The fate of human populations within these areas is also an integral consideration in securing their long-term future, for the character of even the upland areas is dependent upon the continuation of low intensity management. However, the rural areas have their own special social and economic problems. They have a long history of depopulation coupled with a decline in the importance of agriculture to the rural economy. Fewer people than ever before are directly or indirectly employed in agriculture-related occupations. Even in parts of Mid Wales, agriculture now accounts for fewer than 10 per cent of the available jobs.[10]

Both the LFA and ESA policies seek to sustain the rural economy through payments of cash subsidies. There are, however, important differences between the schemes related not only to the basis for legal support, but also to the targeting of the payments. The LFA is a relatively old policy dating from 1975. It provides for payments which are largely subsidies on production. As such, the policy can be regarded as merely a continuation of the basic CAP philosophy with respect to

---

[8] T. N. Jenkins, *Future Harvests*, Department of Economics and Agricultural Economics, University College of Wales, Aberystwyth, 1990.

[9] Ministry of Agriculture Fisheries and Food, *Agriculture in the UK, 1988*, HMSO, 1989.

[10] G. Sinclair, *The Upland Landscape Study*, Environmental Information Services, Narbeth, Dyfed, 1983.

subsidies. The policy was adopted initially by means of a directive.[11] The ESA policy, however, represents somewhat of a revolution in the way that payments are made to farmers *pro rata* on their land holding for a variety of services and activities. The ESA policy was adopted as part of an EC regulation.[12] Before considering these two policies in detail, however, it is important to appreciate the nature of EC policy-making and the characteristics of its various legislative devices.

EC Policy Formation and Implementation

Within the EC, the power to legislate is vested in the Council of Ministers. This is an institution where the Ministerial representative of each of the twelve member states has equal status. Since the decision to ban the use of hormone growth regulators in livestock farming in 1985, the Council of Ministers has been *de facto* a majority voting institution. Prior to that time, new provisions could only be adopted on an unanimous vote, effectively conferring a veto on each member state.

The Council of Ministers has an array of instruments that can be adopted to give force to EC policy. The strongest of these is a Community regulation which enables EC law to become directly applicable within every member state. In practice, it can only operate in those areas of policy where there is conformity between member states. It is used primarily, but not exclusively, in the regulation of agricultural support prices where it is important that member states operate in concert. Regulations have also been used, for example, to incorporate international conservation treaties into Community law.[13]

In policy areas where there are major differences in administrative procedures between member states, regulations would be ineffective. The precision necessary in drafting a regulation to ensure unequivocal coverage of each member state would be unachievable in practice. In these situations, Community directives are favoured as they have the necessary flexibility to accommodate the differences in administration and policy style between member states. A directive defines policy objectives which are binding throughout the Community, but leaves the means of achieving these objectives to each member state.

Once a regulation has been adopted by the Council of Ministers, member states have no alternative but to comply with its provisions. Consequently, the formulation stage represents the only opportunity for individual member states to influence the scope of a regulation. In contrast, member states can also affect the outcome of a directive in the

[11] Council of the European Communities, Directive on Mountain and Hill Farming in certain Less Favoured Areas, *Official Journal*, 18, L128 (19 May 1975), 231–66.

[12] Council of the European Communities, Regulation on Improving the Efficiency of Agricultural Structures, *Official Journal*, 28, L93 (30 March 1985), 1–18.

[13] Haigh, *EEC Policy*.

procedures that are adopted to implement it. Indeed, a member state antagonistic to the objectives of a particular directive may adopt procedures which effectively nullify it. Assessing the impact of a directive, therefore, is a complex process involving a systematic review to ensure that legislation is in place to give effect to the directive, that appropriate procedures are adopted to implement it and finally that the outcome is in accordance with its policy objectives.[14]

The Less Favoured Areas Scheme

In April 1975, the Council of Ministers adopted a directive for the designation of areas considered less favoured because natural features place constraints on agricultural production.[15] The preamble to the directive indicates that the provenance of the LFA policy is an agricultural initiative falling under the agricultural provisions of the Treaty of Rome, namely articles 42 and 43. This has persuaded one environmental lawyer to argue that it should not be evaluated in environmental terms.[16] Indeed, the interpretation of the provisions of the LFA policy in the UK in strictly agricultural terms would tend to lend credence to this line of argument. Notwithstanding, a more strictly accurate interpretation of the directive is as a policy employing support for farmers as a means of achieving non-agricultural objectives, namely sustaining a minimum rural population or conserving the countryside within areas having severe natural constraints on agricultural production.

Under the terms of the directive individual member states are responsible for defining the extent of their own area regarded as less favoured (article 2.1). The directive, however, specifies the three types of criteria which may be considered. These are detailed in article 3.

First, mountain areas 'characterised by a considerable limitation of the possibilities for using the land and an appreciable increase in the cost of working it, due:

either to the existence, because of the altitude, of very difficult climate conditions, the effect of which is substantially to shorten the growing season,
or, at a lower altitude, to the presence, over the greater part of the district in question, of slopes too steep for the use of machinery or requiring the use of very expensive special equipment,
or to the combination of these two factors where . . . this combination gives rise to an (equivalent) handicap' (article 3(3)).

[14] P. Wathern, S. N. Young, I. W. Brown and D. A. Roberts, 'Assessing the Environmental Impact of Policy: a Generalised Framework for Appraisal', *Landscape and Urban Planning*, 14 (1987), 321–30.
[15] EC Directive on Mountain and Hill Farming.
[16] Haigh, *EEC Policy*.

Secondly, member states may designate areas 'in danger of depopulation and where the conservation of the countryside is necessary [and] which . . . must simultaneously exhibit all the following characteristics:

(a) the presence of infertile land, unsuitable for cultivation or intensification, with a limited potential which cannot be increased except at excessive cost, and mainly suitable for extensive livestock farming;

(b) because of this low productivity of the environment, results which are appreciably lower than the mean as regards the main indices characterising the economic situation in agriculture;

(c) either a low or dwindling population predominantly dependent on agricultural activity and the accelerated decline of which would jeopardize the viability of the area concerned and its continued habitation' (article 3(4)).

Finally, small areas with special problems may be designated. These must be areas which exhibit 'specific handicaps and in which farming must be continued in order to conserve the countryside and to preserve the tourist potential of the area or in order to protect the coastline' (article 3(5)). In order to avoid these special provisions being used unfairly to subsidize large sectors of the farming community, the area that can be designated under Article 3(5) was limited to 2.5 per cent of the total area of the member state.

There is no limit to the extent of Less Favoured Area that can be designated as long as the criteria in article 3 are adhered to. Currently, 53 per cent of agricultural land in the UK is classified as LFA. This is, for example, comparable to the situation in the Federal Republic of Germany, prior to reunification, at 54 per cent, but significantly lower than the 78 per cent of agricultural land that has been designated LFA in Greece.[17]

In the UK, it is the criteria designated in article 3(4) which have been mainly used for designating areas eligible for assistance under the scheme. The 1984 amendment to the designated LFA details how the UK meets the policy objectives of the directive. Most of the LFA in the UK comprises infertile hill and mountain land where more than 70 per cent of the total utilized agricultural area is grassland with a stocking rate of one livestock unit per forage hectare. A livestock unit is calculated on the basis of animal equivalents, namely bulls, cows and other bovine animals over two years (1 unit); bovine animals from six months to two years (0.69); sheep (0.15), and goats (0.15).[18]

[17] Jenkins, *Future Harvests.*
[18] EC Directive on Mountain and Hill Farming.

Farm rents and unit farm labour income are taken as the indices indicative of rural areas with economic activities appreciably lower than the mean for the country. Thus, the LFAs are characterized by rents and incomes not exceeding 65 per cent and 80 per cent of the national averages respectively. Low population density also influences designation, with regions defined as LFA having fewer than fifty-five inhabitants per square kilometre (urban and industrial areas lying within the area are excluded from the calculation). The percentage of the total working population engaged in agriculture must exceed thirty. Although this figure seems incompatible with the very low numbers of people employed in agriculture in most rural areas today, the definition of LFA excludes any urban and industrial inliers.

In 1984, the definition of LFA in the UK was extended to encompass some area complying with article 3(5). These included not only areas with adverse natural production conditions, namely steep slopes, very strong winds and poor drainage, but also areas with handicaps resulting from geographical location, specifically islands. The latter category clearly has regard for the coastline protection criterion.

Responsibility for defining LFAs within the UK lies with the Ministry of Agriculture, Fisheries and Food (MAFF), in conjunction with its sister organizations the Welsh Office Agriculture Department (WOAD) and the Department of Agriculture for Scotland (DAFS). The criteria employed in the UK have even been acknowledged by one MAFF official as probably stricter than article 3(4) requires.[19] When LFAs in the UK were first designated, livestock farmers received uniform production subsidies, again involving a rather narrow interpretation of the terms of the directive.

This contrasts markedly with the situation in the Netherlands, where LFA status has been used as a means of compensating farmers to farm amongst the natural constraints on agriculture, rather than paying them to remove or overcome them. These LFAs have been designated under the terms of article 3(5), with countryside conservation the primary objective. In France, some LFAs have been designated under the terms of article 3(5), with countryside conservation the primary objective. In France, some LFAs have been designated under article 3(3) with a differential level of financial support related to the intensity of the natural constraint on production faced by farmers. Under these arrangements those most severely affected, that is those in areas where removal of the constraint is technically not feasible, attract the highest level of payment.[20]

[19] P. Wathern, S. N. Young, I. W. Brown and D. A. Roberts, 'The EEC Less Favoured Areas Directive: Implementation and Impact on Upland Land Use in the UK', *Land Use Policy*, 3 (1986), 205–12.
[20] M. Smith, *Agriculture and Nature Conservation in Trust*, Arkleton Trust, 1985.

The Countryside Commission asserts that 'in terms of its effect on the environment, agricultural policy in the UK has continued to be implemented in a blinkered fashion, too often simplistically pursuing narrow economic objectives'.[21] This criticism is equally valid of implementation of the LFA provisions as it is of other facets of agricultural policy in the UK. Indeed, implementation of the LFA Directive can be regarded as a continuation of the status quo in policy related to agriculture in the hills and uplands. Adoption of the directive did not occur in a vacuum, but rather against a thirty-year history of livestock subsidies to hill farmers. In 1975, the LFA provisions were simply absorbed into existing national programmes, a device often encountered in UK implementation of EC policy.[22] The area initially designated coincided with the previous boundary defining eligibility for hill land subsidies, under the Hill Livestock Rearing Act 1951. The exact limit of the LFA in the UK, however, is difficult to establish as this is considered confidential by MAFF. Only lists detailing parishes (community council areas in Wales) wholly or partly within the LFA are published. Since the initial stringent definition of LFAs in the UK, there have been several revisions of the boundaries, with the most recent extension occurring in 1990.

The directive enables member states to grant 'an annual compensatory allowance for the permanent natural handicaps' experienced by farmers in order to assist specified activities, essentially livestock farming (article 5). In the UK, Hill Livestock Compensatory Allowances (HLCAs) are intended to encourage farming and to raise farm incomes in order to give effect to the policy. The HLCA is a system of annual headage payments for sheep and for cattle kept for breeding purposes. In view of the overproduction of milk within the EC, payments to farmers for dairy cattle under this scheme may not exceed ten livestock units per holding (article 7(1)(a)). Indeed, the UK is even more stringent over this issue with a reduction in payments for cattle producing surplus milk for sale. Twenty-five per cent of HLCA payments can be recovered by member states from the EC agricultural budget, the European Agriculture Guidance and Guarantee Fund (EAGGF). The remainder must be found from national sources.

Article 7(1) requires member states to fix the amount of compensatory allowance according to the severity of the permanent natural handicap affecting farming activities. When HLCAs were first implemented in the UK, uniform rates of payment were introduced, irrespective of the degree of constraint experienced by individual farmers or the extent of a farm holding.

---

[21] Countryside Commission, *Evidence to the House of Lords Sub-committee on Agriculture and the Environment*, Countryside Commission, 1984.
[22] Smith, *Agriculture and Nature Conservation*.

The introduction of uniform HLCAs throughout the LFA in the UK in 1975 was clearly in breach of article 7(1). This situation persisted until the 1984 revisions of the LFA. At that time a major extension took place to include areas having lesser constraints on production. The newly designated areas were defined as 'disadvantaged land', with the original LFA being described as 'severely disadvantaged land'. At the same time differential rates of payment were introduced. At present (1 February 1991), HLCA payments in the severely disadvantaged areas stand at £54.50, £7.50 and £4.50 for cattle, ewes within specially qualified flocks, and other ewes, respectively. The rates for disadvantaged areas are £27.25 for cattle and £2.25 for ewes. Maximum rates of payment are £62.48 and £46.86 per hectare for the two types of area. Maximum stocking rates for which HLCA is paid varies from 6.6 ewes per hectare in severely disadvantaged areas to nine ewes per hectare in disadvantaged areas.

The other major feature of the HLCA scheme is the differentiation of sheep according to breed and husbandry practice. Specially qualified flocks, alternatively referred to as 'high rate sheep', are flocks which comprise sheep of twenty-two specified hill breeds or crosses between them. Further, the animals must be kept in at least three regular and successive age groups, the youngest of which are shearlings. Sheep not complying with this definition are often described as 'low rate sheep'.

The only restrictions placed upon HLCA claims relate to the size of holding and a commitment to continue hill farming. The minimum land qualification is 3 ha of eligible land, and farmers must sign an undertaking to continue to farm at least 3 ha of eligible hill land for the following five years. Repayment of HLCAs may be required if the latter condition is broken.

The importance of the HLCA sheep payments to farming in the sparsely populated areas cannot be overstated, particularly at a time of declining sheep prices. It has been estimated that HLCAs may form up to 40 per cent of the sheep sector's gross output. Further, a 20 per cent drop in sheep numbers in the LFA in Wales, for example, would lead to a £17 million cut in sheep sector income, with an additional decrease of £7 million in the income of the rest of the economy.[23] There is clear evidence that the limits on HLCA payments at 6.6 ewes per hectare are taken as targets by farmers in order to optimize their income, rather than maxima determined by sound agronomic practice. The HLCA paid for sheep in Clwyd, North Wales, for example, indicates a stocking rate close to six ewes per hectare across the whole LFA within the county.[24]

[23] G. O. Hughes, *Support Structures for Sheep Farming*, Department of Economics and Agricultural Economics, University College of Wales, Aberystwyth, 1988.
[24] P. Wathern, S. N. Young, I. W. Brown and D. A. Roberts, 'Recent Land Use

These bald figures, however, give no picture of the environmental consequences of the LFA policy in general, nor specifically how it has been operating in the UK. The influence of sheep grazing upon the upland environment is well known.[25] It is clear that continuation of the uplands in their present form is dependent upon extensive sheep grazing. The livestock carrying capacity equivalents of different vegetation types still eludes plant scientists, so that acceptable stocking levels are almost impossible to determine. Lack of these guidelines is important, for semi-natural is probably the second most important factor, after topography, in determining landscape quality. Heathland and heather moorland vegetation is especially prized in the upland areas. It appears that moorland dwarf shrub communities are eliminated by stocking densities in excess of 1–2 sheep per hectare.[26]

HLCAs, however, are paid for up to 6.6 ewes per hectare. In real terms, this figure must substantially underestimate the grazing intensity on upland systems given the multiple lamb births commonly achieved with good husbandry today. Poached land is not an uncommon sight on hill farms at present, indicating the heavy pressure on the uplands. The more subtle changes in vegetation composition with high levels of grazing[27] go unnoted in the absence of detailed botanical monitoring. Thus, environmental impact from this source is unquantified at present.

The demise of some dwarf shrub communities in the uplands,[28] however, is a consequence of a related aspect of the LFA policy. The semi-natural vegetation of the uplands is incapable of sustaining the high numbers of sheep currently encountered. Lowland fodder crops, especially silage, provide one means of maintaining sheep numbers through periods of low natural production. A recent development becoming more widespread in the uplands is feeding sheep on concentrates. Farmers in the uplands have always attempted small-scale improvements in order to increase the productivity of their holdings. The scale of improvement, however, accelerated rapidly through the early 1980s as new technology offered farmers an opportunity to upgrade land previously considered unimprovable. The

Change and Agricultural Policy in Clwyd, North Wales', *Applied Geography*, 8 (1986), 147–63.

[25] D. F. Perkins, 'Snowdonia grasslands', in O. W. Heal and D. F. Perkins (eds.), *Production Ecology of British Moors and Montane Grasslands,* Springer Verlag (Berlin), 1978, pp. 289–95.

[26] D. Yalden, 'Sheep densities on moorland — a literature review', in J. Phillips, D. Yalden and J. Tallis (eds.), *Peak District Moorland Erosion Study Phase I Report*, Peak District Planning Board, 1981, pp. 125–31.

[27] R. G. H. Bunce and O. H. Heal, 'Landscape Evaluation and the Impact of Changing Land Use in the Rural Environment: the Problem and an Approach', in R. D. Roberts and T. M. Roberts (eds.), *Planning and Ecology*, Chapman & Hall, 1983, pp. 164–88.

[28] As note 24.

technological advances were associated with substantial grand-aid for agricultural improvement.

Under the terms initially of the Farm and Horticulture Development Scheme (FHDS) and later the Agriculture and Horticulture Development Scheme (AHDS), farmers received grants to carry out agricultural improvements. The AHDS was the programme formulated by the UK to give effect to the EC directive on farm modernization.[29] Twenty-five per cent of such grant payments can be recovered from the EC agricultural fund, the EAGGF. Although the scheme was formally withdrawn at the end of 1985, some of its provisions are still operative. Under the AHDS, farmers claim improvement grants for items included in a development plan approved by MAFF. The approved development plan runs for a period of one to six years; consequently some do not terminate until December 1991. The types of works which could be aided under this scheme included field drainage; road and path construction; hedging, walling and fencing; reseeding and clearance of reclamation of land. Grant-aid ranged from 50 to 70 per cent for these works, with higher rates within LFAs. The scheme favoured large farmers. In 1981/2 over 22 per cent of the total grant was paid to 3.7 per cent (the largest) farms, while 51 per cent (the smallest) received only 14.5 per cent.[30]

The environmental impact of this scheme has been immense. One of the most contentious issues was grant-aid for the construction of farm roads which attracted a 50 per cent subsidy. These were constructed to provide access to the remoter parts of farms, often opening up previously inaccessible land for improvement. The subsequent improvements were also grant-aided. There were unsupported allegations that construction grants were used to generate farm income through the use of outside contractors on a reciprocal basis. Undoubtedly, the grant-aid available in the early 1980s did much to degrade the scenic and wildlife interest of upland areas. Whether this should be regarded as intensification within the terms of the LFA Directive seems a moot point.

However, consideration of the intense sheep grazing encouraged by the unrealistically high ceilings on HLCAs, in conjunction with the grant-aid available to farmers for improvements within the LFA, allows an assessment of the ability of the directive, as implemented in the UK, to achieve its policy objectives. One of the primary objectives of the directive is to protect the countryside. Yet the 1980s were characterized as a period of progressive degradation in the quality of the upland environment.

[29] Council of the European Communities, Directive on the Modernisation of Farms, *Official Journal*, 15, L96 (2 March 1972), 1–8.
[30] M. MacEwen and G. Sinclair, *New Life for the Hills*, Council for National Parks, 1983.

The influence of the overall LFA policy upon environmental quality is difficult to isolate from all of the other factors operating in upland areas, especially as no new major initiatives were adopted to implement it. However, it is possible to make some general assessment of the impact of production subsidies. First, the recent history of store cattle in the uplands is one of decline. The adoption of the LFA policy has done little to stem that decline, with numbers continuing to dwindle.

The second factor seems to be the influence of current farming practices on the extent of semi-natural vegetation in the uplands. The extent of rough grazing has been inversely related to sheep numbers since at least the early 1950s.[31] In this context, the term 'rough grazing' approximates to unimproved vegetation, but it is not possible to relate this precisely to any particular vegetation type. However, the introduction of the LFA policy had no influence upon the trend. The inference is clear: farmers convert the semi-natural vegetation of their holdings to improved pasture in order to provide forage.

Another influence of the LFA policy has been detected in an intensive study of one area of Clwyd, North Wales. This concerns the composition of flocks. With virtually maximum numbers of sheep being kept on holdings, the only way that a farmer can increase income from subsidy is by changing from 'low rate' to 'high rate' sheep. In 1981 a significant widening of the price differential between the two types of sheep was reflected in a marked decline in 'low rate' sheep numbers and an increase in 'high rate' sheep, probably indicating a switch.[32]

The second policy objective of the LFA Directive, namely sustaining a minimum population level in the uplands, is also difficult to assess. One consequence of increased efficiency is to reduce the need for hired farm workers. This category has undergone a substantial decline across the whole of the agricultural sector with about 250,000 male full-time jobs disappearing between 1960 and the mid-1980s.[33] Most upland farms are now wholly family farms with pluriactivity increasingly important. The LFA at best has had no influence on the decline. The worst scenario is that the LFA and related policies may have contributed to it.

HLCA payments may have been an inducement to lowland livestock farmers to take over upland holdings. For example, in Snowdonia, North Wales, it is 'common practice for hill farms to be acquired by lowland farmers who sell off or abandon the farmhouse and run the land from as far away as Anglesey or the Lleyn Peninsula'.[34] Indeed, hill farming support has had little impact in arresting the decline in the

[31] As note 24.
[32] As note 24.
[33] Wathern and Baldock, *Regulating the Interface.*
[34] A. MacEwen and M. MacEwen, *National Parks: Conservation or Cosmetics,* Allen & Unwin, 1982.

number of upland farms.[35] Numbers have fallen in certain Welsh study areas by 40 per cent, with farm size increasing from 66 to 81 ha. For example, a decline in part-time and full-time holdings of 8.3 and 19.3 per cent respectively between 1976 and 1981 in Clwyd has been shown.[36] This covered a period when the LFA was in operation. It is argued that the benefits accruing from LFA headage payments and from grants fall disproportionately upon large holdings generating revenue which can be used to purchase neighbouring farms. The outcome of this process of farm amalgamation is an inevitable decline in rural populations and, with a lack of opportunities for young people to enter farming, an ageing population.

Although the AHDS programme is drawing to a close, some farmers with approved improvement plans will still be able to claim grant-aid for environmentally damaging operations until the end of 1991. The sum of £25.9 million was allocated to this scheme in 1998/9.[37] The proportion of this figure that can be attributed to the LFA is not known, as the scheme operates throughout the UK. The adverse impact of the AHDS upon the environment was tacitly acknowledged in the programme that was drawn up to replace it in 1985.

The agricultural structures and farm training directives adopted in 1972 were scheduled to have only a ten-year life before being reviewed and modified. The review of these directives, along with the 1975 LFA Directive (essentially part of the same package of measures), eventually came to fruition in 1985 when the regulations on improving the efficiency of agricultural structures was adopted.[38] This is generally referred to as the 'new agricultural structures' regulation. One outcome of these deliberations was the incorporation of the LFA Directive almost unchanged within articles 13–15 of the regulation. The slight changes represent some relaxation of the restrictions on the LFA scheme. Thus maximum permissible payments were raised to 101 ECU per hectare, and the extension of the proportion of any member state that could be designated LFA under the provisions of article 3(5), special areas, increased from 2 to 4 per cent. The regulation has had no impact on the way HLCA, the key element of the LFA policy, is paid to farmers. Consequently no modifications to UK procedures have had to be adopted to give effect to the LFA provisions of the regulation. The regulation, however, has not been without impact. Article 8(2) provides for the payment of grant-aid for energy-saving projects and for the protection and improvement of the environment. The latter aspect is of note, given the attack on the capital grant provisions of the AHDS. Henceforth, increasing farm efficiency would have to be set

[35] Sinclair, *The Upland Landscape Study*.
[36] As note 24.
[37] As note 9.
[38] As note 12.

within the context of its likely environmental consequences. The new regulation in effect paved the way for a new grant programme. The Agricultural Improvement Scheme (AIS) encompassed a variety of measures related not only to changes in agricultural practice, increasing energy efficiency and environmental protection and improvement, but also revenue generation through tourism and craft industries on the farm. All measures were designed to improve the income of eligible farmers, defined as those spending at least 1100 hours per year working in the business and deriving a minimum of 50 per cent of income from the farm business, with at least 25 per cent from agriculture. While conditions may be regarded as rightly excluding the 'hobby' farmer, it does mean that those who are more accurately regarded as 'part-time' farmers are also excluded from grant-aid. The AIS programme became operative on 1 January 1986. Grant-aid is available for conservation and environmental protection measures with or without an approved development plan as long as capital works for grant-aid exceed £750.

There are several important differences between the AHDS and the scheme that replaced it. First, the intensification measures causing severe impact upon the quality of the upland environment were excluded from all grant-aid. Thus, for example, assistance for farm road construction ceased. Secondly, the full impact of livestock farming as a source of environmental, especially water, pollution, was acknowledged. The main pollution threats are silage effluent, slurry storage, muck spreading under the wrong weather conditions and parlour washings. Under the AIS programme grant-aid for pollution prevention measures were reinforced. Thus, farmers were eligible to claim grant-aid for a variety of facilities including storage tanks, storage compounds and dung steads for effluent and slurry, anaerobic digesters, waste treatment plant and silage effluent storage and treatment facilities. In addition, local authority charges levied for connecting agricultural buildings to the mains sewer were also grant-aided.

The enhancement of pollution control measures left a fundamental weakness in the scheme. Annual charges for discharge of farm waste as trade effluent to sewers is not grant-aided, and grant is explicitly excluded for general maintenance and repairs to plant. At a time of low profitability in the agricultural sector, it is precisely those components of the farm business which are considered marginal to the main production activities which are the first victims of economies. Thus, even farms which have received substantial capital grants constitute a potential threat to environmental quality in the long term if maintenance grants continue to be excluded from aid schemes.

The other main difference between the AHDS and AIS programmes relates specifically to the LFA. The original scheme showed some bias towards the LFA with higher rates of capital grant available within these areas. For example, field drainage attracted a 70 per cent grant within the LFA, but 50 per cent elsewhere; for road construction, reclamation and reseeding, rates were 50 per cent and 32.5 per cent respectively. The provisions of the AIS extended the differential in favour of the LFA with the rate for most capital works twice, and in some instances four times, as high within such areas.

Agricultural grant schemes, however, are rarely stable for long and the AIS itself has fallen victim to further reform. In 1989, a new programme, the Farm and Conservation Grant Scheme (FCGS) was introduced, again under the provisions of article 8(2) of the new agricultural structures regulation. It embodies most features of the AIS programme with respect to conservation and environmental protection, but has been broadened to reflect the growing concern for environmental compatibility across almost the whole spectrum of agriculture. It encompasses a few new measures, such as grant-aid for fencing to promote the regeneration of broadleaved woodland and heather moorland. In general, it has also redressed somewhat the heavy bias towards the LFA so that rates differ by only 10 per cent for most capital works. To achieve this greater equitability, rates for the LFAs have mostly been reduced, with a few non-LFA rates increasing.

The Environmentally Sensitive Areas Scheme

Contemporary agriculture and its environmental impact became a major political issue in the UK in the early 1980s, stimulated by four considerations. First, consumers became acutely aware that they were paying way above world prices for agricultural commodities. Furthermore, there were large 'mountains' and 'lakes' of commodities in intervention store which were periodically 'sold off' to other countries at bargain prices. Secondly, certain sections of the public perceived current agricultural practices as incompatible not only with countryside conservation but also with animal welfare objectives. Thirdly, the Treasury recognized environmental arguments as an effective way of reining in the high and increasing level of public expenditure on agriculture. Finally, politicians realized that few Parliamentary seats now depend upon the agricultural vote and that even fewer can be regarded as marginal. In an increasingly market economy, politicians began to question whether the public support denied to the 'lame ducks' of industry, such as coal and steel, should continue to go to farmers who had no market for their overpriced and overproduced commodities.

The notion of the farmer as the custodian of the rural landscape was increasingly seen to be at variance with reality. Rather, it was often a case of protecting the environment from the farmer. While measures to protect individual sites of wildlife and archaeological value were in place, the protection of whole landscapes remained an intractable problem. It became clear, however, that many wildlife and scenic conservation issues could be resolved only through such landscape management.

Deterioration in the quality of many environments is often the result of incremental change. The aggregate effect of piecemeal change becomes apparent only when the whole character of an area has altered significantly. In such situations, it is impossible to implicate one specific event, such as the removal of an individual hedgerow or the ploughing out of a particular meadow as the watershed of change. Such incremental change is difficult to control, yet its regulation remains one of the major challenges currently facing landscape management.

The first attempt to confront this problem in the UK was on Exmoor when the National Parks Authority inaugurated a voluntary scheme, 90 per cent funded by the Countryside Commission, to stem the conversion of heather moorland to grassland. The model eventually adopted, involving payments for 'loss of profit forgone', has become the general model for management agreements in the UK, and is discussed in more detail in Chapter 7.

It soon became clear that Exmoor was not an isolated example of conflict between farming and landscape and wildlife conservation. Within a couple of years, a similar problem arose in the Broads. Here small-scale wet meadows and pastures of great scenic and wildlife value were going under the plough at an accelerating rate as farmers sought to achieve the high returns from conversion to cereals using the grant-aid available from MAFF. The Broads Authority was so concerned about these conversions that an attempt was made to establish an Article 4 Direction Order under the Planning Acts to establish mandatory controls over certain agricultural activities subject only to compensation being paid. The matter reached a politically embarrassing head when one farmer in the Halvergate Marshes ploughed a large 'V' in the middle of one of his fields in a gesture designed to express the frustration felt by many local farmers.

During 1984 the Government moved quickly to establish a voluntary compensation scheme similar to that devised for Exmoor. The Broads Grazing Marsh Conservation Scheme, established under section 40 of the Wildlife and Countryside Act 1981, was administered by MAFF but jointly funded with the Countryside Commission. Under the voluntary Broads scheme, farmers were required to enter into a three-year agreement to retain low-intensity grazing, limit fertilizer applications and restrict the use of herbicides to scheduled weeds in exchange for an annual payment of £120 per hectare.[39]

In 1985, 80 per cent of the eligible land was registered for the scheme, even though the payment was far below the projected profit achievable on conversion. Clearly, local farmers were predisposed to the scheme on other than strictly financial considerations. In its special payments to farmers within the section 40 area, the Broads scheme was almost certainly in breach of the competition provisions of the Treaty of Rome. However, it was a political expedient, designed as a stopgap measure to maintain the status quo while a long-term solution was sought. It was clear that the Government already knew what the alternative would be, for at that time it was engaged in discussions over the new agricultural structures regulation. Relatively late in these negotiations, the UK proposed a new mechanism for rationalizing Halvergate and the other problematic areas that were emerging.[40]

For areas where environmental protection was in conflict with agricultural intensification, article 19 of the regulation provides the key measures. Under these provisions, member states are authorized to establish national schemes for the 'introduction or continued use of agricultural production practices compatible with the requirements of conserving the natural habitat ensuring an adequate income for farmers' within specially designated environmentally sensitive areas (article 19(1)). These areas are generally referred to as ESAs and are defined as being 'of recognised importance from an ecological or landscape point of view' (article 19(2)). Farmers entering the scheme must undertake to farm ESAs 'so as to preserve or improve their environment'. In particular 'no further intensification of agricultural production will occur and the stock density and the level of intensity of agricultural production will be compatible with the specific needs of the area concerned' (article 19(3)). Thus, for the first time an attempt was made to target payments according to the environmental needs of individual areas and to move away from blanket provisions which, in general, have stimulated intensification. As with HLCA and grant-aid, 25 per cent of ESA payments can be recovered by member states from the EC agricultural budget.

Paradoxically, although the UK government had originally proposed the ESA provisions, indeed had even established a *de facto* scheme for the Broads, only *ad hoc* provisions for designating ESAs existed. Appropriate legal measures were promulgated with the Agriculture Act 1986. There was, however, an important amendment

[39] K. Turner, 'The Broads Grazing Marshes Conservation Scheme', *Landscape Research*, 10(2) (1985), 28–9.

[40] D. Baldock, 'Farm structures in Europe: the British Initiative' *Ecos*, 6(3) (1985), 2–6.

to the designation criteria specified in article 19(2). Under the 1986 Act, ESAs are recognized not only on their ecological and landscape importance, but also taking account of their archaeological, architectural and historic interest. The unilateral extension of designation criteria for ESAs by the UK has never been challenged.

Slightly different ESA implementation procedures have been adopted in the various semi-autonomous parts of the UK. While the Agriculture Bill was still before Parliament, three separate working parties were set up in Scotland, Northern Ireland, and England and Wales. In England and Wales the working party consisted of the Countryside Commission, the Nature Conservancy Council (NCC) and either English Heritage or its Welsh counterpart, Cadw. In Scotland, the Department of Agriculture for Scotland played the lead role with the Scottish Development Department, the Countryside Commission for Scotland and NCC. In both Scotland and Northern Ireland there were extensive consultations with outside organizations representing different sectoral interests. A detailed account of the period of review leading up to designation is reported elsewhere.[41]

From the outset the Government attempted to exert an influence on the ESA programme. Even before the working parties had completed their deliberations the Secretary of State for Agriculture announced a cash limit of £7 million on the scheme, adequate to designate only five or six ESAs. The working party operating in England and Wales refused to be intimidated by this announcement. It appraised forty-six areas which might be suitable for designation, and on the basis of consultants' reports recommended to the Minister that fourteen areas 'would benefit from early designation'. Furthermore, the working party refused to rank them, thereby implying that the proposed budget was inadequate. This probably prevented the ESA scheme from becoming a mere token gesture. In Scotland twenty areas were investigated and short-listed to two priority areas and three of lower priority. Only one of the nine areas short-listed in Northern Ireland was considered suitable for designation.

The ESA programme has continued to suffer political interference as the initial designation scheme was tailored to fit the £7 million budget. It had been feared that the Council of Ministers would impose a limit on the total area that could be designated ESA in the regulation, as happened with article 3(5) LFAs, but none was specified. Thus, the cash limit was purely a nationally imposed one. During autumn 1986 the proposed designation of nine ESAs was announced. Six were to be designated in England and Wales; five coincided with the boundaries recommended by the working party, namely the Broads, the Somerset Levels and Moors, West Penrith and the North Pennine Dales in

---

[41] P. Wathern, *Environmentally Sensitive Areas*, IIUG (Berlin), 1987.

England and the Cambrian Mountains in Wales. However, only half of the South Downs area recommended by the working party was designated. This area was arbitrarily divided in half (along a main road neatly bisecting the area) because of the high numbers of farmers likely to join the ESA scheme and hence the high cost. In Scotland, one of the two priority areas, Breadalbane, was designated along with one of lower priority, Loch Lomond. The sensitivity of the second priority area, the Machair Lands of the Uists and Benbecula, coupled with potential conflict with another EC grant-aided development programme, the Integrated Development Programme, have been suggested as possible reasons for non-designation at this time.[42] The ESA programme came into operation on 1 March 1987.

The ESA programme has been an important innovation, and even before the scheme came formally into operation, the Secretary of State announced a doubling of the available budget. This was probably a response, not so much to the potential value of the scheme, but rather the unprecedented vote of no confidence by the National Farmers' Union hanging over him at that time.

One consequence of the Secretary of State's interjection was a rapid reappraisal of the undesignated areas, with the result that in early May a further round of designation was announced. Described by *Big Farm Weekly* (21 May 1987) as 'Electorally Sensitive Areas', these encompassed the Suffolk River Valleys, the Test Valley, Breckland and the Shropshire Borders, along with a doubling of the South Downs in England. In Wales, the Cambrian Mountains area was extended and the Lleyn Peninsula designated. The previously discounted Uists and Benbecula in Scotland was designated along with one of the lower priority areas, Whitlow and Eidon. Orkney, the other lesser priority area was once again rejected, but a new area, the Stewartry of Dumfries, was included. Thus as at 1 February 1991 eighteen areas had been designated.

Individual schemes specific to the environmental and conservation needs of each ESA have been drawn up by the appropriate agriculture departments. The schemes are administered locally by the agriculture departments and, in contrast to the previous programmes for Exmoor and Halvergate, funded entirely from the agriculture budget. The ESA schemes have a number of features in common. First, the ESA programme is voluntary, with both full-time and part-time farmers eligible as long as their land is being worked as a farm business. Secondly, farmers are required to enter into an agreement to comply with the provisions of the scheme over a five-year period. This agreement would normally transfer automatically to the next owner; in effect it is covenanted upon the holding.

[42] Ibid.

The schemes devised for Scotland differ from those adopted elsewhere in that they lay greater emphasis upon positive conservation rather than mere protection. Thus, for example, in the Loch Lomond ESA farmers undertake: to avoid grazing semi-natural vegetation at more than 0.5 livestock units per hectare; not to plough, level, reseed or cultivate semi-natural vegetation; to use herbicides and pesticides only in approved situations; to maintain and manage heather; to avoid pollution; to retain hedges, dykes and walls and maintain them in a specified manner; to avoid damage to any archaeological feature; and to obtain guidance and approval for any tree planting, felling, vehicular tracks and major work on farm buildings. Finally, farmers must prepare and agree a farm management plan.

On joining the scheme, a farmer receives two staged payments. First, for the agreement described above there is a flat-rate payment of £15 and £2.50 per annum per hectare for enclosed land and for rough grazing respectively up to a maximum of £1500 per annum per holding. In addition, there are set payments for works carried out as part of the conservation plan at standard costings for particular items of work such as hedge planting, wall construction and stock fencing. One consequence of this approach is that it places a responsibility on DAFS to be closely involved in the ESA programme on a day-to-day basis, with its implications for the cost of administering the scheme.

In drawing up its advice for the Government, the working party in England and Wales was conscious of the need to keep administrative costs low, and recommended a series of flat-rate payments to farmers. As in Scotland, farmers undertake to operate within a system of constraints in return for annual hectarage payments. There is some variation between ESAs. The situation in the West Penrith ESA is of particular note as much of the concern here relates to its great historical interest, with fossilized field patterns and the remains of many prehistoric settlements. Consequently, there are many specific constraints related to the maintenance and protection of historic features such as walls, gate posts and lynchets, as well as the more normal provisions related to the use and management of semi-natural vegetation by grazing. West Penrith farmers within the scheme receive an annual payment of £60 per hectare.

The Lleyn Peninsula ESA has a two-tier system of payments. Tier 1 payments of £15 per hectare require farmers to: maintain existing field boundaries; keep hedges, banks and walls in good order; protect historic features and retain broadleaved trees and scrub. Tier 2(1) payments of an additional £15 per hectare are dependent upon further constraints with respect to rough grazing in order to prevent its improvement or damage by overgrazing. Tier 2(2) allowances of a further £55 per hectare apply only to hay meadows, and place restrictions on improvement and cutting dates. Two-tier payments exist also, for example, in the Somerset Levels and Moors, the Broads and the South Downs. The latter scheme is somewhat unusual in that payments are available to encourage conversion of some arable land to grassland. One outcome could be to re-create the former downland landscape of extensive open grasslands.

Conclusions

The verdict on the current LFA policy must be one of a resounding failure to achieve its stated policy objectives. The main explanation lies in the insistence of MAFF to tie aid to a system of subsidies on production. The pressure has been for farmers in upland areas to intensify with a concomitant loss of environmental quality. MAFF's implementation procedure has been criticized because it 'not only evades the intention of the Directive, but also avoids the need to give agricultural policies objectives that go beyond the production of food or the increase of farmers' incomes. Neither the maintenance of the rural population nor the conservation of the countryside are objectives of MAFF's policy.'[43] Even in 1990 production subsidies were still being singled out as the main weakness of the LFA policy on environmental grounds. Further, it has been arued that both environmental and financial benefits would accrue from a reorientation of the scheme.[44] Suggested changes include first defining stocking rates on a regional basis rather than the blanket categories employed at present. Secondly, tiered payments could be made with a maximum payment established on a per farm basis. This approach, however, does run the risk of farm subdivision in order to maximize benefit for large holdings. Thirdly, a most attractive option would be to establish payments on a hectarage basis rather than as headage payments. This would greatly benefit farmers adopting low stocking rates. Finally, making compensatory payments on some basis related to employment, such as a labour unit basis, would favour labour-intensive small farms. Jenkins further argues that when placed on some basis which provides no incentive for expansion of output, compensatory payments could be used to preserve traditional methods of livestock husbandry and the associated landscape, social and cultural values.

The ESA programme on the other hand has produced a system for subsidizing farmers which does not encourage them to increase production, but rather to continue to manage their farms in an environmentally benign way. Indeed, in the South Downs ESA and in the Scottish ESAs a more positive approach has been adopted which

---

[43] MacEwen and Sinclair, *New Life for the Hills.*
[44] Jenkins, *Future Harvests.*

goes beyond merely maintaining the status quo by seeking to improve environmental quality. That the working party in England and Wales was able to consider the 32 areas not included on its shortlist as being 'not unsuitable for designation' indicates that not all of the undesignated areas of the UK are totally wrecked from an environmental point of view. Thus, there is considerable scope to extend the scheme to others areas. There is no impediment in the new agricultural structures regulation to doing so. However, there appears to be a reluctance on the part of the Government to replace a subsidy on productivity with a subsidy on unproductivity.

During 1990 there was a review of the working of the ESA. In Wales, for example, WOAD has commissioned research on take-up rates within the Cambrian Mountains ESA. The results have not yet been published but it appears that the rate of uptake is increasing, but still only stands at about 30 per cent of farmers. Ministerial statements seem somewhat at variance with this figure, indicating rates as high as 70–80 per cent, but the data to support this assertion have not been published, indeed it is not even known whether these values relate to area of land or numbers of farms within the scheme. What the outcome of the review will be, is unclear, although the Secretary of State for Wales has already announced that there will be no increase in levels of funding. Whether this indicates that an increased total budget is unnecessary because of low uptake rates, or that rates will not be increased, is also unclear.

It is important not to rhapsodize about the ESA scheme prematurely. Clearly, it does have great potential. However, in 1988/9 a mere £9.1 million was allocated to the ESA programme within a total agricultural budget of £12.8 billion.[45] Most of the remainder was a subsidy on production. Even the LFA budget was of an order of magnitude greater than for HLCA payments alone. Until there is greater equitability in the resources available to manage the countryside for features such as wildlife and scenic quality and recreation value compared with the subsidies and grants currently applied to encourage overproduction of agricultural commodities, the prognosis for the quality of the rural environment cannot be good.

[45] As note 9.

Index

This Index includes Cases, Statutes, Statutory Instruments and EC legislation